"Southern Baptists are at a critical mor[...] our membership is declining, our cooper[...] ary force is being downsized, and our bap[...] are signs of spiritual renewal among us, e[...] [...]ongoing theological renaissance and missional revitalization taking place in SBC congregations all over our nation. This is a time for hope, not despair. I'm grateful that *The SBC & the 21st Century* brings together some of the wisest voices among us to help Southern Baptists think through how we can best pursue faithfulness for the glory of God, the health of our churches, and the sake of this lost world that God so loves."

Nathan A. Finn, *dean of the School of Theology and Missions and professor of Christian thought and tradition, Union University*

"Here is a collection of prescient essays on the Southern Baptist Convention, America's largest Protestant denomination, written by a superb team of scholar-activists. Beyond the analysis and perspective offered here, there courses through this volume a common theme: the urgency of declaring the gospel of Jesus Christ to all persons everywhere. This is the historic mission of the SBC and its future."

Timothy George, *founding dean and professor of divinity, history, and doctrine, Beeson Divinity School, and general editor, Reformation Commentary on Scripture*

"Baptist and evangelical movements have historically embraced fidelity to the timeless truths of God's Word, as well as flexibility about the best means to reach the current generation. But there is always a temptation, especially for a denomination as large as the Southern Baptist Convention, to become stagnant and nostalgic. Thus, it is heartening to see SBC leaders tackling such hard questions and contemporary challenges as those in Jason K. Allen's stimulating book. I recommend it highly."

Thomas S. Kidd, *Distinguished Professor of History, Baylor University*

"I got saved in a Southern Baptist church, went to a Southern Baptist university and graduated from a Southern Baptist seminary. Jason Allen nails why my heritage is a force for the future. I believe that the SBC's best days are ahead, and this book is the map."

Darrin Patrick, *lead pastor, The Journey; vice president, Acts 29 Church Planting Network; and chaplain, St. Louis Cardinals*

"Dr. Jason Allen has assembled a remarkable collection of articles by a wide range of current Southern Baptist leaders. The articles pretty much cover the landscape of Southern Baptist life and where the Convention may be headed. Southern Baptist pastors and laypeople need to be aware of current trends and projections for the future of the SBC. In these days of a changing culture and a need for revival in our churches, this volume will be of great value. You will be profited and challenged as you read it."

Jerry Vines, *pastor-emeritus, First Baptist Church, Jacksonville, Florida; two-time president, Southern Baptist Convention; and president, Jerry Vines Ministries, Inc.*

The SBC
and the
21ˢᵗ Century

REFLECTION, RENEWAL, & RECOMMITMENT

The SBC
and the
21ST Century

edited by JASON K. ALLEN

With *Contributions by* RONNIE FLOYD, R. ALBERT MOHLER JR., FRANK PAGE,
PAIGE PATTERSON, DAVID PLATT, THOM RAINER, *and* OTHER LEADING SCHOLARS

FOREWORD BY RUSSELL MOORE

B&H
ACADEMIC
ASHVILLE, TENNESSEE

Dedication

This book is affectionately dedicated to my five children:

Anne-Marie, Caroline, William, Alden, and Elizabeth—

with the realization that they are precious to me beyond measure

and the greatest stewardship God has given me and Karen;

and with the prayer that they will, in their generation,

see and serve vibrant, biblical, Southern Baptist Convention

churches as followers of our Lord Jesus Christ.

Contents

INTRODUCTION

SOUTHERN BAPTIST CONVENTION AND COOPERATION

SOUTHERN BAPTIST DOCTRINE AND DISTINCTIVES

SOUTHERN BAPTIST MINISTRY AND MISSION

◇   ◇   ◇   ◇

Foreword

Russell D. Moore

Novelist William Faulkner once famously told students at the University of Virginia that the southern evangelicals so prevalent in his Bible-Belt ecosystem were not religious. Surprised, the students asked, "If they're not religious, then what are they?" Faulkner replied, "Well, they're Southern Baptist."

What the great man of letters meant was that, in his view, to be a Southern Baptist was a matter of cultural orientation, not a matter of a set of theological precepts or ethical practices or even political stances. For him Southern Baptist identity wasn't primarily about believer's baptism or local church congregationalism or the priesthood of all believers or religious liberty. It wasn't even about God or Jesus or the Bible. It was primarily about an "emotional condition" that was inseparable from the experience of life in the poor and rural American South. To be a Southern Baptist wasn't, he argued, to identify with a particular intellectual or liturgical condition but rather to simply be a type of person born in a particular place in a particular time.

As much as I hate to take issue with a fellow Mississippian, especially one now long dead, Faulkner was wrong to underestimate the theology and lived church life of Baptist Christians in the South. After all, no matter how captive the churches or the institutions of Southern Baptist life have been to the spirit of the age, and that is all too often, the gospel was always there, if sometimes obscured or even submerged. The gospel, of course, has a way of beating its way out of our jars of clay and then knocking us down off of our feet of clay. Faulkner was right, though, that Baptist Christianity has too often, where it is the dominant religion, traded away the inheritance of gospel distinctiveness for the mess of pottage of cultural civil religion. At its worst, this sort of cultural Christianity meant captivity of the denomination to the Antichrist views of racial supremacy and with that to the state-sponsored terrorism of the regimes of human slavery or the Jim Crow order. Too often our proclamation looked like little more than a southern-fried social gospel, inviting our neighbors to receive the "good news" of the 1950s American dream. That was true even when we used Bible language such as "revival" and "awakening" or when we spoke of areas of Southern Baptist saturation, audaciously, as our "Zion."

As I've argued elsewhere, that form of cultural Christianity can only thrive where the civil religion it maintains is useful in securing oneself a place in the earthly order.[1] If a revival of biblical orthodoxy does not tear down these golden calves, then a secularizing culture surely will. We should not lament such loss. We should instead be warned by it and prepare ourselves for the opportunity to be the people of Christ in a new era brimming with gospel opportunities.

Organizational consultants tell us that an institution is on the precipice of dying when it sees itself perpetually in the past. That tendency is, of course, always with us. Some would set the "golden age" that they look to as the high point of Southern Baptist programs and cultural dominance. Texas pastor Bart Barber once noted (rightly, in my view) that the Baptist General Convention of Texas's past tension with the rest of the Southern Baptist Convention, a tension that resulted in the formation of a new state convention, was quite different in one important aspect from the rest of the inerrancy controversy of the 1970s through the 1990s in Baptist life. The Texas moderates, he argued, did not want to go the way of the contemporary Cooperative Baptist Fellowship. They weren't eager to embrace, for instance, the sexual revolution or the extremes of mainline Protestant theology. At the same time, he noted, they didn't want to go the way of the contemporary Southern Baptist Convention, toward confessional clarity on biblical inerrancy and contemporary debates on human sexuality and gender. They didn't want to go toward the contemporary expressions of each of these options, he argued. They wanted simply to return to the Southern Baptist Convention, circa 1978, and freeze it there. But the era of the 1950s or the 1970s cannot be held for us in amber—whatever our theological commitments.

Others will look to the necessary correcting of the ship, the Conservative Resurgence begun with the election of Adrian Rogers as SBC president in 1979, as the "golden age." Some do so with the nostalgia that naturally comes to all of us as we age. Some see every issue as coming with the same existential threat that theological liberalism posed to the convention in those days and wish to see the convention in the same sort of upheaval perpetually, even where theological aberrancy doesn't exist. This comes with its own sort of peril. David was a mighty man of war, and Israel was right to celebrate his conquests at the direction of the Spirit of God. But David was chosen by God to fight only necessary battles, ones

---

[1] Russell Moore, *Onward: Engaging the Culture without Losing the Gospel* (Nashville: B&H, 2014), 1–2.

of God's own choosing. David's descendants were right to seek to emulate his fighting spirit in the defeat of the giant of Gath or of the Philistine armies that threatened the camps of Judah. They would not do well to emulate his bloodshed of Uriah the Hittite or his militaristic (and egotistic) census of his people. We should emulate the courage and conviction of the Conservative Resurgence, but we should do so because that fight was rooted in biblical truth. We should not valorize fighting for the sake of fighting. David's bloody years pointed to King Jesus's conquest of sin and death and the devil, to be sure. But the peaceful reign of Solomon also pointed to Christ in the "rest" of having all enemies under his feet, of the building of God's temple. We ought to be prepared for when doctrinal deviancy might tear us apart, but we ought to be grateful when we exhibit the kind of missional unity and confessional consensus, grounded in inerrant biblical revelation, for which the leaders of the Conservative Resurgence prayed and worked.

We should be looking forward to a new era with new challenges and new opportunities. This does not mean, though, that we have not been here, at least in some ways, before. Our ancestors in England and in colonial and Revolutionary America crafted a Baptist identity bound to what historians Thomas Kidd and Barry Hankins have called a sense of being "intentional outsiders."[2] Thomas Helwys and Roger Williams and Isaac Backus and John Leland knew what it meant to be voices crying in the wilderness, and their voices helped shape the future for us even if it meant jail time for them. The Baptist future may look much like the Baptist past—scrappy outsiders willing to face cultural marginalization for holding to the distinctives of a believers' church ruled by King Jesus alone.

This means we must train the next generation to know and love the Bible, to hear in it the Spirit speaking to the churches. It means we must guard the Baptist contributions to the larger body of Christ—baptism reserved for confessing believers alone, a church that reflects and models the kingdom of priests, a gospel that comes not through coercion of state power or cultural pressure but through the sovereign working of the Spirit through the addressing of free consciences.

There are, of course, several pitfalls to this calling. The first is what many in our older generations (rightly) lament in the passing of a close tie between church and culture. The Bible was easy for me to learn as a child because I was present in my Southern Baptist church each week for Sunday School, two worship services each Sunday, Sunday night Training Union, Monday night visitation, and Wednesday night Royal Ambassadors, at the very minimum. In a time when churches increasingly meet only for Sunday morning worship, perhaps with a home community group hosted at some point in the week, the saturation of

---

[2] Thomas S. Kidd and Barry Hankins, *Baptists in America: A History* (New York: Oxford University Press, 2015), 244.

children with the Bible poses real challenges that must be met by more than just forty-five-minute sermons that are compilations of Bible commentary quotes.

The second pitfall is that no one and no people enjoy a prophetic calling that requires careful distance from the "tribes" as they are set up at the moment. We can see this with the Baptist distinctive of religious freedom. The Baptist Left often accused Baptist conservatives of abandoning religious liberty. Sometimes they were right, as Baptists fell in line for state-sponsored writing of prayers or for zoning out of existence the houses of worship of unpopular religious minorities. But then again often these Baptist progressives forgot all about "soul freedom" as soon as the question was of a politically similar set of politicians forcing nuns to violate their consciences in purchasing contraceptive drugs and devices.

The Baptist future will require faithful, conservative, confessional Baptists to see ourselves as the best of our ancestors saw themselves—as the people of Christ before we are anything else. The Baptist future will require us to teach why we believe such strange things as bodily resurrection and miracles and the forgiveness of sins. The Baptist future will require us to stop trying to reach our "target demographics" and see congregations where carnal divisions are torn down. The Baptist future will require us to model for our children what it means not to fear man as we stand for our principles against our enemies and against our allies. The Baptist future will require the courage to say to a dying world, "You must be born again." In that I have hope and indeed more than hope. I have a sense of exhilaration. The world needs the gospel. The almost gospels will not keep their promises. And the body of Christ needs the contribution of the cantankerous, Bible-believing, freedom-loving Baptists.

We should pray that 100 years from now our descendants are reaching new generations, sloshing new believers in and out of baptisteries in the name of the Father and of the Son and of the Holy Ghost. When some ask why they "waste" so much water on such a rite, let's pray that their witness is so clear that the answer will be, "Well, they're Baptists." And when some ask why they would "waste" their time on the sort of miserable sinners and cultural outcasts they are receiving with the gospel, let's pray that their witness is so clear the answer will be, "Well, they're Christians."

Preface

Southern Baptists do not call councils; those are the pope's business. Throughout our history, however, there have been times when wisdom demanded that Southern Baptist leaders come together to consider our collective work and how best to conceptualize our future together.

That is why I invited key Southern Baptist stakeholders to gather in the fall of 2015 on the campus of Midwestern Baptist Theological Seminary for a symposium entitled The SBC and the 21st Century: Reflection, Renewal, and Recommitment. This gathering was the first of what will be a triennial symposium on the Southern Baptist Convention hosted by Midwestern Baptist Theological Seminary.

The presenters provided insightful assessments of the Southern Baptist Convention's past and present and hopeful exhortations for our future. As each person spoke, I was encouraged by the thoughtfulness of their work and became increasingly confident that the symposium—and this book—would contribute to the future of the Southern Baptist Convention.

Not every invitee was able to come to Kansas City for the symposium, but I am grateful that many additional SBC leaders were able to contribute a chapter to this book even if they could not attend in person. Collectively we have undertaken this responsibility with the hope that God's greatest work through Southern Baptists is before us—not behind us—and with the prayer God will use our meager contributions in this book toward this great end.

Southern Baptists do not call councils, nor do we issue encyclicals. Contained within this book are descriptions of, and prescriptions for, our denomination's future—not dictates. Nonetheless, I pray God will use this book to enhance his glory among and through Southern Baptists and that our churches will be pleased to receive the counsel and encouragement contained herein.

Acknowledgments

I am deeply indebted to many who have given much in order for this project to come to completion. First, as always, I am deeply indebted to my wife, Karen, and our five children for their encouragement and support throughout this entire project. Humanly speaking, they make life worth living. It makes completing a project like this so much more doable when I know I have my precious family rooting for me.

I am also very thankful to the many contributors, both those who were present at the SBC and the 21st Century Symposium, and those who were not able to attend but contributed a chapter to this work. Each one of these men is an individual I respect greatly, and it is an honor to partner with them in such a joint effort.

I am especially appreciative of Thom Rainer, Jim Baird, Audrey Greeson, Dean Richardson, and my other friends at LifeWay Christian Resources and B&H Academic, who saw this project worthy of publication and who have been a joy to work with every step of the way. Thank you.

I also want to express my most sincere gratitude to those at Midwestern Seminary who have played an indispensable part in this project's completion. First, in the president's office, Patrick Hudson, Catherine Renfro, Teresa Moody, Dawn Philbrick and Jake Rainwater have all provided tireless support and great encouragement. Additionally, my colleagues Jason Duesing and John Mark Yeats both provided wise counsel and timely input as well. More broadly, I am grateful to God for the stewardship I have to serve as president of Midwestern Seminary, and for the many ways this institution rallied around the symposium itself and this subsequent book.

Finally, and most of all, I am indebted to my Lord Jesus Christ, who has strengthened me because he considered me faithful, putting me into service.

INTRODUCTION

A Never-Changing Witness in an Ever-Changing World: The Enduring Southern Baptist Mandate

Jason K. Allen

Radiating the denominational optimism of his era, in 1948 an ebullient Alabama pastor named Levi Elder Barton mused, "I am more tremendously convinced than ever that the last hope, the fairest hope, the only hope for evangelizing the world on New Testament principles is the Southern Baptist people represented in that Convention. I mean no unkindness to anybody on earth, but if you call that bigotry then make the most of it."[1]

When Barton penned those words, Southern Baptists were approaching their zenith. The postwar era would be good to Southern Baptists, like most every other Protestant denomination. Numerically the SBC enjoyed dramatic expansion. Denominationally the SBC became more cohesive and organizationally mature. Culturally Southern Baptists neared the apex of their social influence and political clout. Christ appeared to be building his church, and an angel appeared to be riding over the denominational dust cloud.

Nonetheless, in hindsight Barton's assertion might invite a smile or even a wince. It may appear as denominationally prideful and self-absorbed. But, if one can overlook his apparent hubris, Barton projects a sentiment—an almost romantic desire—which has been the SBC's unifying theme since 1845 and its primary catalyst into the twenty-first century—fulfilling the Great Commission.

---

[1] Levi Elder Barton, "God's Last and Only Hope: The Fragmentation of the Southern Baptist Convention," *Alabama Christian Advocate,* June 29, 1948, vi

Now, nearly seven decades after Barton's assertion, the numbers still impress. The Southern Baptist Convention boasts more than 15 million members in nearly 50,000 churches. In the deep South the numbers are even more impressive.

Yet all is not well within the Southern Baptist Zion. Nearly fifty years ago, Dean Kelley's insightful *Why Conservative Churches Are Growing* documented the correlation between a denomination's acceptance of liberal theology and the numerical decline that always followed.[2] Kelley's argument was clear enough—if a church does not believe in the full truthfulness of Scripture, the exclusivity of the gospel, and the eternal realities of heaven and hell, it feels no urgency to evangelize. Denominational decline always follows doctrinal compromise.

Similarly, Kelley demonstrated how conservative churches—including Southern Baptist churches—that still held conservative doctrine, tended to grow numerically. Sound doctrine led to evangelistic urgency.

Kelley's research produced a stark study in contrast, and it served as a *causus belli* for conservatives during the Southern Baptist Convention's inerrancy controversy. As a convention of churches most concerned with missions and evangelism, the logic was airtight. The only way to ensure vibrant evangelism and missions, conservatives argued, was to recover their theological foundations.[3]

Yet for Southern Baptists, past pride in our relative strength contra mainline denominations has given way to the realization that we are currently on a similar but, thankfully, slower path. Southern Baptists are not impervious to the fate of the mainline denominations. Recent denominational statistics have made this clear. However, while trend lines document the past, they do not have to determine the future.

The optimism of previous generations has given way to concern over how well we are reaching the world and what role we will play in it. The deeper into the twenty-first century we go, the more acute our challenges will likely become. Indeed, the decades before us will likely present the SBC with unique, even unprecedented, challenges on most every front.

Denominationally, indicators such as baptisms and giving through the Cooperative Program cause ongoing concern. The near unbounded optimism of previous generations is now buffeted by the realities of declining denominational statistics. These realities force us to confront pressing questions like:

- Will we reimagine our structures, programs, and efforts to most effectively reach the world for Christ, or will we retrench and risk being a past-tense denomination?

---

[2] Dean Kelley, *Why Conservative Churches Are Growing: A Study in Sociology of Religion* (New York: Harper & Row, 1972).
[3] Ibid.

- Will we recommit ourselves to funding our collective Great Commission work through the Cooperative Program, or will we choose to endlessly downsize?
- Will we grow more unified around shared convictions and mission, or will we fragment over secondary concerns and tertiary doctrinal differences?
- Will we see the generational transition that is upon us as an opportunity to seize or a change to resist?

Theologically, the SBC's doctrinal recovery, as captured and codified in The Baptist Faith and Message 2000, has now been fully implemented in all of the national entities. The Southern Baptist Convention stands in the year 2016 as a tower of theological certainty and convictional clarity. No one wonders what Southern Baptists believe on the big theological and social issues of the day. But this strength invites its own series of questions:

- Can we maintain intergenerational theological faithfulness, successfully projecting these gains deeper into the twenty-first century?
- Will we recover a regenerate church membership, comprised of baptized believers, covenanted together in a disciplined church?
- Will we be able to maintain a distinct Baptist identity while we engage and partner with the broader evangelical community?
- Will the recovery of the doctrine of inerrancy lead to a renewal of biblical authority, sufficiency, and a renewed commitment to biblical exposition?
- Will the theological uniformity of the SBC's entities lead to more confessionally aware and theologically informed churches?

Culturally, Southern Baptists, especially in the deep South, enjoyed unique influence for more than a century. An uneasy church-state alliance reinforced social and moral expectations and fostered an ambient Christianity. That influence is giving way to mere tolerance, which, in some corners, is morphing into intolerance. Our cultural moment, including real and growing threats to religious liberty, should press Southern Baptist churches closer toward unity in belief and mission. These realities invite still more questions:

- Can we be content as a distinct cultural minority and remain faithful to the dictates of Christ in the face of social marginalization?
- Will we have the courage to hold firm on pressing cultural issues, such as opposition to same-sex marriage, against increased public agitation to the same?
- Will we be content to view ourselves, as Russell Moore has argued, as "communitarian instead of majoritarian?"

This book's contributors take up these issues and many more. And it brings me back again to Levi Elder Barton, who was "more tremendously convinced than ever that the last hope, the fairest hope, the only hope for evangelizing the world on New Testament principles is the Southern Baptist people represented in that Convention. I mean no unkindness to anybody on earth, but if you call that bigotry than make the most of it."[4]

Nearly seven decades later, Barton's assertion still rings with a certain element of truth, and I resonate with his hopeful assessment—to a certain degree.

More soberly, though, I am inclined to invert Barton's words.

As for me, I am now more tremendously convinced than ever that the SBC's last hope, fairest hope, and only hope is for God to grant us careful reflection, spiritual renewal, and recommitment to the Word of God, the gospel of Jesus Christ, and the Great Commission. If you call that desperation, then make the most of it.

Though our world is ever changing, one thing is clear—the Southern Baptist witness is never to change. Whether delivered in Galilee by our Lord himself, preached by the apostles in the book of Acts, considered by 309 gathered messengers in Augusta, Georgia, in 1845, flowing from the pen of Levi Elder Barton in 1948, discussed over beignets and coffee at Café du Monde in 1967, affirmed in The Baptist Faith and Message 2000, pondered anew in 2016, or projected deeper into the twenty-first century—Southern Baptists are called to be a people standing on the Word of God and moving forward together to reach the world with the gospel of Jesus Christ. As we do, surely Christ will be pleased to build his Church through us, and an angel will continue to ride over our denominational dust cloud.

May, by God's grace, the pages that follow further this cause.

---

[4] Barton, "God's Last and Only Hope," 2.

SOUTHERN BAPTIST CONVENTION
AND COOPERATION

The Cooperative Program and the Future of Collaborative Ministry

Frank S. Page

THE INCEPTION

In *One Sacred Effort*, Chand Brand and David Hankins correctly point out that there was a problem in the 1920s in regards to supporting the missions and ministries of the Southern Baptist Convention. Though the Convention at this time was eighty years old, it was struggling to fulfill its resolution of "organizing a plan for eliciting, combining, and directing the energies of the whole denomination in one sacred effort, for the propagation of the gospel."[1]

The number of denominational enterprises and institutions was growing. Each was seeking contributions from the congregations without regard to the needs of the others. Sunday by Sunday, fund-raisers or agents from seminaries, colleges, orphanages, hospitals, mission boards, and benevolent organizations would travel across the country asking churches for their help. Some speakers were better than others. Some efforts were more fruitful than others. Each speaker sought the best Sundays on which to present their case. Each wanted a significant amount of time in the service to make maximum impact for their financial appeal.

The cost of raising money sometimes approached 50 percent of the proceeds. The way the system worked in those days was that the salary of the "agent" was to be fulfilled before money actually went to the agency or entity requesting their services. The system was broken, and churches began to call for help.[2]

---

[1] "Preamble and Constitution of the Southern Baptist Convention," 1845 SBC *Annual* (Richmond, VA: H. K. Ellyson, 1845), 3; cited in Chad Owen Brand and David E. Hankins, *One Sacred Effort: The Cooperative Program of Southern Baptists* (Nashville: B&H, 2005), 2.

[2] Brand and Hankins, *One Sacred Effort*, 91.

In 1925, at the Southern Baptist Convention annual meeting in Memphis, Tennessee, the convention adopted a recommendation from its Future Program Commission, chaired by Louisiana pastor M. E. Dodd. It called its new plan for giving the "Co-Operative Program of Southern Baptists."

In its report at the Cooperative Program's (CP)'inception, the Future Program Commission remarked, "The very difficulties which we have encountered and the testing time through which we have passed have revealed to the denomination its dependable financial resources and strength and have demonstrated beyond question the wisdom and necessity of the Co-Operative plan of Southern Baptists."[3] Thus, in 1925 Southern Baptists adopted a revolutionary model for funding its missions and ministries. It was not met with universal acceptance at first. There was great resistance from various corners of the Southern Baptist globe. However, within a few years people began recognizing the efficiency and genius of this new organization. Over the years millions upon millions of dollars have been given through this collaborative effort to support missions and ministries at every level. Begun as a partnership between the national and state entities and conventions, the amount raised during the first full year of the CP was $4,128,188. The CP has continued to function until this very day. To date, nearly $17 billion ($16,737,922,656) has been given through this collaborative form of ministry.

Decades later, Albert McClellan, longtime Baptist leader with the Executive Committee of the Southern Baptist Convention, called the Cooperative Program "a significant fulfillment of the one sacred effort clause of the 1845 constitution."[4] This ministry-support tool caused Southern Baptists to come of age as a denomination. It allowed them to accomplish a world-changing mission they had embarked upon eight decades earlier.

CURRENT STATUS

During the last complete fiscal year, October 1, 2013, to September 30, 2014, churches forwarded to their respective states $478,700,850 for the CP. Of that amount, $180,971,579 was sent on to the national level. The percentages state conventions have forwarded to the national level have changed over the past few years. Following is a breakdown of how that has changed over the past decade.[5]

---

[3] "First Annual Report of Future Program Commission to Southern Baptist Convention," *1925 SBC Annual* (Nashville: Marshall & Bruce, 1925), 27, cited in Brand and Hankins, *One Sacred Effort*, 2–3.

[4] Cecil and Susan Ray, *Cooperation; The Baptist Way to a Lost World* (Nashville: The Stewardship Commission of the Southern Baptist Convention, 1983), 54, cited in Brand and Hankins, *One Sacred Effort*, 3.

[5] "History of the Division of Cooperative Program Funds Between All State Conventions and the SBC," historical chart maintained by the Executive Committee of the Southern Baptist Convention, http://www.sbc.net/pdf/cp/CPStatistics/HistoryOfDivisionCPFundsBetweenAllStates.pdf. Accessed September 23, 2014.

CP FISCAL YEAR	STATE %	SBC %
2004–05	63.90	36.10
2005–06	63.27	36.73
2006–07	62.66	37.34
2007–08	63.45	36.55
2008–09	62.66	37.34
2009–10	62.33	37.67
2010–11	61.80	38.20
2011–12	61.23	38.77
2012–13	61.97	38.03
2013–14	62.20	37.80

A complete breakdown of the state convention/SBC percentage split since 1925 is printed in an appendix.

The Executive Committee received another $5.59 million in direct gifts for the 2013–14 Cooperative Program Allocation Budget. The breakdown of how the total of $186.5 million was disbursed is as follows:[6]

SBC ENTITIES	CP ALLOCATION BUDGET
International Mission Board	$ 94,048,733
North American Mission Board	$ 42,518,758
Golden Gate Seminary	$ 3,917,738
Midwestern Seminary	$ 4,547,493
New Orleans Seminary	$ 7,095,349
Southeastern Seminary	$ 7,805,315
Southern Seminary	$ 8,959,754
Southwestern Seminary	$ 8,569,970
Historical Library and Archives	$ 447,762
Ethics & Religious Liberty Commission	$ 3,078,366
SBC Operating	$ 5,578,372

This humble beginning in 1925 has truly made a significant difference in the life of Southern Baptists. It has become the primary source of funding the

---

6 "Eighty-Eighth Annual Report of the Executive Committee of the Southern Baptist Convention," *2015 SBC Annual* (Nashville: Executive Committee of the Southern Baptist Convention, 2015), 134.

Convention's collaborative ministries. Yes, other special missions offerings are received each year, such as Lottie Moon Christmas Offering, Annie Armstrong Easter Offering, and state mission offerings. There are a plethora of other calls for funding, but the CP remains the centerpiece and primary means of funding for state and national ministries and missions.

FACTORS WHICH IMPACT COLLABORATIVE MINISTRY

Ethnic Diversity

It is appropriate to highlight the number of churches and church-type missions in our convention. The Annual Church Profile indicated we have 46,499 cooperating churches in 2014. Of those churches note the following diversity:[7]

RACIAL/ETHNIC GROUP	CHURCHES
Anglo	38,808
African-American	2,904
Hispanic-American	1,765
Korean	666
Native American	391
Chinese	170
Other Asian	144

The number of ethnic congregations within our convention has grown dramatically over the last few decades.

Level of Participation

Many have been frustrated that a large number of churches do not give cooperatively at all. In fact, in the last year 17,517 churches either did not submit an Annual Church Profile report or reported no CP gifts at all.[8]

Other interesting facts include the following in 2014:

- The top 2,083 CP-giving churches made up 50 percent of all CP funds received. They averaged giving at a 7.6 percent giving level.[9]
- The top 8,701 CP-giving churches made up 80 percent of all CP funds received. They average a 7.2 percent giving level.[10]

---

[7] "Selected 2013 Annual Church Profile Data by Racial/Ethnic Group" (Alpharetta, GA: Center for Missional Research, North American Mission Board, 2015).

[8] Analysis by the Office of Cooperative Program and Stewardship of the Executive Committee of the Southern Baptist Convention using data from the June 2015 release of the 2014 Annual Church Profile Report by LifeWay Christian Resources of the Southern Baptist Convention, July 2015.

[9] Ibid.

[10] Ibid.

- Over the past seven years, *total receipts* reported by Southern Baptist churches dropped 8 percent (from $12.12 billion in 2008 to $11.15 billion in 2014).[11] This is a significant figure. Charitable giving is up but not to churches.[12]
- Over the past five years, the *dollar* amount received for the SBC portion of CP has declined by 3 percent ($186.5 million to $180.9 million).[13]
- Though the dollar amount has dropped, average church CP percentage has leveled out and has hovered in the 5.4 to 5.5 percent range since 2011—5.407 percent in 2011; 5.414 percent in 2012; 5.50 percent in 2013; and 5.47 percent in 2014.[14]
- In the most recent fiscal year (2014–2015), national CP was up over the previous year by 1.39 percent.[15]

We can rejoice that CP dollars are on the increase. Why is this? Much of the discussion has been positive. Our churches have been challenged to review the CP. They are not asked to give simply out of blind obedience but to give after they have studied it and discover it is the most efficient and effective way to support our cooperative missions and ministries on an ongoing basis.

The staff of the Executive Committee works hard to develop strategies with pastors and churches across the convention. Much travel and energy have been spent in the last several years to connect with churches at every level and at every ethnicity. Personal meetings have been occurring with influential pastors across the convention. A number of churches have crossed the one million dollar per year CP contribution mark, and several are moving in the direction to soon pass that mark. For that we are grateful.

However, we also recognize the vast majority of CP funds come from our churches that are smaller and medium sized. This recognition is crucial. One of the corrective steps taken by the Executive Committee is the development of ministry councils. One of those ministry councils is the Bivocational and Small Membership Church Advisory Group. We are seeking information from these

---

[11] Roger S. Oldham, "National CP Shows Signs of Rebounding," *SBC LIFE* 23 (Spring 2015): 1–2, contains a six-year analysis (2008–2013). 2014 data is from the "Eighty-Eighth Annual Report of the Executive Committee of the Southern Baptist Convention," *2015 SBC Annual* (Nashville: Executive Committee of the Southern Baptist Convention, 2015), 135.

[12] Analysis by the Office of Convention Finance of the Executive Committee of the Southern Baptist Convention using data from "An Overview of Giving in 2012," *Giving USA Highlights*, Giving USA 2013; "An Overview of Giving in 2013," *Giving USA Highlights*, Giving USA 2014; and "An Overview of Giving in 2014," *Giving USA Highlights*, Giving USA 2015 (Indianapolis: Lilly Family School of Philanthropy, Indiana University, Indiana University-Purdue University at Indianapolis, 2013, 2014, 2015).

[13] "Eighty-Eighth Annual Report of the Executive Committee of the Southern Baptist Convention," *2015 SBC Annual*, 133.

[14] Ibid.

[15] Staff, "CP Surpasses Budget Projection for Fiscal Year," Baptist Press, October 2, 2015. Accessed October 7, 2015. http://www.bpnews.net/45593/cp-surpasses-budget-projection-for-fiscal-year.

churches as to how we might better connect with and include them in convention processes.

REASONS FOR PARTICIPATION

Biblical Examples

Collaborative ministry follows a New Testament pattern of churches joining together for various kinds of missions and ministries. The concept of collaborative ministry certainly is a biblical imperative. Hebrews 12:1–2 (HCSB) states:

> Therefore, since we also have such a large cloud of witnesses surrounding us, let us lay aside every weight and the sin that so easily ensnares us. Let us run with endurance the race that lies before us, keeping our eyes on Jesus, the source and perfecter of our faith, who for the joy that lay before Him endured a cross and despised the shame and has sat down at the right hand of God's throne.

One of the interesting calls for action in this passage is that *we* run together the race that has been set before *us*. The plural pronoun is used not once but twice in that first verse. God has set out a race before us, and that race is best run when we run it together. The essence of cooperation finds its basis in a biblical imperative that we work together for the sake of the Lord.

There are multiple examples of collaboration throughout Scripture. Perhaps the greatest number of these examples is found in the book of Acts. In Acts 8:14, when the apostles in Jerusalem heard of the work going on in Samaria, they dispatched Peter and John to the city. They wanted to be a part of what was happening. Another example of collaborative ministry is found in Acts 11:21 when the Jerusalem church sent out Barnabas to visit and check on the evangelistic outreach to the Gentiles.

The New Testament also demonstrates other kinds of collaborative ministry. Financial support for other churches is seen in 1 Corinthians 16 and 2 Corinthians 8–9. Again in Acts 11:27–30 we see this kind of cooperative, supportive ministry.

New Testament churches cared for one another, colabored beside one another, and assisted one another in times of difficulty. They truly did believe there was a race we must run *together*. The Great Commission of the Lord Jesus Christ is best done and accomplished when churches work together collaboratively.

Practical Affirmation

The CP ministry is a collaborative way of doing work that gives all churches a seat at the table. When one recognizes the relatively small number of large churches in our convention, we must recognize the importance of collaborative ministry for the smaller church and the medium-sized church. It truly gives everyone an opportunity to be "at the table." The same is true for the ethnic congregation. Some of these churches, often new to the SBC, have struggled to understand the concept of the CP and are now beginning to be involved at heightened levels. They are seeing that the CP allows everyone an opportunity to be involved.

Let it be stated in more explicit terms. Many people in the twenty-first-century are calling for direct funding of missionaries so the churches can have more control and be "part of the mission ministry." The truth is the International Mission Board, the North American Mission Board, and other entities have always sent out missionaries from the local church! However, funding them is the issue. Megachurches can easily fund missionaries directly. In the churches I have pastored in my two previous full-time pastorates, we could easily raise funds to send missionaries and did so when those missionaries could not go through International Mission Board processes. Yet in a smaller church that becomes far more burdensome. Many churches struggle to pay month-to-month bills, and self-funding a missionary is difficult.

This becomes even more problematic among many of the ethnic congregations. A 2011 Pew Research study showed that the average household wealth (net worth, not income) of the average Anglo-American household is twenty times that of the average African-American household.[16] It is almost as stark a contrast with Latino households. The average Anglo household is eighteen to twenty times wealthier than the average Latino or Hispanic household.[17] Therefore, mission volunteers from an ethnic community have to work twenty times harder to raise their own support. This is a clear recommendation of collaborative ministry, and it points out that small and ethnic churches can always be partners in sending, serving, *and* going when they are a part of giving through the CP.

Executive Committee vice president Sing Oldham stated a concept recently that powerfully illustrates this point: "the principle of collective gain." Though he expands this in other ways using an analogy of a river system, the bottom line is that as churches join together, their collective contributions can make a huge difference when totaled together. Just so, state conventions as they share their portions that are forwarded on to the national convention together make a significant difference. The collective gain "downstream" is staggering.

Oldham uses the analogy of the upper Mississippi, fed, of course, by the mighty Missouri River that begins in the high Rocky Mountains of western Montana and flows through or beside seven western states before bisecting Missouri to empty into the Mississippi River. Farther south, the Mississippi is joined by the Ohio River (which is fed first by the Allegheny and Monongahela Rivers then the Cumberland

---

[16] Rakesh Kochhar, Richard Fry, and Paul Taylor, "Wealth Gaps Rise to Record Highs Between Whites, Blacks, Hispanics," Pew Research Center, July 26, 2011. Accessed September 23, 2014. http://www.pewsocialtrends. org/2011/07/26/wealth-gaps-rise-to-record-highs-between-whites-blacks-hispanics.

[17] Ibid.

and Tennessee Rivers) to form the lower Mississippi, which is later joined by the Arkansas River and others. The result is a mighty outpouring of water resources that makes a huge difference in our nation. Similarly, churches and state conventions joining their collective resources make a mighty difference.

CHALLENGES TO COLLABORATIVE MINISTRY

To say there are challenges to the CP is an understatement. The complexity of the Southern Baptist Convention has brought about a new kind of discussion regarding how to fund the missions and ministries. In the second half of the twentieth century, there was uniformity in programming and understanding of mission support. With new methodologies and ecclesiologies, and sometimes new doctrinal beliefs, come much discussion about how one best funds the needed ministries. As the twenty-first century continues to march along, the individualistic nature of our culture has impacted our churches dramatically, and many seek to do their own work in their own way. A large number of ethnic churches seek to support work that is more connected to their particular people group or homeland from which they came.

State Convention Issues

As one travels around the nation, one quickly begins to pick up on concerns about CP giving which might be related to issues in a particular state convention. In other words, our state partners, with whom we have had working relationships since the beginning of Cooperative Program, are in transition. The Great Commission Task Force (GCR) recommendations, some of which were adopted outright and others referred to the Executive Committee by the convention in 2010 (see appendix),[18] encouraged changes in CP giving percentages. Many state conventions have taken that challenge and are moving toward giving a greater portion of their resources to national missions and ministry causes. This has challenged several of our state conventions. Our state conventions have reduced the number of their employees fairly dramatically. In the last decade the number of state convention employees had declined approximately 1,750 to fewer than 1,350, a 25 percent decrease between 2003 and 2013, with additional loss of staff since then,[19] with the Florida Baptist Convention announcing another 47 percent reduction in staff just two weeks prior to the time of writing (from 115 employees to 61 statewide employees) in order to forward a larger percentage of their CP

---

[18] See items 73–97 in "Proceedings," *2010 SBC Annual* (Nashville: Executive Committee of the Southern Baptist Convention, 2010), 77–98.

[19] Telephone and e-mail interviews with state Baptist convention executive directors, research conducted by the Office of Convention Communications and Relations of the Executive Committee of the Southern Baptist Convention, Spring 2013.

contributions to SBC causes.[20] While a few states have decreased their percentage contributions to the national level, the majority have increased the amount they forward to SBC causes.

What are the serious issues involved here? One of the issues that must be understood and discussed is the sheer amount of lostness in our world compared to the lostness in our own country. With thousands of churches in our states, many pastors believe churches should be responsible for winning the lost and discipling the saved in their respective states. They do not view state convention ministries as necessary, as powerful, or as compelling as they were in previous generations.

Another issue is that many of our "old line" southern state conventions, some of which predate the SBC, deeply connect to institutions that require serious funding. While experts disagree in this area, many of the state convention institutions, such as colleges, children's homes, ministries to the aging, and student/collegiate ministries, require funding. This makes it difficult for these states to respond aggressively in formula changes.

Methodological Changes

Across our convention there is a massive change in both demographic and methodological preferences. These preferences are often inaccurately, described as:

- Individual versus Corporate
- Societal versus Cooperative
- Contemporary versus Traditional
- Young versus Old

This methodological divide is impacting our denominational direction. Even in the past few years, this methodological quandary has impacted some of our denominational entities. It has also dramatically impacted our primary funding source, the CP. Pressure is building in this particular area of convention life. Many are seeking new ways for funding missions and ministries. Many are recognizing the demographic force of individualism that is powerfully at work. Some are calling for a more societal form of giving to missions and ministries that they believe to be more "church-centric" or "Holy Spirit driven." Much of this discussion happens in the context of whether one is more relevant in the twenty-first century or one is tied to an outdated, outmoded method of missions support. Again, many of these characterizations and even caricatures are inaccurate.

The status of our convention is best described as a group of churches in transition but looking for divine intervention. There is hope because of our Lord. There is hope because our entities are more focused than ever. There is hope because

---

[20] Barbara Denman, "Fla. Baptist Conv. to Reduce Staff by 47%," Baptist Press, September 18, 2015, http://www.bpnews.net/45497/fla-baptist-conv-to-reduce-staff-by-47.

many of our younger pastors and leaders are beginning to engage and ponder cooperation. Many are asking hard and thoughtful questions. That gives hope to all the denominational executives.

FUTURE STRATEGY

In light of the current situation, the Executive Committee and other national entities and state conventions have begun a process called Great Commission Advance. If we are to experience true Great Commission advance through the CP, we need renewed:

- **Prayer:** We must undergird a renewed commitment to CP missions with coordinated prayer that invites God's blessing and unites SBC churches and entities in Great Commission advance.
- **Vision:** We are seeking to communicate a renewed, clear, and compelling vision of the CP for both current and future generations.
- **Responsibility:** We must teach every willing Southern Baptist in every Southern Baptist church to embrace personal responsibility for the Great Commission through a balanced Acts 1:8 missional strategy that values cooperation with multiple SBC missions partners.
- **Positioning:** We must continue to work together to position the CP as the preferred and foundational means for SBC churches to implement an intentional and balanced Acts 1:8 missional strategy in obedience to the Great Commission.
- **Partnership:** We are striving to rebuild full trust and CP partnership between national SBC entities, state conventions, and our churches.
- **Customization:** We are currently working with ministry partners to translate and customize cooperative missions conviction to key audiences within the SBC, sustaining positive relationships and dialogue with each of those audiences.
- **Stewardship:** We must challenge every Southern Baptist to a biblical standard of tithing and total life stewardship and a renewed culture of generosity, allowing them to break the bond of materialism and follow God's call to help fulfill the Great Commission.

CONCLUSION

The Cooperative Program has passed its ninetieth year of existence. The billions provided have been powerfully used to build:

- The largest permanent, fully funded **mission force** of international missionaries.

- An aggressive **church-planting movement and strategy** with a goal to plant 15,000 churches over the next decade that involves NAMB, our state and associational partners, and hundreds of sending and supporting churches.
- **Six theological institutions** with more than 18,000 full-time and part-time students, with each seminary among the top ten of all theological institutions in the United States when counting total enrollment.
- **State ministries** including colleges and collegiate ministries, children's homes, homes for aging, church health and revitalization ministries, and many other services.

Acts 1:8 (HCSB) states, "But you will receive power when the Holy Spirit has come on you, and you will be My witnesses in Jerusalem, in all Judea and Samaria, and to the ends of the earth." It is imperative that we understand the power of this message. Two things about this passage stand out. First, the source of power is clearly identified. The hope of our Southern Baptist ministries will not come from denominational resources, missiological expertise, or academic excellence. It will come from the power of the Holy Spirit. All attempts to deal with struggles in our convention will always fail when we attempt to only apply logistical answers to truly spiritual problems. That is a truth every believer must remember daily. The power to be a witness, to be great men and women, to be great churches comes not from studied or purposeful development of skills but only from the power of the Holy Spirit. It is *his* power that we are lacking. It is *his* intervention we need. God will bring a Holy Spirit revival to us. Please, Lord, tarry not.

Not only is his *power* clearly pointed out in this passage; his *plan* is also clearly identified. The geographical spread of the gospel is clearly delineated. No matter where one lives, believers begin witnessing at home and then extend into all the world. As Oswald J. Smith used to say, "The light that shines the farthest will shine the brightest at home."[21]

We desperately need to understand that God wants missions and evangelism to be one and the same. The hope of the Southern Baptist Convention is a Holy Spirit touch from God. That will only come when followers are obedient to his command to be witnesses in every sphere he has outlined.

One of the deep needs in this twenty-first century is for us to emphasize evangelism, as well as missions, church planting, and church expertise. This is nothing new. Fifty years ago Billy Graham said, "In many circles today the Church has an energetic passion for unity, but it has all but forgotten our Lord's commission to evangelize."[22]

---

[21] Cited in Warren Wiersbe, *Be Distinct: Standing Out as God's Unique Creation (2 Kings & 2 Chronicles)* (Colorado Springs: Victor, 2002), 119.

[22] Billy Graham, "Why the Berlin Congress?," World Congress on Evangelism, 1966. Archived at the Billy Graham Center, Collection 14, box 2, folder 2.

How true this word is! We must recognize the need for missions involvement and evangelistic endeavor that is balanced and consistent.

Over and over the need for the CP manifests itself. Several denominational executives, including this author, have pointed out a willingness to move to a new modality of funding if something could be revealed that is more efficient and effective for the long term. To this point no one has stepped forth with anything that would come close to the efficiency and effectiveness of the CO. It is still the best way to see missions and evangelism accomplished by individual believers through their individual churches, even as they collaborate with other churches to impact our nation and the world. God does require his followers to be Acts 1:8 people. When that is accomplished, the tensions that threaten to pull a convention apart will be minimized or eliminated. All believers must become persons on fire for the Lord, people who desperately want to be part of a movement of God that sees the world come to Christ.

By the Numbers: What SBC Demographics Tell Us About Our Past, Present, and Future

Thom S. Rainer

Learning about the history of our families has been in vogue for several years. Millions of people, now aided by such resources as Ancestry.com, are delving into the eras of their previous generations. The past informs our present and possibly projects our future.

Indeed I have found myself somewhat fascinated about my own family history. But even more than I, my brother and other family members have spent hundreds of hours learning more about our past. For those who have never undertaken such endeavors, a word of caution is in order. Be prepared for news about your ancestry that is not so pleasant. Such is the reality of confronting our past.

My hope was to discover I came from the lineage of kings, presidents, and heroes. For the most part, however, I saw more slave owners and swindlers. It was not always a pretty sight.

LEARNING FROM THE NUMBERS OF THE PAST

It is that caution I bring to this chapter. If you are fearful of confronting the brutal facts of your past and present, stop reading now. It will be overall disappointing. But if you are here with the hopes of informing our present with thoughts for the future, please continue reading.

My perspective is a macroview of the Southern Baptist Convention by the numbers since its inception. It does not tell the millions of stories of faithful missionaries, conversions, disaster relief, reunited families, doctrinal faithfulness, steadfast preaching, dynamic discipleship, and community impact. That is the problem with numbers. We know there are stories behind them, but the raw numbers rarely reveal those stories.

The advantage of numbers is their sheer objectivity. Numbers are nothing more than numbers. For sure, they can be interpreted and misinterpreted, but their pure quantitative character does lend a sense of objectivity.

The challenge with the numbers to which I have access is their magnitude. How do I choose from millions of data points submitted since 1845?[1] In that year 4,126 churches of the Southern Baptist Convention submitted a variety of statistics, including baptisms and membership. From 1846 to 1871, reporting was sporadic. Such inconsistencies are understandable. Though the Civil War technically lasted from April 12, 1861, to May 9, 1865, the years before and after were fraught with tension and then rebuilding.

Over the years SBC congregations slowly added items to their annual reports. Here are the first years for different statistical categories:

- Baptisms: 1845
- Total membership: 1845
- Total receipts: 1968
- Sunday school/small group: 1972
- Worship attendance: 1991

There are many other statistical categories on what is now called the Annual Church Profile. In order to provide a reasonable statistical analysis, however, I have limited my research to those five categories plus the total number of churches in the SBC.

The journey has been fascinating if not addictive. I now understand how many people dedicate countless hours of their lives to genealogical discovery. The more you learn, the more you want to learn. But learning implies a willingness to confront brutal facts. Such is the primary lesson I learned on this journey.

The Southern Baptist Convention began in 1845 with a healthy numerical membership. A total of 4,126 churches reported a membership of 351,951. In that same year, the churches reported 23,222 baptisms, approximately one baptism per year for every fifteen members.

The next 170 years have been mostly positive for Southern Baptists, at least from a numerical perspective. But the historical path can provide us insights to our struggles today and perhaps hint toward positive paths forward.

---

[1] The numerical data are derived from the statistical reports of the Southern Baptist Convention from 1845 to 2014. Though it has had several different names in the past, today it is called the Annual Church Profile. State conventions of the Southern Baptist Convention collect the data and send it to LifeWay Christian Resources for consolidation and reporting. As I indicate in this chapter, the statistical categories have changed over the years. All information is submitted voluntarily by individual congregations of the convention.

We will follow the historical path of these numbers to the modern era. In doing so, we will attempt not only to learn from our past but also to see our present and to project our future. In order to provide as much clarity as possible, I limited my historical excursion to five of the most important numerical historical issues. The first of these deals with an extended period where the SBC started few churches.

THE SILENT ERA FOR NEW CHURCHES: 1920 TO 1949

One of the more remarkable strategies of the Southern Baptist Convention has been the historical and modern emphasis on starting new churches. Over the past century that emphasis has come from different organizations. Many local churches have taken the initiative to plant churches. Similarly, new church emphases have emanated from state conventions, some associations, and the North American Mission Board, formerly the Home Mission Board. Many times different combinations of these organizations have worked together to start churches.

New church work has been a major contributor to the lifeblood of the SBC. From a not-so-modest beginning of 4,126 churches, the denomination now has more than 50,000 churches. Though our denomination may show signs of struggle today, it would be immeasurably worse without this emphasis on new churches.

Let us fully grasp the import of new churches. These congregations reach new members who will become our missionaries, pastors, and key lay leaders. They will become our seminary professors and denominational leaders. Without a determined emphasis on starting new churches, the entire denomination suffers.

Such is the reason it is difficult to fathom that the SBC had zero new net churches for a roughly thirty-year period, from 1920 to 1949. Net churches, of course, is the arithmetic totals of new churches started less churches closed. In 1920 the Southern Baptist Convention had 27,444 churches. Thirty years later the number was 27,285, a net growth of negative 159 churches.

The impact of such anemic church planting efforts cannot be overstated. For three decades our total number of churches was stagnant. In the years that followed, church planting yielded an average of 3,000 net new churches per decade. Applying those numbers to the missed opportunities of those thirty years suggests we missed the opportunity to have an additional 9,000 churches in our denomination today.

Those 9,000 churches could have been the homes to hundreds of thousands of new baptized converts, to thousands of missionaries, to countless pastors and church staff, and to even more new churches. Why did one of the largest denominations in history become virtually silent in church planting for thirty years?

Unfortunately, the data are insufficient to determine the precise numbers of church closings versus new churches started. Obviously, there were slightly more closings than plants during this era, but the specific mix cannot be determined.

One can always form hypotheses to test possible reasons for the lack of growth in the number of SBC congregations from the 1920s through the 1940s. For example, were resources depleted after World War I, which preceded this era, or World War II and the Great Depression, which took place during this era? Was this a case of simply inadequate funding or lack of people resources?

I have reservations about this historical explanation. First, our churches typically are more robust and vibrant during difficult times. During times of affluence and calm many of our members are not motivated to evangelize and start new churches.

Second, two other data points suggest that the SBC was reaching people during this time. Annual baptisms increased 93 percent from 1920 to 1949. And church membership increased by 114 percent. There was no shortage of people to start churches. And Southern Baptists historically have not needed significant dollars to plant new congregations. The denomination and its churches had the ability to become a church-planting force, but it did not.

One tidbit of Southern Baptist history may, however, provide some hints into this historical anomaly. In 1919 the convention launched the "$75 Million Campaign." The purpose of the campaign essentially was to fund the national entities in a pre-Cooperative Program era. One of the entities to be funded was the Home Mission Board, with an explicit purpose of starting new churches on behalf of the convention. Is it possible that church leaders viewed this funding as the new alternative to starting churches? Did church leaders relinquish their responsibilities in church multiplication to the national entity?

Then, in 1919, C. S. Carnes, the treasurer of the Home Mission Board, embezzled $909,461 from the entity. To put it in perspective, that amount is equivalent to $12.6 million in today's dollars. It was more than one year's budget of the HMB.[2] A plausible hypothesis, then, is the combination of local churches forsaking church planting and the failed trust in the HMB led to a dearth of new churches. Ultimately, though, a certain answer remains elusive.

THE EVANGELISTIC DENOMINATION OR NOT?

Southern Baptists, perhaps more than most denominations, have touted their convictions about the importance of evangelism. We rightly call ourselves a Great Commission denomination. For certain, the International Mission Board is the

---

[2] Albert McClellan, *The Executive Committee of the Southern Baptist Convention, 1917 to 1994* (Nashville: Broadman, 1985), 98–101.

major international mission agency in the world. Even with the recent financial challenges of the IMB, the mission efforts of Southern Baptists have few peers.

The denomination and international missions are intricately related. The Board of Foreign Missions, later the Foreign Mission Board, was established in 1845, the same year the Southern Baptist Convention began.[3] That year would not end without the appointment of the first missionary for the SBC, Samuel C. Clopton. China was chosen as the first mission field.

Similarly, the denomination has been clearly identified as an evangelistic force in North America. Since SBC churches began reporting statistics, baptisms have been one of the few common metrics. Denominational organizations of the SBC at the national, state, and associational level have historically had personnel specifically emphasizing evangelism. Some of the largest meetings of Southern Baptists historically have been evangelism rallies.

It would thus be unfair to label our denomination as nonevangelistic, even with the declining baptismal statistics of recent years. You will rarely see an organization sustain a Great Commission emphasis as long as Southern Baptists have.

Nevertheless, we cannot ignore the baptismal decline. The numbers shout a reality that is both uncomfortable and challenging. While acknowledging that baptisms are not a perfect metric for conversion growth, they do tell a fascinating story about our denomination.

There are essentially two ways to look at baptism metrics. The most obvious is total baptisms, whether the total is for a church or for the denomination. The second is per capita baptisms, where the number is related to membership or attendance. I prefer the latter metric. For example, you would expect a church of 3,000 members to have more baptisms than a church of 100 members. You can compare the churches easier if the baptismal statistics are expressed as a ratio related to members.

In 2014 the Southern Baptist Convention congregations baptized one person a year for every fifty-one members. Stated more colloquially, it took fifty-one of us a year to reach one person for Christ! In 1950, one of our best years for baptismal effectiveness, it took only eighteen Southern Baptists to reach one per for Christ in a year. According to these metrics, therefore, our denomination was three times more effective at reaching people for Christ sixty years ago than it is today.

The metric of total baptisms tells a similar story. In 1972 the SBC had a total of 445,725 baptisms. In 2014 total baptisms had fallen to 305,301. You would have to go back to 1948 to find baptisms at this low level.

Explanations for the decline are conjecture, but there is sufficient evidence to make educated conjectures. Here are eight possible reasons for the decline in baptisms in the Southern Baptist Convention:

---

[3] James T. Draper with John Perry, *LifeWay Legacy* (Nashville: B&H, 2006), 47–48.

1. *Decline in "cultural baptisms."* Over the past few decades, cultural Christianity has been waning. It is no longer necessary to be a part of a church to be accepted as a good-standing member of a community. We have sufficient anecdotal evidence that suggests many of our baptisms were of unregenerate members.

2. *Greater economic affluence.* Affluence of church members and conversion growth are typically inversely related. While correlation cannot prove causation, there is good reason to believe we stop evangelizing as actively when we have a more comfortable lifestyle. Of course, Southern Baptists have moved more and more to become a suburban and urban denomination from its more modest rural economic roots.

3. *Failure to replace programmatic evangelism.* Programmatic evangelism has been discarded by many congregations as its effectiveness has waned. The problem is that the programmatic approach was not replaced with something else. A church that does not have an intentionality about evangelism is unlikely to be evangelistic.

4. *Busyness of churches.* Church calendars are often filled with more activities than hours in the day. As a consequence, church members can be so busy doing good things that they fail to do the best things, such as evangelism.

5. *Busyness of church members.* Our busy culture does not lend itself toward the intentionality of evangelism. Too many church members have passively disobeyed the Great Commission with calendars filled with temporal activities.

6. *Unbiblical concepts of church membership.* For too many church members, church life has been inwardly focused: What have you done for me lately? The church has become more like a country club than a biblical congregation. Members who are obsessed about getting their own preferences met are not likely to be evangelizing others.

7. *Dissension and conflict.* Church conflict has become normative. Many pastors and church leaders are not tired *of* church, but they are tired *from* church. Conflict and criticisms deplete physical and emotional resources that should be used toward reaching people for Christ.

8. *Prayer deficits.* Evangelism is on the front lines of spiritual warfare. We must not assume we have the charisma or persuasion skills to convert people. The Holy Spirit convicts. We must be praying to the Triune God for his strength, power, and authority.

Though some pundits may suggest the culture is no longer as receptive to the gospel as it was a few decades ago, I am not sure that argument has merit. My research indicates receptivity to the gospel or to a simple invitation to church is high.[4] We may not be reaching people for Christ because we are not trying to reach people for Christ.

So is the Southern Baptist Convention evangelistic? An objective answer would be "yes, but." The numbers tell us we have much for which to be grateful. And the numbers tell us we have much more to do.

ARE WE THEN A SUNDAY SCHOOL DENOMINATION?

We have never been a quiet denomination. At times our spirited temperaments work toward our favor. We can direct our enthusiasm toward evangelism and missions. At other times, however, we focus our energies on disagreements and fight among ourselves. Instead of obeying a Great Commission, we create a great distraction.

One of the more contentious issues in the early history of the Southern Baptist Convention was the decision to form a Sunday School Board. Attempts at this effort failed initially. Indeed, many felt the failed efforts before 1891 were a clear indication the project should be abandoned. Still others maintained a loyalty to the American Baptist Publishing Society.

Eventually, however, the convention decided to present the issue to a vote. The 1891 convention was held in Birmingham.[5] The site was the O'Brien's Opera House on First Avenue. It was the first time in the history of the Southern Baptist Convention the annual meeting was not held in a church facility. Planners anticipated a meeting too large to hold in a church because of the contentious issue of starting a Sunday school entity. They were right.

Even the opera house was not sufficiently spacious for the meeting. James M. Frost, the chairman of the committee to present the recommendation, described the room as "packed to suffocation." A reporter estimated 2,000 people crammed into the theater with 300 more jammed onto the stage. Frost approached the podium to make the recommendation. Many people expected divisive pandemonium to break forth at the moment he concluded his report. After all, starting a new Sunday School Board was one of the most divided decisions the convention would make to this point in its history.

Frost read the report. At his conclusion he put the report down. To the surprise of everyone, there was a surreal quiet and calm in the room. The order of business allowed Frost to speak to the recommendation first. Then the anticipated and acrimonious points and counterpoints were likely to take place.

Instead, someone unexpectedly approached the podium. He was a distinguished man of sixty-four with and neat and flowing beard. Though he held no official position in the convention at that time, everyone knew the man. He was

---

[4] Thom S. Rainer, *The Unchurched Next Door* (Grand Rapids: Zondervan, 2003).
[5] The following story is excerpted from Draper with Perry, *LifeWay Legacy,* 1–19.

Dr. John A. Broadus, cofounder and president of The Southern Baptist Theological Seminary. He had been a proponent of an independent Sunday School Board for years.

No one dared question the breached protocol of the moment. "I have seen for 20 years that we were divided in our preference as to where we should get our Sunday School literature," Broadus began. "And now if a majority favor a Sunday School Board to take in charge our Sunday school literature, let it be done." Broadus paused and then continued in the unusual quiet of the moment. "People have come here feeling that there is to be excitement and a heated debate. I hope they will be disappointed. Orders have been issued for full reports and discussion. I hope there will be nothing to report. I shall be happy if no hot words are said. If anyone says anything about sectionalism he will regret it and, after he has said it, he will wish he had not done so."

The room fell into total silence. No one had expected this development. After a few more moments of awkward silence, a voice came from the crowd: "Question!" When the momentous vote took place, only thirteen persons voted no. Broadus fell back in his chair and, in a moment of relief and joy, cried unashamedly. The Baptist Sunday School Board was born.

This historical excursion into the birth of the Baptist Sunday School Board must end. The assignment of this chapter is simply to try to interpret what the numbers mean. But the numbers of this organization provide potentially helpful insights.

We must first ask what the Sunday school numbers tell us. First, the numbers tell us about men, women, boys, and girls in a small group studying the Bible or, at the very least, biblical truths. One would hope Sunday school growth would be indicative of overall health in the denomination. Unfortunately, we do not have Sunday school or small-group attendance numbers until 1972. Though Sunday school enrollment numbers grew steadily until the 1980s, we can only surmise that attendance followed that same healthy pattern.

One of the more profoundly influential people in Southern Baptist life the first half of the twentieth century was Arthur Flake.[6] Flake headed the influential Sunday School Department of the Sunday School Board from 1920 to 1937. The nearly two decades of leadership he provided shaped our denomination for a half a century. He is best known for his five-step growth process called "Flake's Formula":

- Know the possibilities.
- Enlarge the organization.
- Provide the space.
- Enlist and train the workers.
- Go after the people.

---

[6] A good summary of Flake influence can be found in David Francis, *The 5-Step Formula for Sunday School Growth* (Nashville: LifeWay, 2005).

What is not commonly known about Flake is his insistence on the right teaching of doctrine. He implemented through the Baptist Sunday School Board a class on doctrine for all teachers. No Sunday school teacher, he felt, should begin his or her role without a thorough understanding of the doctrinal truths of Scripture.

The genius of the Flake concept was its trifold emphasis on strong doctrinal teaching, insistence on involvement in a small group, and intentionality about reaching beyond the church's doors. Though the evidence is circumstantial, I am convinced that the best numerical half-century of the SBC, 1920 to 1970, was shaped significantly by Flake.

His approach addressed the issue of the "front door" for churches: intentionality in Great Commission behavior. But he also had the right emphasis on closing the "back door": get people involved in groups and train them in right doctrine. Though Flake's Formula may seem old and antiquated today, his principles are pervasive through generations.

The numerical evidence of Flake's influence is best seen in Sunday school enrollment, which increased from one million in 1920 to over seven million in three decades. Indeed, the Sunday school movement seems to be the primary driver of SBC growth for the twentieth century. But there is good evidence that indicates the Sunday school movement lost its influence around 1970. In the years where we have Sunday school or small group attendance data, 1972 to the present, there has been virtually no growth. To the contrary, average group attendance has remained in a tight range of 3.6 million to 4.1 million for more than forty years. The most recent average attendance for groups is 3.8 million.

Simply stated, the numerical evidence indicates we have not truly been a robust Sunday school denomination for the most recent four decades. It seems as though Southern Baptists follow a common fourfold pattern. First, we have the ingenuity to devise a helpful methodology such as Flake's Formula and Sunday school. Second, we often declare the program to be methodologically salvific with much fanfare. In other words, the program, once the means, becomes the end. Third, after time we discard the program because we deem it irrelevant or because we do not want to be labeled as program driven. Fourth, we do not replace the discarded program with anything else.

There may be a supposition at this point that my solution to the SBC's struggles is simply to return to methodologies of the past. To the contrary, I am not advocating dated methodologies or stale programs. I am seeking the principles behind these approaches to see if they have relevance today.

Neither Flake's Formula nor Sunday school had intrinsic value. Their true value was in what they pointed churchgoers to do: to be intentional about reaching people and to have a place where community and discipleship took place. Many of the churches of the Southern Baptist Convention have lost such intentionality. They, therefore, have closed their front doors and opened their back doors widely. Decline is thus inevitable.

THE INFLUENCE OF AFFLUENCE

Sociologically, religions tend to weaken as wealth increases among its adherents. Theologically, wealth can be a god we worship or an idol we covet. In either case, affluence can potentially be a negative influence on a body of Christians. We rest in the false comfort and assurances of our material possessions and bank accounts.

Though we cannot conclude with causative statements about the growing wealth of Southern Baptist church members and commensurate declines in attendance and membership, the numbers can tell us two realities that need little interpretation. Our challenge, though, is that the Annual Church Profile did not request data on church finances until 1968. Another challenge is that we can only surmise that greater giving among church members is a sign of increased affluence of those families.

The first reality is that Southern Baptist church members are giving to their respective congregations at a much healthier rate today than in years past. For example, the average amount given per member has more than doubled from 1968 to 2014 after being adjusted for inflation. The second reality is that the level of giving per member has not increased in a decade, after proper adjustments for inflation.

So how do we interpret this paucity of financial information? I suggest we do so carefully. Though the raw data of the SBC cannot yield definitive conclusions, it would appear that the growing affluence of the SBC church members can at least partly explain the growth in inflation-adjusted giving. The second conclusion is that for the past decade the SBC has been headed for decline or in decline. Thus total membership giving is declining commensurately.

If our hypothesis is mostly true, then the affluence of our congregational members was a decidedly negative influence on the growth trajectory of our denomination. To what extent this factor affected the SBC would be mostly conjecture. But the evidence, circumstantial as it may be, seems to indicate it has played more than an insignificant role in our decline.

WHERE DO WE GO FROM HERE?

This chapter has numbers, a lot of numbers. Indeed, the accumulation of data since 1845 can lead to analysis paralysis. So let us return to the basics of our issue. We are attempting to make sense of these numbers to understand the past so we can move forward in the future.

What these numbers may hide are the individual congregations behind them. We really should not be speaking of denominational issues as much as we do local church issues. Though the denomination has large organizational structures at the national, state, and associational level, the Southern Baptist Convention is at its core some 50,000 churches and missions.

In some ways it seems we are trying harder to do those things that are not working. While denominational entities at all levels can seek greater efficiencies and stewardship, the real issue is with the local churches. We do not need an improved denomination. We need healthier churches. How can we accomplish that reality?

I have worked with and researched thousands of churches. Though I cannot oversimplify the characteristics of these congregations, I have seen four consistent characteristics of healthy churches.

First, these churches have a strong biblical foundation. The primary purpose of the Conservative Resurgence was to return our denomination and seminaries to the truthfulness of Scripture. We are now training leaders for our churches who believe in the inerrancy and infallibility of the Word of God.

Second, healthy Southern Baptist congregations have been intentional about evangelism. The gospel not only should be believed; it should be shared. I am saddened by the paucity of evangelistic intentionality I see in many of our churches. When Southern Baptists were reaching the culture, there was intentionality about sharing the gospel and inviting people to church to hear the gospel. While programmatic evangelism may have lost its luster in our churches, we must find ways for our members to be intentionally involved in sharing their faith in today's culture. We should not abandon one approach until we have an effective plan for a new approach.

Third, our churches are well above average by almost any metric when we stress the importance of getting members into a small group. In small groups relationships are developed, the Bible is discussed, community takes place, and assimilation is effective. The Sunday school model was effective for a long season. What are we doing to move our people to groups today? What is the plan for the millennial era?

Fourth, and in conclusion, the healthiest congregations are vibrantly intentional about prayer. As was in the early church, they devote themselves to prayer. The members understand that human power is woefully inadequate. When our churches demonstrate complete dependence on God and his power, the congregations have health and power because the Triune God is its source.

So, what are the numbers telling us? Perhaps it is simplifying the issue too much, but it appears that the numbers are telling us we have lost our focus. We have become complacent and comfortable. That is the bad news we have learned from our ancestral study. Perhaps we can turn these bad trends to good, but it will not come because we are doing the same things we have been doing with greater zeal. The time has come for new wineskins. How can we help our churches evangelize the culture of today? What models can we create in our church where more members are in groups together? How can we encourage a new and renewed emphasis on the power of prayer?

These are the questions we must be asking. These are the questions we must be answering. And these are the actions we must be taking. Then, in the hope and power of God, we may see a new and healthy trend in the numbers. And, by the grace of God, those numbers will tell us that we are truly rebuilding the house of God.

From Babylon Baptist to Baptists in Babylon: The SBC and the Broader Evangelical Community

Collin Hansen and Justin Taylor

M y (Collin) conversation with this Southern Baptist leader concerned evangelicals in elite private universities. Curiously, at least to me as a young journalist, he did not personally identify with evangelicals. Those Yankee evangelicals adopted an adversarial posture toward the university administration, he said, as if students needed to choose between Christ and mainstream acceptance. But where he came from, Southern Baptists and the establishment were one and the same. You do not need to choose between Christ and culture when Christians are the culture.

This Southern Baptist leader and I spoke in 2005 in the wake of the "values voter" election when Southern Baptists and evangelicals helped propel President George W. Bush to reelection on a platform that included seeking a constitutional amendment banning same-sex marriage. Neither of us knew it at the time, but this election marked the end of a remarkable era of Southern Baptist influence in presidential politics. In the previous quarter-century, Southern Baptists had elected two of their own in Jimmy Carter (1976–1980) and Bill Clinton (1992–2000). In part due to buyer's remorse over the liberal social policies of these Democratic presidents, they supplied electoral muscle to candidates favored by the nascent Religious Right, including Ronald Reagan (1980–1988) and later George W. Bush (2000–2008). Even before then, the most famous Southern Baptist of them all—Billy Graham—became a close adviser during turbulent times to Lyndon Johnson (1963–1968) and Richard Nixon (1968–1974).

But starting in 2006 with a midterm electoral rebuke to George W. Bush, and continuing under the presidency of Barack Obama (2008–2016), Southern Baptists no longer play White House kingmaker. So long a fixture of mainstream America, Southern Baptists have been marginalized by the culture's sharp liberal turn, especially in sexual morality.

Much like evangelicals.

Between the late 1970s and early 1990s, as the battles raged over theological direction in the Southern Baptist Convention, many leaders on both sides could still find agreement on one point: we are not evangelicals. Foy Valentine, who served on the eve of Carter's election as executive secretary of the Southern Baptist Christian Life Commission (now the Ethics & Religious Liberty Commission) talked to *Newsweek* magazine for its landmark "year of the evangelicals" cover story. The moderate Baptist leader, noted for his support of the *Roe v. Wade* decision in 1973, told Kenneth Woodward, "We are not evangelicals. That's a Yankee word. They want to claim us because we are big and successful and growing every year. But we have our own traditions, our own hymns and more students in our seminaries than they have in all of theirs put together."[1]

Adrian Rogers, an unlikely ally to Valentine as one the leaders of the Conservative Resurgence in the SBC, shared this perspective. Duane Litfin, who would later become president of Wheaton College, recalls: "We lived for almost a decade in Memphis, and one of my good friends there was Adrian Rogers. Adrian would always make a point of it: 'We are not evangelicals,' he would say. 'We are Baptists.'"[2]

In 1979, the same year Rogers was elected SBC president for the first time—a watershed event in twentieth-century American religion—the Southern Baptist Theological Seminary in Louisville, Kentucky, hosted the liberal World Council of Churches. By contrast, as Southern Baptist theologian and historian Timothy George observes, the flagship SBC seminary never hosted some of the most distinguished evangelical advocates for biblical inerrancy, the cause that propelled Rogers to denominational leadership. Such noted evangelical theologians as J. I. Packer, Kenneth Kantzer, and Carl F. H. Henry were not invited to Southern Seminary.[3]

Had Southern Baptists at places like Southern Seminary always differentiated themselves from evangelicals? Not according to Southern Seminary historian and dean Gregory A. Wills: "The popularity and influence of the faculty went far

---

[1] Quoted in Kenneth L. Woodward, "Born Again! The Year of the Evangelicals," *Newsweek* 88 (October 25, 1976), 76.

[2] Duane Litfin, "The Future of Evangelicalism (and Southern Baptists)," in *Southern Baptists, Evangelicals, and the Future of Denominationalism,* ed. David S. Dockery (Nashville: B&H, 2011), 100.

[3] Timothy George, "With David Dockery Among Baptists and Evangelicals," in *Convictional Civility: Engaging the Culture in the 21st Century: Essays in Honor of David S. Dockery,* ed. C. Ben Mitchell, Carla D. Sanderson, and Gregory A. Thornbury (Nashville: B&H Academic, 2015), 16.

beyond the borders of the Southern Baptist Convention." Wills cites J. P. Boyce speaking at the New York Chautauqua in 1880 and 1881 as an example. John Broadus was in higher demand in the North than the South, even turning down consideration as president of the new University of Chicago, funded by John D. Rockefeller. He stayed at Southern Seminary and became its president in 1889.[4]

The relationship, then, between Southern Baptists and evangelicals has never been static. Sometimes SBC moderates have distanced themselves from evangelical theology they regarded as too conservative. And sometimes SBC conservatives have distanced themselves from evangelical theology they regarded as too moderate. Sometimes evangelicals have downplayed their Southern Baptist credentials. And sometimes evangelicals have played up their Southern Baptist credentials as the thing more evangelicals need.[5]

We will assess various approaches in four pairs of representative Southern Baptist evangelicals from the latter half of the twentieth century and the first decades of the twenty-first. Writing as evangelicals who are not Southern Baptists but who have greatly profited from our relationship with Southern Baptists, we aim to show why evangelicals need Southern Baptist conviction and why Southern Baptists need evangelical experience. The journey begins at Babylon Baptist Church and ends with Baptists in Babylon.

SOUTHERN BAPTIST BY NAME, EVANGELICAL BY REPUTATION: CARL F. H. HENRY AND BILLY GRAHAM

Among all the varied and conflicted spiritual influences of Carl F. H. Henry's childhood on Long Island (b. 1913), Baptists were not among them. But after his conversion in 1933 and subsequent matriculation at Wheaton College, Henry developed baptistic convictions, and he was immersed at the unforgettably named Babylon Baptist Church on Long Island in 1937. He later enrolled at Northern Baptist Seminary in Chicago.[6]

Henry is probably best known to history as the first editor of *Christianity Today*, where he started in 1956. Working in offices near the White House as a symbolic gesture of evangelical intent to rub shoulders in the halls of power, he joined Capitol Hill Baptist Church. He retained that membership until his death in 2003. As Southern Baptists following the Conservative Resurgence have

---

[4] Gregory A. Wills, *Southern Baptist Theological Seminary, 1859–2009* (New York: Oxford University Press, 2009), 179.

[5] For various perspectives on the relationship, see Leo Garrett Jr., E. Glenn Hinson, and James E. Tull, *Are Southern Baptists "Evangelicals"?* (Macon, GA: Mercer University Press, 1982), followed by David S. Dockery, ed., *Southern Baptists and American Evangelicals: The Conversation Continues* (Nashville: B&H, 1993).

[6] Carl F. H. Henry, "Fifty Years a Baptist," in *Why I Am a Baptist*, ed. Tom J. Nettles and Russell D. Moore (Nasvhille: B&H, 2001), 210.

sought to achieve academic respectability and cultural relevance while maintaining biblical fidelity, the late Henry continues to mentor young scholars through his writing.[7] But during his lifetime Henry was known more as pioneer of the postwar neoevangelical movement than as a Southern Baptist churchman. The location of his archives at Trinity Evangelical Divinity School (TEDS), affiliated with the Evangelical Free Church of America, indicates his primary association with the major evangelical institutions in the Chicago area. For most of his life, he was a prophet without honor in his chosen denomination as he fought theological drift among Northern Baptists and at Fuller Theological Seminary, where he was a founding faculty member.

Born to Presbyterian parents, Billy Graham was baptized as an infant in 1919. He was saved as a teenager in 1934 under the preaching of influential Southern Baptist evangelist Mordecai Ham and then baptized by immersion as a college student. He was baptized again by immersion in 1938 when he realized that his ministry would be hindered if he were not baptized as a professing believer in a Southern Baptist church.[8] Graham in those days was still sorting out his future; he also attended two fundamentalist schools before settling on Wheaton College. There he met his wife, Ruth Bell, daughter of Presbyterian missionaries to China. In more than sixty-three years of marriage, she never joined Graham in Southern Baptist church membership.

Graham's autobiography devotes two chapters to Southern Baptist presidents of the United States (Jimmy Carter and Bill Clinton) but none to the battles over the Bible that tore through his denomination between the late 1970s and mid-1990s as his ministry increasingly focused on international affairs such as ending nuclear proliferation. Graham never hid his Southern Baptist ordination, hard earned in his youth under scrutiny from a collection of country preachers. But with a parish the size of the globe, Graham transcended denominational politics and geography as he put a charming smile on the face of global evangelicalism.

Neither man will be primarily remembered for his work in denominational machinery. But Henry and Graham each loaned considerable authority to young Southern Baptists at crucial turning points. And those leaders would rise to key positions of influence inside the convention and beyond in the wider evangelical movement.

---

[7] See, for example, Gregory Alan Thornbury, *Recovering Classic Evangelicalism: Applying the Wisdom and Vision of Carl F. H. Henry* (Wheaton: Crossway, 2013). Thornbury earned his PhD at Southern Seminary under Albert Mohler and later served as dean under David Dockery at Union University, a college in the Southern Baptist tradition located in Jackson, Tennessee. He is now president of King's College in New York City. See also Matthew J. Hall and Owen Strachan, eds., *Essential Evangelicalism: The Enduring Influence of Carl F. H. Henry*, ed. Matthew J. Hall and Owen Strachan (Wheaton: Crossway, 2015). Hall and Strachan are professors and administrators in Southern Baptist Schools (Southern Seminary and Midwestern Baptist Theological Seminary, respectively).

[8] Billy Graham, *Just As I Am* (New York: HarperCollins, 1997), 56.

While serving on faculty with Henry at TEDS, New Testament scholar D. A. Carson served as a carrier for an important letter from Henry to Mark Dever, a Cambridge University student completing doctoral studies on the Puritan theologian Richard Sibbes. Henry wanted Dever to be considered as pastor of his home congregation, Capitol Hill Baptist Church, a couple blocks from the Supreme Court building. Dever would assume the role of senior pastor in 1994, and his subsequent influence as an evangelist, preacher, networker, writer, and ecclesial theologian has extended far beyond the SBC.[9]

Around this same time Graham offered his support to Mohler as the young Southern Seminary president struggled to consolidate leadership and enforce the Abstract of Principles adopted by the school's founders in 1858. During his inauguration, Mohler announced plans to launch the Billy Graham School of Missions, Evangelism, and Church Growth. At a time when Southern Baptist churches throughout Louisville closed their doors to Mohler and his family, Graham preached his inauguration service at Freedom Hall in October 1993. According to Wills,

> Graham's support gave the school credibility and momentum. . . . The Billy Graham School also afforded Mohler the opportunity to recruit conservative scholars to compose the faculty of the growing school. The Graham School professors were an important counterweight to the faculty's moderate majority during the years of transition.[10]

To illustrate just how much conservative Southern Baptists owed to the broader evangelical movement led by Graham and Henry, consider the schools from which Mohler recruited his new faculty: TEDS, Gordon-Conwell Theological Seminary (cofounded by Graham), Dallas Theological Seminary, Taylor University, and Wheaton College. Mohler and other Southern Baptist conservatives could never have reformed their convention without help from fellow evangelicals.

EDUCATIONAL PIONEERS INSIDE AND OUTSIDE THE SBC: DAVID DOCKERY AND TIMOTHY GEORGE

As far as David Dockery (b. 1952) and Timothy George (b. 1950) are concerned, there has never been a debate about whether Southern Baptists should be regarded as evangelicals. George recounts:

> One of the things that drew David and me together in the early days of our friendship was a clear sense that this dichotomy was unhealthy, unnecessary, and based on a fallacious reading of Baptist history. It seemed obvious to us that,

---

[9] Personal correspondence from D. A. Carson to the authors, February 18, 2016.
[10] Wills, *Southern Baptist Theological Seminary, 1859–2009*, 544–45.

of course, Southern Baptists were evangelicals—admittedly evangelicals with their own Southern-fried distinctives, one of which was the very denominational cocooning that downplayed their affinity with other like-minded evangelical believers.[11]

Arguably no other leaders in the last half century have straddled the fence between Southern Baptists and evangelicals with such balance as George and Dockery. Both are active Baptist churchmen and have contributed to Baptist life and scholarship, beginning with their first scholarly collaboration on Baptist theologians.[12] Both men served with Chuck Colson on the Prison Fellowship Board, and both held the Carl Henry Chair of the theology committee for the organization.

George has been a longtime member of *Christianity Today*'s editorial board and an advisory life trustee of Wheaton College. In 1988 he became the founding dean of the interdenominational Beeson Divinity School in the heavily Southern Baptist state of Alabama, and he has recruited faculty from Wheaton and TEDS. He previously taught church history at Southern Seminary, where he instructed both Dever and Mohler.

Dockery has served as a board member for *Christianity Today*'s parent company, Christianity Today International, and was one of the first Southern Baptists to become active in the Evangelical Theological Society in the 1980s. He is now president of TEDS after a long and illustrious stint in charge of Union University, a school affiliated with the Tennessee Baptist Convention and located in Jackson, Tennessee. A native of Birmingham, Alabama, he previously served as chief academic officer of Southern Seminary, an appointment that came in the middle of the most heated battles between moderates and conservatives over control of the school.

The move from Southern Baptist to evangelical schools illustrates an ongoing trend in the historical relationship between these overlapping Protestants. While Graham and Henry built an evangelical foundation that supported the recovery of Southern Baptist institutions, George and Dockery earned their stripes in Southern Baptist institutions so they could strengthen evangelicals in their current positions.

As evangelicals, Dockery and George have great appreciation for gospel believers of various denominations. They are both known for their efforts at fostering church unity. But as Southern Baptists they critique evangelicals for neglecting the centrality of the local church. Dockery writes:

---

[11] Timothy George, "With David Dockery Among Baptists and Evangelicals" in *Convictional Civility*, 17.

[12] David S. Dockery and Timothy George, *Baptist Theologians* (Nashville: Broadman, 1990), updated as David S. Dockery and Timothy George, *Theologians of the Baptist Tradition* (Nashville: B&H, 2001). Both men are also profiled in their own right as Baptist theologians in James Leo Garrett Jr., *Baptist Theology: A Four-Century Study* (Macon, GA: Mercer University Press, 2009) 696–700, 704–9.

If I were to ask you, "What is the connection between Rick Warren, Chuck Colson, Carl F. H. Henry, Harold Lindsell, and Billy Graham?" the answer would probably not be obvious to some, but all had or have their membership in Southern Baptist churches. Yet hardly anyone thinks of them as Southern Baptists. Their identity comes from a parachurch group, a social network, or an organization, rather than a denomination.[13]

Dockery does not just want more credit for Southern Baptists. He recognizes a weakness in the evangelical generation of Henry and Graham. He says evangelicals have fallen short in their teaching on ecclesiology. Local churches have a place in God's plan of discipleship that parachurch organizations can only supplement, never supplant. Likewise, George says, "Ecclesiology is the new frontier of evangelical theology in the 21st century," and "In the future, I do not think anything is going to be more urgent than the question of the church. What is the church? How are we as faithful, believing Christians to relate the church and the gospel?"[14]

As leaders of evangelical seminaries, George and Dockery are in prime position to help future pastors answer just these questions. As Southern Baptists and other evangelicals feel increasingly marginalized from a culture like Babylon, ecclesiology might seem less important than apologetics or evangelism. But without visible, vibrant communities of faith that teach believers to obey everything Jesus commanded, the Great Commission cannot be fulfilled (Matt 28:18–20). As George and Dockery know from experience, Southern Seminary could never have been recovered without the leadership of local churches. An evangelical movement that relies too much on parachurch institutions such as colleges and universities, which depend heavily on federal funding, is vulnerable to collapse under sustained social and political pressure. In part due to the influence of George and Dockery, ecclesial theologians such as Dever have offered some of most biblical, balanced reflection on how to survive our cultural crisis.[15]

SOUTHERN BAPTISTS TRIED AND TRUE: ALBERT MOHLER AND RUSSELL MOORE

Russell Moore (b. 1971) grew up in Biloxi, Mississippi, the proud son of Woolmarket Baptist Church. They loved the Bible. They revered Billy Graham. They fought in business meetings. What could be more Baptist than this trinity?

---

13 David S. Dockery, "So Many Denominations: The Rise, Decline, and Future of Denominationalism," in *Southern Baptists, Evangelicals, and the Future of Denominationalism*, 21.

14 Timothy George, "The Faith, My Faith, and the Church's Faith," in Dockery, ed., *Southern Baptists, Evangelicals, and the Future of Denominationalism*, 88.

15 Mark Dever, "How to Survive a Cultural Crisis," *The Gospel Coalition* (May 27, 2013). Accessed February 20, 2016. http://www.thegospelcoalition.org/article/how-to-survive-a-cultural-crisis.

Soon Moore would discover that he had much to learn about the state of the SBC in the mid-1980s.

> I remember the day, however, when as a college student I began to question whether my home congregation was even Baptist at all. A bright, articulate Baptist minister told me that the doctrinal convictions I had been taught were not distinctively Baptist, but instead were "evangelical," maybe even "fundamentalist." Real Baptists, he insisted, did not believe in an "old Princeton" concept like biblical inerrancy. Baptists, he said, held to the Baptist distinctives of soul competency, the priesthood of the believer, believer's baptism, separation of church and state, and religious liberty. Baptists were not "creedalists," like my home church seemed to have been.[16]

Moore had stumbled into the Baptist identity debates between moderates and conservatives that would continue to dominate the next decade of denominational politics. He did not know that his denomination had become the chief front in a war over inerrancy that had turned evangelicals against one another and divided schools in the previous two decades.

Eventually he would become dean of the School of Theology at Southern Seminary (2004–2013) and now serves as president of the Ethics & Religious Liberty Commission (2013–present). For much of Moore's childhood, evangelicals ran a number of schools such as Beeson, TEDS, and Gordon-Conwell that were more conservative than Southern Seminary. By the time he would earn his PhD at Southern in 2002, the school would be more conservative than nearly any other evangelical school. At one point almost invisible at such meetings as the Evangelical Theological Society, Southern Baptists would fill the program pages by the early 2000s.

The school's conservative ascendancy and Moore's move to the ERLC would coincide with the waning influence of the Religious Right, which had been led in part by his predecessor, Richard Land. As Southern Seminary would become a kind of Jerusalem for conservative evangelicals, America would feel more like Babylon. Tested and triumphant in battles that threatened to send the SBC down the same path as moribund mainline denominations, Moore and his generation of Baptists know that compromise with the world will always be tempting but never true to the teaching and example of Jesus Christ (John 16:33).

Probably no conservative evangelical today has more consistently warned against the Babylonian takeover than Albert Mohler (b. 1959), current president of Southern Seminary.[17] A former assistant to retiring moderate president Roy

---

[16] Russell D. Moore, "Baptist After All: Resurgent Conservatives Face the Future," in *Why I Am a Baptist*, 234.
[17] See, for example, his books *Culture Shift: The Battle for the Moral Heart of America* (Colorado Springs: Multnomah, 2011) and *We Cannot Be Silent: Speaking Truth to a Culture Redefining Sex, Marriage, and the Very Meaning of Right and Wrong* (Nashville: Thomas Nelson, 2015).

Honeycutt, Mohler was initially suspected by some of harboring liberal tendencies. But he dispelled those notions with his aforementioned faculty hires and eventually his outspoken views on cultural issues.

Mohler's influence among evangelicals as a cultural commentator and leader in such interdenominational initiatives as Together for the Gospel and The Gospel Coalition does not detract from his primary identity as a Baptist. As Wills recounts in his history of Southern Seminary, Mohler faced pressure to turn the school into a mainstream evangelical seminary. Some professors lobbied for uniformity on inerrancy but latitude on gender roles. In other words, they wanted a school like Beeson, TEDS, or Gordon-Conwell. In response Mohler said Southern Baptist had founded and funded the school and that he had no mandate to broaden its doctrinal basis, even to include other evangelicals. "The Southern Baptist identity functioned to prescribe the character of the school," Wills writes, "whereas evangelical identity could function only descriptively."[18]

So as social pressure on evangelicals increases and some prominent leaders abandon traditional evangelical beliefs, Mohler sees his Baptist identity as necessary ballast for an evangelical movement lacking accountable leadership. One can see his "confessional evangelical" perspective in his rejoinder to "generic evangelical" John G. Stackhouse Jr.:

> There is no evangelical high court. In the end, this is one of the limitations of evangelicalism as a movement.
>
> All this reminds me how thankful I am as a Baptist before I am an evangelical. As a member of a Baptist church and as a professor within a Southern Baptist seminary, I am held accountable, with all of my fellow members and colleagues, to certain definite beliefs that are explicitly stated in confessional form. John may be right that there is no evangelical magisterium that can prevent anyone from claiming to be an evangelical, no matter how divergent his or her theology may be. But my church can and should impose its discipline, even as my denomination should protect its membership and my seminary must ensure the orthodoxy of its faculty. In other words, John's essay helps me to affirm even more energetically my belief that the only way evangelicalism can be retained as a definable theological movement is by means of a glad and eager confessionalism. The largely parachurch character of evangelicalism ensures that this will be difficult. That is why, at the end of it all, John's fascinating essay reminds me that evangelical, no matter how well defined, is just not enough. The term is essential as it points to a movement, but that may well be the extent of its usefulness.[19]

---

[18] Wills, *Southern Baptist Theological Seminary, 1859–2009*, 537.

[19] R. Albert Mohler Jr., "A Confessional Evangelical Response," in *Four Views on the Spectrum of Evangelicalism*, ed. Andrew David Naselli and Collin Hansen (Grand Rapids: Zondervan, 2011), 154–55.

Moore and Mohler might be the two preeminent voices among evangelicals on cultural developments at a time of unprecedented social change. They intend to lead evangelicals by being Baptists.

BAPTISTS FOR WORLD EVANGELISM:
MATT CHANDLER AND DAVID PLATT

Thus far we have focused on Southern Baptist leaders—Graham and Henry, Dockery and George, Mohler and Moore—whose primary vocation and identity reside outside the local church. While all have been committed to the local church, they became widely known in their capacities as leaders of institutions and organizations (CT and BGEA, TEDS and Beeson, SBTS and ERLC) designed to serve and strengthen the local church. In addition, the preceding three pairs have not made foreign missions and church planting a major focus of their attention. Matt Chandler (b. 1974) and David Platt (b. 1979)—two of the best-known Southern Baptists in the thirty-something to forty-something age range—are different in all of these regards. They not only see themselves as Daniels in Babylon but also operate with a sense of urgency to multiply Daniels in the Babylons around the world. They represent two possible trajectories for a younger generation that is somewhat ambivalent about denominations but recognizes their utility for advancing the Great Commission.

Chandler, raised as a military brat with a difficult home life, was converted to Christ in high school through the witness of a football teammate. Ever since that time, his vocational ministry has been associated with Southern Baptists. After graduating from high school, he served as the youth pastor of a small Southern Baptist church, Highland Baptist Church (LaMarque, Texas), before enrolling in Hardin-Simmons University (Abilene, Texas), associated with the Baptist General Convention of Texas. Having earned a bachelor's degree in Bible, he joined the pastoral staff for a few years at another Southern Baptist church, Beltway Park Church (Abilene, Texas). He also led a growing interdenominational Bible study and began to receive invitations for itinerant speaking.

Given that Chandler was still a relatively new Christian with an increasingly popular ministry, the question of seminary was natural. But further formal theological education was not in his future. Chandler, now newly married to his wife, Lauren, started seminary twice—once at Logsdon School of Theology (at Hardin-Simmons) and once at Southern Seminary, but dropped out both times. "Seminary," he writes, "felt to me like I was laying a foundation in a house I was already living in."[20]

---

[20] Matt Chandler, "Thoughts Concerning Seminary," *The Village Blog*, February 12, 2009. Accessed February 20, 2016. http://www.thevillagechurch.net/the-village-blog/thoughts-concerning-seminary.

Chandler next moved to Dallas, where he focused on his itinerant speaking ministry. In 2002 he was approached by Highland Village First Baptist Church (Highland Village, Texas), a baby boomer congregation of 168 people willing to invest their future in this confident and charismatic twenty-seven-year-old. Chandler accepted the invitation and became their lead pastor.

Highland Village First Baptist Church was the result of Southern Baptist churches planting churches—a church plant of a church plant of a church plant, to be exact, dating back to 1869. Though the Baptist church is still incorporated under its full original name, Chandler wanted to change its public presentation and reputation. Since 2002, it has operated publicly as "The Village Church." Dropping the Baptist nomenclature was seen as "a means of eliminating obstacles that prevent people from exploring the claims of Christ through a local church." The church explains: "This in no way separates us from our Baptist heritage but enables us to be more effective for the Lord Jesus Christ."[21]

With five campuses spread throughout the Dallas–Fort Worth metroplex, the church now has about fifteen thousand attendees each weekend, making it one of the ten largest churches in the SBC.[22] But Chandler is not a church-growth pragmatist. When he arrived at the Village Church, two of his strong points of emphasis were unpopular among boomer Southern Baptists: covenant membership and Calvinistic soteriology. Chandler insisted on both, and the church grew exponentially.

In the fall of 2002, Chandler met with a group of leaders at the Village Grill restaurant. Sitting at a table covered with butcher paper and crayons for doodling, Chandler began to sketch his vision for the church. He began with a circle in the middle, with several lines emanating from it. The center represented The Village Church, and the lines emanating from it represented churches they would plant for the glory of God. The Village Church would be a Great Commission church—not merely multiplying in size through evangelism but multiplying exponentially through church planting.[23]

One manifestation of this vision is Chandler's involvement with the Acts 29 church-planting network.[24] Chandler states that The Village Church joined Acts

---

[21] The Village Church, "What Is Our Denominational Affiliation?," February 2, 2009, http://www.thevillagechurch.net/sermon/what-is-our-denominational-affiliation.

[22] Thom Rainer, "2014 Update on Largest Churches in the Southern Baptist Convention," Thomrainer.com (blog), July 12, 2014. Accessed February 21, 2016. http://thomrainer.com/2014/07/2014-update-largest-churches-southern-baptist-convention. At time of writing, The Village Church has about eight thousand members. The large ratio of attendees to members is the inverse of many Southern Baptist churches, whose member roles far exceed the number of those who come each week.

[23] The Village Church, "The Village Church Campus Transition." Accessed February 21, 2016. http://www.thevillagechurch.net/the-village-church-campus-transitions.

[24] Acts 29 is a network of church-planting churches that embrace five distinctive theological foundations: they (1) are passionate about gospel centrality; (2) enthusiastically embrace the sovereignty of God's grace in saving sinners; (3) recognize and rest upon the necessity of the empowering presence of the Holy Spirit for all of life

29 in 2004 because of their desire to plant churches and because at that time the SBC had a failure rate of about 70 percent with its church plants. He did not want to entrust the young men of their church to what he perceived to be poor assessment, training, and coaching.[25] Where the SBC is perceived to be weak, Chandler will use other means to further the Great Commission. But where it can help, he will partake, promote, and invest.

In 2012 Chandler was appointed president of the network, succeeding its controversial and beleaguered founder Mark Driscoll. Chandler immediately insisted that the network become known for four things: (1) planting churches that plant churches; (2) holiness and humility; (3) radical diversity; (4) seriousness about evangelism and conversions. When asked if Acts 29 plans on becoming a denomination, Chandler responds: "No intention. I'm already involved in the Southern Baptist Convention."[26]

Chandler and The Village Church's involvement in the SBC represents another form of cooperation with the broader evangelical community. The church remains in partnership with the Denton Baptist Association, the Baptist General Convention of Texas, and the Southern Baptist Convention—all three of which contributed financial support to establish the church. When asked why they do not become an independent church, The Village Church responds that they are already autonomous, just like every SBC church. While they do not send "messengers" to the annual convention, they do participate in the Cooperative Program, allowing them to be a part of the largest missionary organization in the world.[27]

Chandler can be viewed as a friendly critic of the SBC, a grateful beneficiary, and an increasingly popular influencer. Although his personal and ecclesiastical lack of engagement with denominational politics necessarily limits his formal influence within the denomination, he is widely respected—especially among younger, Reformed-leaning evangelicals in the SBC. His availability to speak at SBC seminaries and events, his willingness to self-identify with the SBC as a denomination, and his engagement with organizations like the ERLC, ensure that Chandler (and by extension Acts 29) will continue to influence and be influenced by the SBC.

---

and ministry; (4) are deeply committed both to the fundamental spiritual and moral equality of men and women and to men as responsible servant-leaders in the home and church; (5) embrace a missionary understanding of the local church and its role as the primary means by which God chooses to establish his kingdom on earth. Further, they hold to the Lausanne Covenant Statement of Faith. See Acts 29, "About." Accessed February 21, 2016. http://www.acts29.com/about.

[25] Acts 29, "2015 Annual Report." Accessed February 21, 2016. http://www.acts29.com/wp-content/uploads/2015/06/A29-AnnualReport-2015.pdf.

[26] Joe Maxwell, "Matt Chandler, the Preacher Stung by Joy," *Christianity Today*, May 13, 2014. Accessed February 21, 2016. http://www.christianitytoday.com/ct/2014/may/matt-chandler-preacher-stung-by-joy.html.

[27] The Village Church, "What Is Our Denominational Affiliation?" The use of the word "delegates" instead of the preferred term "messengers" tends to reinforce the point.

In many ways David Platt—the current president of the SBC's International Mission Board (IMB)—appears to be very different from Chandler. Unlike Chandler, Platt grew up in a Christian home. And unlike Chandler, Platt seemed determined to pursue every educational degree available. After graduating from the University of Georgia with two BAs, he went on to earn an MDiv, a ThM, and a PhD from New Orleans Baptist Theological Seminary. After completing his doctorate, he remained at the SBC school as dean of chapel and assistant professor of expository preaching and apologetics.

Platt's vocational involvement with the local church began at Edgewater Baptist Church in New Orleans, only to have all of his earthly goods within their parsonage destroyed by the flooding from Hurricane Katrina in August 2005. From there, at the age of twenty-eight, Platt became the pastor of the Church at Brook Hills in Birmingham, Alabama. John Vaughn—the researcher who helped to coin the term *megachurch*—said he was unable to recall hearing of such a young minister becoming the senior minister of such a large church.[28] Platt may have become the youngest megachurch pastor in modern evangelical history.

As the church grew, Platt became increasingly known in Southern Baptist circles through his speaking engagements at SBC seminaries, churches, conferences, and mission endeavors. But Platt also seemed to share some of Chandler's denominational ambivalence. Like The Village Church, Brook Hills did not use the word *Baptist* in its name. Early in his days at Brook Hills, Platt told *Christianity Today* that he did not believe "loyalty to a denomination is a biblical priority for the church." He affirmed the value of denominations like the SBC but primarily in an instrumental sense: "If it helps the church better accomplish missions goals, it's a good thing. . . . Denominations can be helpful, particularly in organizing for overseas work."[29]

Platt's perspective was increasingly shaped by his passion to see the gospel preached where Christ has not yet been named (Rom 15:20). He was deeply humbled and challenged as he taught Christians in underground churches in Asia, where underresourced pastors implored him to teach the Bible book by book day after day, late into the night. He became increasingly disillusioned with the American Dream, culminating in his *New York Times* best-selling 2010 jeremiad, *Radical: Taking Back Your Faith from the American Dream.*

In this book Platt recounts the growing tension in his soul as he took the helm of a wealthy American megachurch. He contrasted his first Sunday behind the pulpit of the affluent Birmingham congregation with his teaching at underground house churches in Asia just three weeks earlier: "As a new pastor comparing the images around me that day with the pictures still fresh in my mind of brothers

---

[28] Greg Garrison, "At 28, Pastor Has Five Degrees and a 4,300-Member Flock," *Christianity Today,* August 15, 2006. Accessed February 21, 2016. http://www.christianitytoday.com/ct/2006/augustweb-only/133-22.0.html.

[29] Ibid.

and sisters on the other side of the world, I could not help but think that somewhere along the way we had missed what is radical about our faith and replaced it with what is comfortable."[30] Platt channeled this incongruity into a publishing sensation, a prominent role as his generation's leading mission advocate, a series of marathon teaching sessions called "Secret Church," replicating the devotion of churches in the majority world, and a pathos in preaching that allowed his hearers to see and sense his unceasing burden for the lost peoples of the world.

Few who knew Platt's personality and passion would have been surprised if he had announced that he was resigning his pastorate in order to move to Nepal as a missionary. The draw for Platt was real. But in August 2014, he instead accepted the presidency of the IMB, the world's largest missionary-sending agency, dedicating to uniting fifty thousand Southern Baptist churches in "one sacred effort to fulfill the Great Commission among all peoples."[31]

Though widely recognized as one of the most visible and successful missions advocates of his generation, Platt's appointment still attracted controversy among some within the SBC. Although Brook Hills contributed generously to the IMB (the latest budget under Platt's tenure earmarked over $1 million in contributions), $100,000 was sent directly to the SBC Cooperative Program Allocation Budget, bypassing the typical path of giving through Alabama State Convention, which retains approximately half of the money for state missions and ministries. Brook Hills contributed only $25,000 to the Cooperative Program through the state convention. Pastor Bart Barber, a trustee at Southwestern Baptist Theological Seminary, summarized his concerns as follows: "The IMB President's salary comes from the Cooperative Program. Whoever draws that salary ought to have been supportive of the Cooperative Program. For me, it's no more complicated than that. We need not an IMB President who wrestles with the Cooperative Program, but one who has embraced it."[32] After Platt's election, Barber wrote a post explaining that though he had opposed Platt's candidacy, his desire for the flourishing of the Cooperative Program entailed that he would now support his IMB president.[33]

Platt, like Chandler, views the SBC as an important but not indispensable means of advancing the Great Commission: "If it doesn't help us more effectively

---

[30] David Platt, *Radical: Taking Back Your Faith from the American Dream* (Colorado Springs: Multnomah, 2010), 7.

[31] Southern Baptist Convention, "International Mission Board." Accessed February 21, 2016. http://www.sbc.net/aboutus/entities/imb.asp.

[32] Bart Barber, "Why David Platt Should Not Be the Next IMB President," *Praisegod Barebones* (blog), August 25, 2014. Accessed February 21, 2016. http://praisegodbarebones.blogspot.com/2014/08/why-david-platt-should-not-be-next-imb.html.

[33] Bart Barber, "David Platt Is My IMB President, Too," *Praisegod Barebones* (blog), August 27, 2014. Accessed February 21, 2016. http://praisegodbarebones.blogspot.com/2014/08/david-platt-is-my-imb-president-too.html.

make disciples of all nations . . . then it would not make sense to come together. This is why we exist."[34] But while Chandler has become the president of an evangelical-Reformed network of churches (while retaining his own church's dual affiliation with the SBC), Platt has become the president of a key SBC institution. These two men represent different trajectories for a younger generation of SBC pastors: those who are involved, but more at a distance, and those who are increasingly becoming invested in the institutional structure. Both are united in their overarching desire for the nations to be glad in Christ (cf. Ps 67:4), and both operate with a missionary mind-set of using any biblically permissible means possible to save the lost (1 Cor 9:22)—including supporting the SBC.

BABYLON AND BEYOND

When Southern Baptists have declined their evangelical credentials, they have not hesitated to tout their denomination's superior numbers and influence. For much of the twentieth century, regional and cultural unity differentiated Southern Baptists from evangelicals wandering in the northern wilderness as exiles from their denominational homes, now captive to Babylon.

But now that regional and cultural unity works against Southern Baptists eager to see the gospel of Jesus Christ proclaimed with different accents. And the numbers, while still impressive by comparison, have stagnated and even begun to decline. In 2015 the SBC endured its largest single-year numerical decline since 1881.[35] Denominational leaders such as Daniel Akin, president of Southeastern Baptist Theological Seminary in Wake Forest, North Carolina, sound the alarm: "We must confront the sobering reality that the Southern Baptist Convention remains a mostly middle-class, mostly white network of mostly declining churches in the South."[36]

When combined with the waning influence of conservative Christians on national politics, the declining numbers suggest that younger Southern Baptists envision Babylonian exile as their future in the twenty-first century.

"Older Southern Baptists are more likely to see the U.S. as Israel," writes Trevin Wax, managing editor of The Gospel Project, a widely used curriculum

---

[34] Southern Seminary, "Interview with David Platt," March 9, 2009. Accessed February 21, 2016. http://www.sbts.edu/resources/interviews/interview-with-david-platt-complete-audio/. For the video segments on the SBC and the CP, see http://www.sbts.edu/media/video/interviews/interview-platt-09-sbc.flv and http://www.sbts.edu/media/video/interviews/interview-platt-10-cooperative.flv. Accessed February 21, 2016.

[35] Bob Smietana, "As Church Plants Grow, Southern Baptists Disappear," Christianity Today, June 12, 2015, http://www.christianitytoday.com/gleanings/2015/june/southern-baptist-decline-baptism-church-plant-sbc.html.

[36] Daniel Akin, "The Future of the Southern Baptist Convention," in Southern Baptists, Evangelicals, and the Future of Denominationalism, 270.

from the SBC publisher, LifeWay. "Younger Southern Baptists are more likely to see the U.S. as Babylon."[37]

Compared to other evangelicals, however, Southern Baptists seem equipped in at least one key way to survive and even thrive in Babylon. The Conservative Resurgence of the 1980s did not resolve every theological dispute in America's largest denomination, but it settled the question of authority and power. The churches would rule. Denominational executives served at the pleasure of ordinary Southern Baptist church members. If seminary leaders and agency heads wanted to negotiate peace with Babylon, they would need to answer to the people. And for better or worse, it will always be difficult to change the collective will of more than 15 million Southern Baptists. Indeed, the testimony of the twentieth century suggests that not even the decades-long output of moderate and liberal pastors from Southern Baptist seminaries could change the essentially conservative character of the convention.

By contrast, evangelical identity in the movement inherited from Graham and Ockenga hinges in no small measure on the decisions of elites in publishing, education, and fund-raising. There may be no official evangelical gatekeepers, but these editors, college presidents, and nonprofit CEOs set the standard for what their movement will regard as acceptable. The pressures to conform to the world are enormous. Publishing tends toward the new and the transgressive, with felt-needs marketing aimed at younger generations. Colleges and seminaries must prove themselves to accrediting agencies while shifting the burden of higher administration costs onto students that increasingly depend on federal loans. Nonprofits likewise seek federal grants that constrain their sectarian beliefs in a never-ending pursuit of greater ministry reach in a world with countless needs. Even theologically conservative organizations must ward off the inevitable temptations to progress beyond their original intent and motives.

"As long as evangelicalism remains a parachurch-driven coalition, Southern Baptists will remain nervous about certain types of cooperation with the broader evangelical movement,"[38] wrote Southern Baptist historian Nathan Finn in 2011. This perspective helps explain why Union University separated in 2015 from the largely evangelical Council for Christian Colleges and Universities, which did not dismiss two schools that approved of homosexuality.

SBC leaders for the twenty-first century see themselves as part of a greater evangelical tradition under considerable pressure from an increasingly hostile world. But they brandish their Southern Baptist credentials and primary allegiance

---

[37] Trevin Wax, "5 Observations About Younger Southern Baptists," *The Gospel Coalition*, May 5, 2014. Accessed February 21, 2016. http://www.thegospelcoalition.org/blogs/trevinwax/2014/05/05/5-observations-about-younger-southern-baptists.

[38] Nathan Finn, "Passing on the Faith to the Next Generation," in *Southern Baptists, Evangelicals, and the Future of Denominationalism*, 243.

to the local church as firewalls against the theological declension their denomination miraculously reversed in the twentieth century.

"If 20 years ago I believed that the imperative was to say to Southern Baptists that we really are evangelicals, then the imperative that now falls on us is to say to Southern Baptists that we really are Baptists," Mohler writes. "The younger generation already knows that the Southern Baptist Convention is located somewhere within the great evangelical tradition. The issue today, however, is that the evangelical movement is now in more trouble than the SBC."[39]

Southern Baptists increasingly exiled from mainstream American culture in the twenty-first century have rediscovered evangelical ambivalence with their earthly home. The question remains whether evangelicals who confuse mission with seeking the world's approval will learn from the Southern Baptist experience of the twentieth century. Numbers do not guarantee success. And movement leaders must be accountable. We believe the leadership of places like Babylon Baptist Church will be crucial in equipping evangelicals for mission among their neighbors in our Babylon and far beyond.

"Keep yourselves biblically grounded," Litfin counsels the SBC. "Stay Christ-centered, gospel-centered, Word-centered. This is what will keep you useful to the Lord. If you do this, and you do it as part of the larger evangelical movement, the Lord may use the SBC to help keep American evangelicalism relevant deep into the 21st century."[40]

---

[39] R. Albert Mohler Jr., "Southern Baptists, Evangelicals, and the Future of Denominationalism," in *Southern Baptists, Evangelicals, and the Future of Denominationalism*, 283.
[40] Litfin, "The Future of Evangelicalism (and Southern Baptists)," 111.

The Future of Baptist State Conventions

Paul Chitwood and John L. Yeats

S tate Conventions, like most every other aspect of SBC life, are experiencing a season of unique fluctuation. This season of transition is not likely to abate in the near future. Yet state conventions remain an integral part of Southern Baptist work. As set forth in this chapter, state conventions have proven integral to Southern Baptist work in every era—past, present, and, as we contend, in the future.

The future of denominational work is inextricably tied to the past. What is the history of the state convention as a denominational structure?

CHITWOOD: The history of the Southern Baptist Convention (SBC) is inseparable from not only the history of state conventions but, specifically, the history of the Kentucky Baptist Convention (KBC). Kentucky Baptists created our state convention in 1837, some eight years before the Southern Baptist Convention was formed in 1845.

Of course, Kentucky was home to Baptist work long before the KBC was organized. The first evangelical church organized west of the Alleghenies was Severns Valley in Elizabethtown, Kentucky, founded June 18, 1781. The first association started west of the Alleghenies is Elkhorn, now known as the Central Kentucky Network of Baptists, organized on September 30, 1785. Kevin Ezell, a Kentucky native who now presides over the North American Mission Board, would be pleased to know, if he does not already, that the idea for the plan of the American Baptist Home Mission Society was developed in Shelbyville, KY by John Mason Peck and Jonathan Going in September 1831.

The idea of the Cooperative Program also originated in Kentucky. On November 16, 1915, the General Association of Baptists in Kentucky (now the

KBC) met at Jellico, Tennessee, in my home church about a hundred yards from the Kentucky state line, and adopted a budget plan for the support of all denominational work in the state and across the country. This was a decade before the SBC, meeting at Memphis in 1925, adopted the Cooperative Program. The Kentucky plan was fashioned after that of First Baptist Church of Murray beginning around 1900.

The SBC owes its existence and its primary funding mechanism to the state conventions that preceded it. Kentucky Baptists enjoy a rich history intertwined with the history of the SBC, but they also enjoy a work still thriving today. In fact, the 2,400 churches of the KBC are planting more churches today than at any time on record. They are currently in a growth trend in baptisms, overall church membership, and in missions giving through the Cooperative Program and through each of the major missions offerings, including the Lottie Moon Christmas Offering for International Missions, the Annie Armstrong Easter Offering for North American Missions, and the Eliza Broadus Offering for State Missions.

We have a rich history. And we undertake our work today and will do so in the future standing on the shoulders of those who have gone before us.

YEATS: In 1835 Missouri Baptists adopted a constitution for the newly formed "Central Association," forerunner of the Missouri Baptist Convention (MBC). The association's stated goal was to "adopt means and execute plans to promote the preaching of the Gospel in the destitute churches and settlements within the bounds of the state."[1] From that day forward, the Missouri Baptist Convention has existed to make disciples, multiply churches, and develop leaders.

Missouri Baptists always have been an independent bunch, upholding the Baptist distinctives of the infallibility and veracity of God's Word, believer's priesthood, and autonomy of the local church. We have learned the hard way that we can accomplish more for the kingdom of God by working together than we could ever accomplish alone.

Today, Missouri Baptists are nearly half a million strong, serving in nearly 1,900 churches, and pooling our resources to advance the gospel message in Missouri, throughout North America, and around the world.

Then a few decades ago something happened. "Mission drift" began to occur. Mission drift happens in your church, too. It is a natural tendency to move slowly away from the historic purpose for which the MBC was founded. In an attempt to provide an ever-growing slate of programs and resources, our missionary staff and our activities have, at times, expanded to keep pace and in the process we lost focus.

What we must learn to do is sharpen our focus on why our churches brought us into existence. That is not hard to understand. We must clarify our mission and

---

[1] R. S. Duncan, *A History of Baptists in Missouri* (Saint Louis, MO: Scammel and Company, 1883), 340.

stay on mission and fiercely defend it from the good things that people want us to do and stay true to our mission of cooperating with heartland Baptists to make disciples, multiply churches, and develop leaders.

Why does the state convention still exist today?

YEATS: The state convention is part of the strategic methodology for reaching the world for Christ. Some have used the Acts 1:8 model to describe the state jurisdiction as a "Judea" ministry. Judea is the jurisdiction that was like the province where Jerusalem was located. Similarly a state convention or regional convention serves to drill down into the cultural context of a particular jurisdiction with relational and authentic ministry that transforms lives and communities with the gospel in ways a global or national ministry cannot.

Cooperating churches in any given state/region have assigned seven unique functions to conventions:

1. Sound the trumpet. In Old Testament times leaders in a particular jurisdiction were given the privilege, the permission, and the power to convene the people—to sound a trumpet and assemble the people for a common purpose. Old Testament prophets were called on to assemble the people. Joel 2:15–16 (HCSB) says, "Blow the horn in Zion! Announce a sacred fast; proclaim an assembly. Gather the people."

Acts contains examples of leaders who assembled to make determinations about various issues facing the early church. Church history bears record of numerous councils formed by church leaders from various geographic locations for the purpose of seeking wisdom and determining perspective. There are times when the people of God need to be convened to consider the purposes of God and how collectively to fulfill the mission.

In the context of Southern Baptist life, this is the role of the state convention. No one church or national entity can summon the people called Southern Baptists who live in a particular state or region. The state convention can do so because of a principle called "jurisdictional leadership."

Here is how jurisdictional leadership works: Churches summon their local members. Associations call together the people that live in their particular area. State and regional conventions call Southern Baptists living in that jurisdiction together to determine the protocols of their cooperative ministries. Southern Baptist leaders call together Southern Baptists on a national scale to determine the scope and practice of the national and international ministries. Every level has the power to convene the people.

Southern Baptists use the term *jurisdictional leadership* rather than *jurisdictional authority*. Southern Baptists have a history of resistance to hierarchical structures in our ecclesiology. In Southern Baptist life four levels of jurisdictional leadership are founded on the Acts 1:8 model. Every level cooperates in shared ministry. Every level values the other levels for the significant contributions they make to the work of the kingdom. There is the sense of partnership and fraternity, not dominance, over one another.

Effective state conventions understand that part of leadership means they work with the associations to convene the people in a local area to accomplish a particular goal. State convention missionaries do this with an attitude of service and partnership, not authoritarianism. Effective national entity leaders understand that partnering with state convention leaders maximizes the capacity to encourage the people in a given jurisdiction to join in an initiative. This is sometimes referred to as consensus building, a vital component of organizational life.

The state conventions convene the people in their respective jurisdictions at annual meetings for the primary purpose of reporting on the previous year and setting goals and policies for cooperative work in the future. The state convention also networks with its churches and church leaders through personal relationships, writing, events, supply preaching, and other methods of communication to tell the story of God at work in and through the cooperative churches in their jurisdiction.

This is part of how we do our work as cooperating Southern Baptists. Someone must lead the cooperative work in a state or region. State conventions and their respective state missionaries have that particular assignment.

2. Strengthen churches. State conventions are only as strong as the churches in their jurisdictions. The key to healthy churches is healthy leadership. State convention leaders are constantly equipping church leaders. This makes for stronger churches and healthier ministries that impact local churches, local associations, and the greater cooperative global work. State conventions assist churches with equipping and organizational structuring so local churches become more effective in disciple-making, multiplying churches, and developing leaders.

3. Support pastors and servants of the Lord serving the local church. The most important key to healthy, disciple-making and missions-minded churches is effective leadership. State conventions facilitate the work of pastors and staff members by providing leadership training, strategic planning, and personal mentoring initiatives. It does not matter if the pastor is in a traditional congregation or a congregation birthed in the last six months or six years. Leadership equipping is vital for twenty-first-century ministry.

When relational trauma erupts in a congregation or association, the state convention is a primary resource for navigating the potential hostilities. Most state conventions have some level of coordinated care ministries for pastors and staff members who experience forced termination. Many local churches turn to the state convention for the training of search committees, transitional leadership, and résumés for potential candidates.

4. Multiply churches. Every New Testament church is a Great Commission church. Every church with effective evangelism, discipleship, and missions ministries is engaged in starting new churches that start new churches. Churches start churches, but who coordinates the churches ready to be part of launching a new church? Who works with churches and associations to launch churches, equip the leaders, and develop standards and benchmarks of accountability? That work is one of the primary tasks of the state convention.

The state convention synergistically works with multiple churches, associations, and a pool of church planters to strategically facilitate churches planting churches in a state or region. It is difficult for a single church of sixty to one hundred attendees to think in those terms. But cooperatively, we can plant hundreds if not thousands of churches.

5. Send the light to the nations. In multiple spheres state and regional conventions are involved in sharing the gospel to the ends of the earth. One of the ways a state convention does this is through its promotion, collection, and distribution of Cooperative Program mission funds received from churches. This requires careful accounting and clear protocols so that funds from churches are moved through the state convention and on to national entities. National entities are dependent on the faithful and trustworthy work of state conventions to fulfill their ministry assignments.

The churches of the particular state or region work through their respective conventions to allocate the Cooperative Program funds. Every state or regional convention I know of is working toward a 50-50 split of those funds where 50 percent is forwarded to national ministries. This demands retooling the state and regional conventions to focus on function and missional goals while discovering more efficient, effective methods for logistics and personnel deployment.

Another way a state convention sends out the gospel light is through strategic planning of multigenerational, multipeople group ministries. Only a small minority of churches has the capacity to provide multigenerational and multipeople group ministries. Such a task can be overwhelming for the majority of local churches, so state conventions orchestrate ministries with churches and associations to accomplish this goal.

For example, every university campus in North America needs an evangelical gospel outreach and discipleship ministry that helps students become discipled, missions oriented, and incorporated into the life a local church. State conventions coordinate Baptist Collegiate Ministries so a comprehensive, on-campus ministry exists.

State and regional conventions also facilitate missions networks for volunteers. Whether coordinating trained disaster relief teams or Baptist Builders, state conventions harness the willingness of volunteers from multiple congregations to make a difference for the sake of the gospel.

Since state and regional conventions have a particular geographic area to reach with the gospel, they facilitate strategies to reach every people group residing in that jurisdiction. It does not matter if that people group has a particular ethnic composition or speaks another language or lives within the parameter of a prison. State conventions partner with local churches and associations to reach all the peoples.

6. *Synchronize the work of entities.* The organizational work of cooperative churches is an amalgamation of state and national entities that are constantly working together toward Great Commission goals. Whether it is a state Baptist college, the International Mission Board, an associational camp, student work on a college campus, equipping conferences, disaster relief ministry, or children's services, there must be a "sychronizer." This is so institutions avoid too much duplication of ministries and minimize holes in the safety net.

The state or regional convention, through its leadership, is the organizational "touch point" that promotes fraternal relationships between churches, associations, state convention entities, and national ministries. This is so Great Commission ministries are accomplished with maximum effectiveness and efficiency.

"Fraternal" and "partnership" are important words that characterize the working relationships between a state convention, the associations, and state entities in its jurisdiction and between a state convention and Southern Baptist Convention entities. This factor is one of the reasons we have the Cooperative Program. Instead of every church, every association, and every state and national ministry acting independently, we can synchronize our work and accomplish far more for the glory of our God than we could ever do on our own.

7. *Shine the light in the public square.* State conventions have a powerful cooperative voice in state legislatures for good and right. Any legislator will tell you that in a congressional hearing a person representing an individual church does not carry the same weight of influence as a person sharing the perspective of 100 churches or 1,000 churches acting in concert. Cooperating churches shine a greater light in the public square.

There was a day when legislators and governmental administrations respected the domain of churches. They understood the invaluable contribution churches made to a community's infrastructure. In many places that perspective has evaporated with the growing secularization of the culture. The state convention is the most effective and efficient means of addressing a state's moral, social, regulatory, and liberty issues with prudence and strategic statesmanship.

So what do state conventions do? State conventions serve at the direction of cooperating Southern Baptist churches in a particular region or state. Churches assign to state conventions these larger scale functions that 99 percent of churches cannot do. State conventions work with small and large churches and local associations to fulfill those functions.

CHITWOOD: State conventions still exist today for the same reason they came into existence: they are a strategic part of church mission strategy. In Kentucky we have sought to acknowledge the reason the KBC exists even in our mission statement, which reads, "The Kentucky Baptist Convention: Created by churches, for churches, to help churches reach Kentucky and the world for Christ."

Baptist churches in Kentucky have chosen to partner together at the state level, the vehicle for their partnership being the KBC. John Yeats has done a great job highlighting the seven unique functions cooperating churches in any given state or region have assigned to conventions. His summary accurately reflects the role of the KBC. Yeats notes that "churches assign to state conventions these larger scale functions that are more than what 99 percent of churches can do." I would go one count further and suggest that the comprehensive functions of state conventions are more than what any single church can do.

Am I suggesting every church needs the state convention? You bet I am! For when a church chooses not to affiliate with and participate in the life of a state convention, there are functions the church could and in most cases should be carrying out that they simply are not, at least not in any effective and efficient way.

For example, I believe every local church should be doing all that the church can do to promote a pro-life agenda and a religious liberty agenda in society and government. But a single church has little impact, particularly on the decisions of state government. To illustrate this point, I recently met with state legislators on these issues. They had invited the pastor emeritus of the largest church in our state, which is in fact one of the largest churches in the world, to join the discussion. As the legislators pleaded with us to mobilize the churches of our denominations to be more active in advocating on these issues, they asked what strategies we could employ to that end. I shared about our platforms for mobilizing the one million Southern Baptists in Kentucky. When asked if the pastor emeritus had a similar strategy for mobilizing the various independent Christian churches across our state, the megachurch pastor lamented that he had no strategy and, because of the absence of a cooperating body, he reported that he would be of no help beyond making calls to a few pastor friends.

If Southern Baptists ever choose to walk away from our cooperative work at the state convention level, we will be left to making calls to a few pastor friends. "But we have Russell Moore and the ERLC!" some may say. Yes, and thank God we do. And while I am grateful that Dr. Moore and his staff take my calls, reply to my text messages and e-mails, and are anxious to help Kentucky in any way we ask, most of their time is spent addressing issues in Washington, D.C. rather than at the state legislative level.

Even if the ERLC had more money and a larger staff, I contend that Dr. Moore's move from Louisville to Nashville means he has little influence, if any, in Frankfort. But when KBC leaders show up in Frankfort, we have been able to stop gambling expansion, the legalization of marijuana, and are finding more and more legislators willing to take on the abortion industry, predatory lending, and defend religious liberty. No church can be as effective as 2,400 churches on these and a host of other issues. That is just one example, among many, of why the Kentucky Baptist Convention still exists today.

Church planting is another great example. While we believe and affirm the biblical model of church planting, i.e., churches planting churches, most churches being planted today in Kentucky are successful not only because of a mother church giving them birth but also because of the 2,400 churches working together to help fund the plants and train the planters through the KBC. When it comes to small churches, and most SBC churches are still small churches, the old adage, "We can do more together," is certainly true regarding church planting. Most of our churches would struggle to birth a new church on their own, but working together what may seem impossible becomes possible. Some may say, "But church planting is why we have NAMB!" NAMB helps plant churches in the SEND cities; NAMB does not help plant churches in Kentucky. The KBC helps churches plant churches in Kentucky.

There is, in fact, a long list of ministries and mission work coordinated at the state convention level that could never be coordinated by national SBC entities and/or mission boards. Orphan care, evangelistic work on state and university campuses, legislative initiatives, Cooperative Program promotion, church revitalization and strengthening, church planting, and disaster relief ministries are but a few examples.

Will the state convention continue to be relevant moving forward? Why or why not?

CHITWOOD: Elton Trueblood first popularized the term "postdenominational" in 1967. In an article appearing in *Christianity Today*, Trueblood stated, "If we are truly conscious of what time it is, one of the chief facts we must know is that, so far as the Christian religion is concerned, we are in a post-denominational age."[2] More than four decades have passed since Trueblood made that statement, and we still have our denominations. The question today is not whether denominations exist. The question is: does anyone care?

I grew up reaping benefits of denominational life without realizing it. For example, my Sunday school literature and offering envelopes were produced by the denomination. The hymnals and pew Bibles were from the denomination. Most of the songs the choir sang were published and provided by the denomination. My pastor was educated by a denominational seminary. My youth pastor was

---

[2] D. Elton Trueblood, "Post-denominational Christianity: What New Church Forms Are Emerging?" *Christianity Today* 12 (November 24, 1967): 3–4.

being educated at a denominational Bible college. Most of my family members who went to college attended a liberal arts college supported by the denomination. I attended summer camps built and staffed by the denomination and youth events sponsored by the denomination. I learned about missions from missionaries supported by the denomination. While some of that has changed, much of it has not.

Well over twenty years ago, the young editor of a state Baptist paper, Al Mohler Jr., wrote in the *Christian Index*: "American religion is experiencing a fundamental restructuring which will transform the landscape of the nation's religious life. Virtually every religious denomination or body is engaged in a process of reorientation, reorganization, or focused on a search for identity."[3] Some things never change!

In fact, the reorientation of American religious life, and of Southern Baptist life, seems to be accelerating. Beginning with the reorganization of the International Mission Board, the North American Mission Board and many of our state conventions, the advancement of the Great Commission Resurgence agenda at the national convention, state conventions, and even in many local Baptist associations, as well as a host of retirements marking the generational transition of leadership, and the shrinking financial commitments of local churches to the Cooperative Program, everything about denominational life seems to be in flux.

I contend, however, that the greatest change we are experiencing is a lack of understanding of and interest in the kingdom role of the denomination. Some see it as irrelevant. Some church leaders see it as financially competing with their local church agenda. Some simply refuse to exhibit the kind of loyalty required for denominational structures and ministries to thrive.

Nevertheless, I believe the state convention will continue to be relevant because the needs being addressed by the churches that formed state conventions still exist and will continue to exist in the future. Baptists still need a voice in the public square, still need to work together to plant churches effective, and can be much more efficient in ministries like disaster relief, orphan care, and higher education as churches organize themselves and partner together on the state level. The need of churches to be a part of a tribe connected with common theological and missional convictions is growing rather than diminishing.

YEATS: I believe that is a question our churches have to answer. Some of the answer rests with those of us who serve state/regional conventions. Will we invest the relational capital in entering the world of our state and regional pastors? While we do that, will we stay focused on the ministry functions and the mission the

---

[3] R. Albert Mohler Jr., "The 1992 SBC: Toward the Denominational Future," *The Christian Index*, June 18, 1992, 2.

churches have assigned to us? Will we lead, or will we simply respond to requests for resources?

I believe the state and regional convention has a great future. One reason: function. Someone has to do the work. Another is the issue of critical mass. When an organization is so small it cannot flourish, it is destined for either a radical transformation or a strategic merger or death. Those state conventions engaged in fulfilling their function and those with sufficient mass will go further into the future to minister with future generations.

How should the state convention determine ministry priorities for the future?

CHITWOOD: I believe the state convention must, in every generation, allow the mission and needs of the local church to determine its ministry priorities. The greatest threat to the relevancy of the state convention is the state convention itself. The ministries of state conventions allowed to become sacred cows that cannot be changed or abandoned when they failed to line up with the mission and needs of the local church are a stench in the denominational camp and cause the convention itself to become a stench.

The stewardship of resources for missions is a sacred task that requires constant evaluation and strategic allocation. To determine the grid for evaluating ministries and allocating resources, state convention leaders must walk closely with pastors and other local church leaders.

Furthermore, the governing structures of state conventions must provide genuine and meaningful opportunities for input and involvement from church leaders so the mission of the state convention is never disconnected from the mission of the church. Where this disconnect has occurred, state convention work has suffered self-inflicted wounds. As a means of bridging this gap, local church pastors have filled many of the executive roles recently occurring within state conventions. This tendency is not only observable at the state convention level. The same has proven true at the national level with the recent hiring of pastors to fill the presidential seats of IMB and NAMB.

YEATS: Dr. Chitwood has clearly articulated the key for understanding state convention priorities. It is the local church. And state conventions must stay "tuned in" to the heart of the leaders of the local churches. Future leaders of state conventions must build on the foundations of the past, seek congruency with the local church leaders in the region or state, cull the irrelevant and nonfunctional ministries, and embrace a common, consensus vision.

How will funding issues impact the state convention's future work?

YEATS: We must face the brutal reality that half of the funding we now have will perish in the next twenty years. If there is not a vision that leads to sacrificial funding, we will perish. If we do not quickly help people see the value of legacy giving, we are in deep trouble for sustaining any measure of support for God's called-out ones.

Our hope is to instill within the hearts of leaders the power of cooperative ministry and how the Lord honors such work. Will the generations behind us see they are part of something grand and we are engaged in something that pleases the Lord? Will they become passionate about the value of working together to fulfill the mission of reaching the world for Christ that starts at the front door of our churches and within the context of the region where God has planted us?

CHITWOOD: Responsible stewardship demands that state conventions remain light afoot as they assess the most critical areas of need in their churches and the greatest opportunities for gospel advance in their state. Conventions must maintain focus on these needs and opportunities and avoid the temptation to branch out into less critical ministries but instead prioritize the funding of mission work among the unreached and unengaged. Therefore, although we may not be able to predict the future, we know the budgets and ministries of state conventions must remain lean, not only to deal with funding challenges but also to ensure the gospel is proclaimed to the ends of the earth.

Historically, state conventions have invested heavily in agencies and institutions within their state to help carry out ministry priorities and goals. Has this changed? What might it look like in the future?

CHITWOOD: Most state conventions have lowered the percentage of funding for in-state agencies and institutions while increasing the percentage of funding for our national entities and mission boards. I do not see this trend reversing. In fact, as ministries like educational institutions and children's homes meet growing cultural, political, and legal challenges, the very existence of these ministries, sadly, has come into question.

In some instances these ministries have grown to the point that they are no longer dependent on the churches for funding. Whether these ministries remain faithful to the theological convictions of the churches in light of the challenges already mentioned is one of the most pressing questions of our generation of denominational work. Some that have become dependent on government funds will no doubt choose to redefine themselves in order to maintain those funds. Others will face significant adjustments to their ministries even if they are able to remain in existence.

Many educational institutions and some children's homes have budgets rivaling or exceeding the Cooperative Program receipts of their state convention. In such instances the state convention could do little if anything to bail out an institution facing financial collapse over the loss of significant government funds.

For this reason and others, a long and growing list of educational institutions have already broken ties with their state conventions. Institutions that still have meaningful relationships with a state convention have either found adequate financial support that does not include government funds or they are rushing to do so even now.

The question of government funds aside, with a few exceptions agencies and institutions once essential to the work of state conventions, primarily in the south, are not nearly as prominent today.

YEATS: Dr. Chitwood articulates clearly the dilemma of the hour. Will institutions be able to function without government support? Now the government is sending signals that there is a new reigning religion, naturalistic secularism, and that religion is intolerant of especially evangelical Christianity and its values.

Unless legislatures move quickly to exempt and protect our religious liberties from coercion from those attempting to force our acquiescence to immorality, the fate of our strategic partnerships with our agencies is but a lawsuit from destruction. Institutional leaders (at least those we still have) in Missouri have expressed their desire to move to a closer relationship to the state convention for protection. They want to be seen as authentic partners with the local churches and the state convention and hence worthy of exemption from overt government control. And in most states the state convention through the Cooperative Program remains the largest private donor year in and year out to these institutions.

Some state conventions have taken an active role in public affairs. From your perspective, how important will the state convention's involvement in public affairs be moving forward?

YEATS: This is an important function for a state convention. If we hold that state conventions have primarily a threefold mission of making disciples, multiplying churches, and developing leaders, we must review this function in light of our mission.

We are to make disciples. What is the benchmark of a disciple? Is a disciple not one who has a Christian worldview revealing the lordship of Christ in every sphere of life and is constantly in a mode of reproducing more disciples who desire Jesus to be lord of every sphere of life? This is the wellspring of leadership.

Consequently, because the Lord has divinely orchestrated our lives to be part of this democratic republic, it is our duty to express his lordship in the pubic square. In this form of government, the people of God need concerted efforts to protect the principles of our nation's heritage such as religious liberty and sanctity of life.

The best approach for concerted efforts depends on the level of public involvement. If a local issue, the pastors or association in that area should pray and team together for the good of the community. If it is a state issue, we must engage appropriately.

For example, when I pastored in Topeka, there was a string of massage parlors between the airport and the state capital building. Someone challenged me that the reason they existed was because the pastors were not exemplifying that they were kingdom-minded men of God.

So several of us got together and prayed for a couple of hours. Then we set a strategy of using telescopic zoom lenses to photograph the license plates of the patron cars. We all showed up one summer evening and divided into teams of two: one pastor to take pictures, the other to drive. We did not communicate with the authorities for fear of alerting the parlors. After the pictures were processed (this is prior to digital cameras and the web), we publicly threatened to run the plates in the local newspaper. We did not need to because our stand motivated the district attorney to do what was right, and the parlors were closed within sixty days.

If you are dealing with a state issue, the state convention should take the lead to coordinate efforts for correction or statutory improvement. Our local church leaders do not have the time to do their work and ours too. Most Baptists have no understanding about how many hours it takes to get a significant bill passed through two houses of state government.

Before the state legislative session starts in 2016, bills of significance are prepared. Several meetings with key political leaders, state legislature leaders, and leading experts on religious liberty are meeting to prepare for what is coming in the spring. There are five areas in need of protection: pastors, churches, schools, ministry institutions, and private businesses. In Missouri accommodation for government workers is already delineated in the law.

This is a desperate need for those historic ministries of education, child care, and care for the aged, as well as the right of private citizens to express their faith while doing business with the pubic. It takes enormous hours of preparation and consensus building to gain statutory protection for our religious liberties.

Or how about keeping government regulators restrained? In 2011 our convention leaders worked hundreds of hours to protect our small, rural churches from government regulators. Every local church that had a water well for flushing or filling the baptistery were to be required to have a particular water filtration system that cost more than the total annual budget of many of our rural churches. However, because our convention lobbyist had longstanding relationships with the legislators, we were able to secure an exemption, much to the chagrin of state regulators.

CHITWOOD: Not since the days of John Leland has the Baptist voice been more needed in American life and government. As in Leland's day, religious liberty has returned as an issue of primary importance for people of faith in America.

Baptists are best positioned to address this issue due both to our history and our theological convictions.

Most challenges to religious liberty are local and are often resolved in the legislative or judicial bodies within their state. Naturally the public affairs arm of a state convention is best positioned to address the issue, often by informing and mobilizing congregants and congregations.

The Ethics & Religious Liberties Commission of the Southern Baptist Convention is always a helpful resource to the state conventions, but as a ministry focused primarily on national issues and federal legislation, the ERLC has neither the time nor the resources to make a significant impact in an individual state, nor should it attempt to do so since the state convention is best positioned.

Should the state convention disappear, the Baptist voice will be silenced. In Kentucky, where Southern Baptists comprise nearly one fourth of the population, state convention efforts to mobilize the citizenry and give the churches a voice of righteousness in state government have proven to be effective on some key issues.

The basic denominational structure of Southern Baptists (i.e., associations, state conventions, national convention) has not changed in 170 years. Thinking creatively, is there a better way for Southern Baptists to reach North Americans and the people of the world with the gospel?

CHITWOOD: The answer to this question is, I believe, dictated by demographics. Where Baptist work is strong and churches are numerous, I believe the traditional denominational structures remain the best way to carry out the Great Commission work of Southern Baptists. That does not mean the denominational organizations themselves are as effective as they could be in every instance. For example, many of our local associations in the south are floundering for lack of an effective vision and strategy in their contemporary context.

Moreover, given the mobility of modern Americans and the benefits technology has brought to communications, many of our associations could easily combine their resources and reorganize into regional networks, staying just as connected and possibly becoming much more effective. The vision and strategy of the association must be formulated as an Acts 1:8 assignment that especially allows smaller churches to be faithful to our Lord's charge. As the culture grows progressively hostile toward the church, and churches find themselves increasingly isolated, the association could play a more vital role than ever before. To put it succinctly, moving forward Baptists will need one another more not less.

While a state convention with thousands of churches could likely not retain its effectiveness by merging with another large convention, I believe many of our smaller state conventions could become much more effective by merging together.

Such moves at the association and state convention level could result in much stronger denominational work.

Moreover, the vision and strategy of associations and state conventions must be refined and communicated in a way that is mission driven and resonates powerfully with the local church. During days of plenty, denominational organizations launched a host of new ministries that may well have been relevant and worthy of investment. The current financial challenges, however, matched by unprecedented opportunities to get the gospel to the unreached and unengaged, require aggressive paring of our ministries at every level of denominational life. This holds true not only for associations and state conventions. Our SBC entities and mission boards have also invested heavily in ministries and projects that are not absolutely essential to their assignment. We quickly must come to the place where every level of our cooperative mission effort is scrutinized critically and organized in a way that maximizes resources for the most essential work.

YEATS: The beauty of Southern Baptists is that no matter the size, every church is valuable. Every association has worth. Every state and regional convention is valuable. Every SBC entity has an immeasurable role to play in the kingdom of God.

Do we need to evaluate those levels? Sure. We need constantly to evaluate our methodologies. However, for a change to take place instead of a spontaneous explosion leading to collapse, we need good civil discussion coupled with solid research and patience for processing. If we succumb to our flesh and become reactionary, we run the high risk of being driven by a lack of understanding and/or someone's preordained agenda. We do not have the luxury of stopping our work, and the lost souls who are waiting on a witness of the gospel from the people God called Southern Baptists need us cooperatively to fulfill our role in the kingdom.

SOUTHERN BAPTIST DOCTRINE AND DISTINCTIVES

Southern Baptists and the Quest for Theological Identity: Unavoidable Questions for the Twenty-First Century

R. Albert Mohler Jr.

The question of identity is a central feature of the modern age. In our culture individuals, institutions, and even business corporations regularly wrestle with the question of their own identity—who are we and how do we know? Yet as central as this question is to our culture, the identity question is a rather recent phenomenon—a gift of modernity. In fact, most people prior to the rise of modernism did not spend much mental energy on the question of identity. In the premodern era, one's identity was an established fact based on sociological factors such as caste, vocation, family, or tribe. Identity was fixed by external sociological, economic, cultural, and religious factors, not by individual choice.

The Enlightenment brought that stability to an end. Now the question of personal identity is unavoidable. Almost everyone now feels the responsibility to construct or negotiate an identity according to a seemingly infinite number of options for self-designation. In fact, psychiatrists, sociologists, and historians have all attested to the fact that the modern identity question creates an enormous burden for individuals and for society. In the modern age the self is a project needing constant attention, maintenance, and focused development.

While the question of identity may be a product of the modern age, Christians would do well to give this issue careful theological reflection. In fact, as Christians, and as Baptists in particular, we must clearly affirm that our identity is unavoidably theological. If we are not careful in terms of how we define our identity, we may put our doctrinal integrity and the strength of our theological convictions at risk.

In this chapter I want to explore our theological identity as Southern Baptists along historical lines, looking at our place within Protestantism and also in the modern era. If we do not understand our own theological heritage, our sense of identity will be greatly impaired, and our theological convictions will be muddled. Additionally, I want to consider ten unavoidable questions we, as Baptists, must consider if we are to retain a self-conscious theological identity in the twenty-first century.

THE REFORMATION AND RELIGIOUS IDENTITY

As Baptists we must recognize that, at least in terms of our theological convictions, we are the heirs of the Protestant Reformation.[1] While Baptists do not recognize any single "founder" of our denomination in the way Lutherans might, we also recognize we are the inheritors of the theological heritage given to us by those who went before us in the Protestant Reformation.

As we consider the Reformation, we should not forget the titanic influence these events had in shaping Western culture and religious experience even up to our current day. In fact, in some sense, our need to reflect carefully on our own theological identity is a product of the Reformation.

This reality is witnessed to by the fact that traditional Catholic historians did not refer to the events of the sixteenth century as the Protestant Reformation but as the Protestant Revolt. In their eyes Luther was doing nothing less than unraveling the fabric of Christendom. To Catholic leaders this revolt represented a decisive statement of individualist theological authority that was in contradiction to the institutional, magisterial authority of the Roman Catholic Church. As a result, Catholics predicted that Luther's revolt would lead to doctrinal dissolution and theological anarchy. In fact, defenders of the Council of Trent regularly point to the proliferation of "thousands" of Protestant denominations as evidence that their predictions turned out to be true.

Furthermore, as many historians have pointed out, the Reformation also led to the separation of throne and altar. The medieval synthesis of faith and reason, along with the unity of the civil magistrate with the church, could not withstand the effects of the Reformation. Indeed, as Catholic apologists at the time predicted, "Christendom" ultimately unraveled—at least in part—because of the Reformation.

This unraveling of Christendom set the stage for our modern consideration of religious identity in the twenty-first century. In other words, the events of the Reformation ultimately led to a consciousness in the West that someone could

---

[1]   For a helpful summary of Baptist origins, see Michael A. G. Haykin, "The Baptist Identity: A View from the Eighteenth Century," *Evangelical Quarterly* 67 (1995): 137–52; and Tom J Nettles, *The Baptists: Key People Involved in Forming a Baptist Identity* (Fearn, Scotland: Christian Focus, 2005).

identify as something *other* than Catholic. These effects were not, of course, immediately apparent, particularly during the first and second generation of the Reformation when much of Protestantism was still inseparably linked to territories and to the civil magistrate. But even in these first generations, the mere fact that Lutheranism presented a rival vision of Christianity to the Catholic Church was a significant break with the past and its settled identities.

As already noted, in the initial generations of the Reformation, the question of religious identity was primarily limited to the prince. But the conditions which tied the magistrates and territories to either Protestant or Catholic versions of Christianity did not continue for long. As the outworking of the logic of the Reformation went forward, the question of identity became more and more acute.

Looking at these same issues, Peter Berger—now in his tenth decade of life and one of the most influential sociologists of our day—wrote decades ago that the "heretical imperative" of the modern era is the imperative *to choose*.[2] In Berger's analysis, in the premodern era one did not need to choose one's beliefs. Instead, in the West virtually everyone was born and baptized into the Roman Catholic Church. In other words, identity was externally fixed for individuals. In the modern secular world, however, this is no longer the case. Choice is endemic in every area of life—we simply cannot avoid it. As a result Berger concludes that in the modern age we must take responsibility for our identity. It is no longer given; it is self-determined.

Baptists in the modern age recognize that what Berger argues is both true and false in terms of our own experience. In one sense Southern Baptists must affirm that Berger is correct when he says that in the modern world we are all responsible for our own identity. In fact, Baptists, of all Christians, must affirm this point since we are unswervingly committed to a conversionist ecclesiology. In other words, Baptist theological conviction is largely built on the notion that one *cannot* be born a Baptist.

Yet it is also the case that for much of its history the SBC, situated in the larger context of the Bible Belt, has been defined tribally. We affirmed that no one could be born Southern Baptist, but many of us operated with the pretense that we were in fact born Southern Baptist in at least tribal terms. For instance, I was enrolled in "cradle roll" as an infant—I still have the certificate. In fact, just a few years ago I learned that I had even been enrolled in "pre-cradle roll" while I was yet to be born. In that instance my certificate of enrollment simply read, "Baby Mohler, due October 1959." If anything indicates the SBC operated with a sense of tribal identity, my own experience at the beginning of life proves the point. I later did indeed believe the gospel at a Vacation Bible School and was baptized,

---

[2] Peter L Berger, *The Heretical Imperative: Contemporary Possibilities of Religious Affirmation* (Garden City, NY: Anchor, 1979).

thus truly identifying as a Christian and joining a Southern Baptist church. But in a real sense my tribal identity as a Southern Baptist was a reality prior to my conversion and baptism.

The point is that as Baptists we must remember the cultural factors that have made the need for a clear theological identity so pressing. The challenges of late modernity make a clear articulation of our convictions more urgent, not less so. Furthermore, we must also remember that even though we have the necessary doctrinal resources to articulate a clear theological identity, Southern Baptists have often defined ourselves more according to our tribe than according to our convictions—a strange phenomenon given our ecclesiological convictions.

BAPTISTS AND EVANGELICALS: BAPTIST IDENTITY IN THE MODERN ERA

In the aftermath of the secular revolution, fewer and fewer people can relate to the experience I had as a boy growing up in an SBC home. For those without that same heritage, the heretical imperative weighs even more heavily upon them than it did on me. For example, the rise of the "nones" (those with no religious affiliation) as a major demographic in America shows that fewer and fewer are born into the world with any tribal identity at all.

The rise of the "nones" in modern America witnesses to a shift in American religious experience that is vastly different even from what many knew at the end of the nineteenth century. In fact, if a choice was then to be made, it was typically a competition between denominations. As evidence of this point, one need look no further than *Baptist Why and Why Not* published by the Southern Baptist Sunday School Board at the dawn of the twentieth century.[3] The chapters systematically worked through why the reader would want to be a Baptist as opposed to a Methodist, an Episcopalian, a Presbyterian, or a member of any other Christian denomination.

A huge shift, however, occurred in the twentieth century that shattered this type of denominational identification. Historically that shift is represented by the publication of *The Fundamentals*, a series of books published between 1910 and 1915.[4] The rise of theological liberalism, at least in the American experience, caused the intense denominational competition that characterized most of the nineteenth century to change radically. Theological liberalism was not a problem confined to one denomination but rather a problem that ran through most major denominations. In this era the most significant theological identity marker shifted from one's denomination to whether one held to traditional orthodoxy or the accomodationist revisionism of the liberal theologians. J. Gresham Machen made

---

[3] J. M. Frost, *Baptist Why and Why Not* (Nashville: Baptist Sunday School Board, 1900).
[4] R. A. Torrey, ed., *The Fundamentals: A Testimony to the Truth*, 4 vols. (Grand Rapids: Baker, 1972).

this point most emphatically in his now famous *Christianity and Liberalism*.[5] As the title suggests, Machen argued perceptively that Christianity and liberalism are not two different streams of the same religion but two entirely different religions.

Mainline Protestantism during this time was quickly coming to embrace the program of theological liberalism. The agenda of the theological liberals was to adopt accomodationist theological convictions in order to maintain cultural dominance. The liberals at the midpoint of the twentieth century believed they needed to change their theology and accommodate themselves to an increasingly secular culture if they were to maintain their cultural significance or influence. As most readers now understand, this project has been nothing short of a disaster. Mainline Protestants have emptied their churches of people, are largely irrelevant in the culture, and worst of all have completely abandoned the gospel of the Lord Jesus Christ.

On the other end of the spectrum, the "fundamentalists" fractured into various subgroups under the umbrella of theological conservatism. One prominent group to emerge from the fundamentalists in the middle of the twentieth century was the movement known as neoevangelicalism. Leaders like Carl F. H. Henry and Harold Ockenga were dedicated to a vision that separated them from theological accomodationist liberals while also avoiding the separatist, doctrinal reductionism of some streams of fundamentalism. The mode of evangelicalism was engagement, and even as it sought steadfastly to maintain fidelity with the faith once for all delivered to the saints, it also sought to engage the increasingly secularized culture on gospel terms. Furthermore, because neoevangelicals were defining themselves over against both liberalism and fundamentalism, early neo-evangelical leaders worked hard at defining their theological identity. This was especially necessary since some of these evangelicals maintained membership and ordination in their own denominational churches.[6]

Yet during this time of great denominational upheaval and the emergence of the neoevangelicals, Southern Baptists found themselves, by and large, at home in Zion—safe in the territory of the Bible Belt. In fact, SBC state papers, books, magazines, and other theological literature during this time hardly even broached the question of the theological identity of Southern Baptists. That all changed in the 1970s, however, when it became clear two rival visions for the future of the Southern Baptist Convention were emerging among the denomination's leaders.

---

[5] J. Gresham Machen, *Christianity and Liberalism* (New York: Macmillan, 1923).

[6] For more on neoevangelicalism, see George M. Marsden, *Reforming Fundamentalism: Fuller Seminary and the New Evangelicalism* (Grand Rapids: Eerdmans, 1987); Matthew Hall and Owen Strachan, eds., *Essential Evangelicalism: The Enduring Influence of Carl F. H. Henry* (Wheaton, IL: Crossway, 2015); Gregory Alan Thornbury, *Recovering Classic Evangelicalism: Applying the Wisdom and Vision of Carl F. H. Henry* (Wheaton, IL: Crossway, 2013).

As in the fundamentalist-modernist controversies of the past, Southern Baptists were split between theological liberalism and faithfulness to the denomination's conservative theological heritage. The more liberal faction, like mainline Protestants before them, adopted an accomodationist approach to theology in order to secure more cultural respectability. The influence of this agenda was so pervasive and dominant in the SBC that in the early 1970s the convention adopted an essentially pro-choice resolution and explicitly supported the legalization of abortion laws in this country.

On the other end of the spectrum, the conservatives claimed continuity, not just with the classical Christian tradition but with the theological convictions of the founders of the SBC. Further, for conservatives inerrancy became a definitional issue for epistemological and theological integrity. Conservatives argued that the abandonment of biblical inerrancy necessarily leads to the type of cultural accommodation that would eventually result in the abandonment of the gospel.

In the midst of this controversy, one of the central identity questions that arose was whether Southern Baptists were evangelicals. The conservatives in the denomination concluded that Southern Baptists were evangelicals and always had been. The intellectual and theological resources that came to define the evangelical movement were shared by conservatives in the SBC. Chief among those resources was the Chicago Statement on Biblical Inerrancy.[7] Furthermore, conservative Southern Baptists were moving with some speed into staple evangelical institutions such as the Evangelical Theological Society. In the early 1980s, Southern Baptists hardly had any presence in the ETS. Now, however, the ETS is flooded with members of Southern Baptist institutions and churches. Again, the reason for this emergence of Southern Baptists into evangelical institutions is ultimately rooted in that in the Conservative Resurgence Southern Baptists recognized that they belonged to a larger theological conversation with evangelicals with whom they shared a basic theological identity. Indeed, conservative Southern Baptists recognized that we not only shared the same vision but also needed to respond with participation and contribute to the leadership of evangelicalism in America.

---

[7] The importance of this issue crystallized with the publication of Harold Lindsell's *The Battle of the Bible: The Book that Rocked the Evangelical World* (Grand Rapids, Zondervan, 1978). For my defense of the Chicago Statement on Biblical Inerrancy, see R. Albert Mohler Jr., "When the Bible Speaks God Speaks: The Classic Doctrine of Biblical Inerrancy" "in *Five Views on Biblical Inerrancy,* ed. J. Merrick, Stephen M. Garrett, and Stanley N. Gundry (Grand Rapids: Zondervan, 2013).

THE COLLAPSE OF CULTURAL CHRISTIANITY
AND THE RISE OF THE BAPTIST MOMENT

In 1987 Richard John Neuhaus published *The Catholic Moment*.[8] Neuhaus's argument was that the Catholic Church, especially in the United States, was best poised to meet the cultural contest and its challenges. What was clear to me when I first read this book was that if there was a Catholic moment, it had already passed by the time the book was even published. I would suggest, however, that we now have every reason to believe that we may be entering "the Baptist moment." As cultural Christianity takes its final breaths, Baptists may be ousted from any place of prominent cultural influence, but our theological convictions uniquely situate us to respond to the challenges posed by late modernity. Our commitment to regenerate church membership, the baptism of believers only, and our understanding of the nature of the church gives Baptists a unique voice in the face of disappearing cultural Christianity. I honestly believe that in coming years evangelicals will increasingly look to Southern Baptists due to the ecclesiological crises created by the collapse of cultural Christianity. The coming generation will urgently need the wisdom and biblical conviction of Baptists on these issues.

But Baptists will only be prepared for this challenge if we retain our theological integrity and remain faithful to our doctrinal convictions. To that end I will conclude this chapter by posing ten questions for consideration as we reflect on the future of Southern Baptist Convention and Baptist identity in the twenty-first century.

UNAVOIDABLE QUESTIONS FOR SOUTHERN
BAPTISTS IN THE TWENTY-FIRST CENTURY

1. Will Southern Baptists embrace an identity that is more theological than tribal? The older I get the more I recognize the value of the tribal inheritance I received as a young boy. This is why I phrased the question "*more* theological than tribal" rather than "theological *instead* of tribal." In fact, I believe it is impossible to survive as a community of conviction without having a certain amount of tribal identity. But, as many young Southern Baptists now realize, tribal identity is not enough. Tribal identity alone will eventually give way to theological accommodation. Our identity must be more theological than tribal, and that requires a change in the logic of the Southern Baptist Convention, certainly a change from the logic employed during the middle and late decades of the twentieth century.

2. Will today's generation summon and maintain the courage to minister Christ in a context of constant conflict and confrontation? In our generation and the

---

[8] Richard John Neuhaus, *The Catholic Moment: The Paradox of the Church in the Postmodern World* (San Francisco: Harper Collins, 1987).

generations to follow, there will never be a faithful ministry that does not face constant conflict and confrontation with the larger culture. If we are seeking peace with the culture, we will abandon the gospel. Are we ready for the challenge? Will we demonstrate theological and moral courage in the face of stiffening cultural opposition?

3. *Will Southern Baptists find a healthy balance between evangelical identity and Baptist conviction?* One of the lessons we can learn from the evangelical movement is that its central weakness was not epistemological. Its central weakness was not its commitment to the core doctrines of the Christian faith. Its central weakness was ecclesiological—an undervaluing of the local church in particular. As Southern Baptists we must be staunchly evangelical, but we must also be unashamedly Baptist. Evangelical is essential, but it is not enough.

4. *Will Southern Baptists maintain the intellectual and moral credibility to speak truth as we live truth?* As Southern Baptists we must not only define what we believe but affirm those same truths with our lives. Southern Baptists must live before the world the convictions we teach, or we will lose all credibility to teach and preach those convictions. Even as Carl F. H. Henry called a generation for the evangelical *demonstration* of our faith, the same call must now be issued to Southern Baptists.

5. *Will Southern Baptists embrace the deep roots and riches of the historic Christian tradition without apology?* Far from being merely of academic interest, our understanding of Baptist origins really does matter. We must remember that while the early Baptists were at pains to demonstrate their differences in matters of ecclesiology from other Protestants, they also went to great lengths to demonstrate that they stood in continuity with confessing, believing Christians throughout the ages. Early Baptists recognized that they had inherited a theological treasure from previous generations that was not distinctively Baptist but was rather, to use Thomas Oden's term, classically Christian.[9]

One of my most important moments at seminary came in the first minutes of my first church history class with Timothy George. He began the class with these words, "My name is Timothy George, and my responsibility is to convince you that there was someone between your grandmother and Jesus and it matters." As Baptists, we need to learn that lesson well. Southern Baptists, particularly SBC pastors, must understand that they are in a long line of godly men that goes back, not just to 1845, but to a room in Jerusalem where Jesus sent his disciples into the world.

6. *Will Southern Baptists preserve the essential gains of the Conservative Resurgence of the last quarter of the twentieth century?* Will we unashamedly and rigorously

---

[9] For a helpful introduction to Oden see his memoir, Thomas C. Oden, *A Change of Heart: A Personal and Theological Memoir* (Downers Grove, IL: IVP Academic, 2014).

hold to inerrancy? Baptists must recognize that Scripture and Scripture alone is the *norma normans non normata*, the norm of norms that cannot be normed. The Bible alone, inerrant and infallible, must remain foundational for our epistemology and always serve as our highest authority—the norm that norms all others.

7. *Will Southern Baptists be comprehensively confessional and not merely anecdotally confessional?* Baptists must recognize that our confession must be more than a document we turn to in crisis or emergency situations. Our confessional identity should shape our articulation of the faith and regulate our theology, teaching, and preaching. If we do not regain a sense of being comprehensively confessional in all we believe, teach, and preach, then we will ultimately fail to be confessional when it matters most.

8. *Will a new generation of Southern Baptists be eagerly and authentically Baptist?* This means Baptists must unashamedly and with theological depth articulate, defend, and live out our ecclesiology. Even as we claim continuity with classic Christian tradition, we also must unashamedly hold our dissenting opinions from other traditions in terms of our doctrine of the church and the ordinances. We must be authentically Baptist because we believe our convictions on these matters are authentically biblical and essential to a right understanding of the church.

9. *Will Southern Baptists produce a generation of pastor-theologians adequate to the challenge of late modernity?* It is not enough that we produce theologians. Of course, we should be grateful for the wonderful theologians and professors faithfully serving our denomination in colleges and seminaries across the world. But the future of the denomination comes down to whether we are producing pastor-theologians—men who can faithfully do the work of theology in local congregations situated in a hostile culture.

10. *In the words of Jesus in Luke 18:8, when the Son of Man comes, will he find faith on the earth?* Though we do not know the future of the Southern Baptist Convention, we ought to at least ask this question of ourselves. When the Son of Man comes, will he find faith in the Southern Baptist Convention? If so, and we must pray that it will be so, it will require us to regain a clear and robust understanding of theological identity. Our responsibility for our denomination and our churches is to be found faithful to that end.

May the Lord, indeed, find us faithful. Amen.

Who Are Southern Baptists?
Toward an Intergenerational Identity

David S. Dockery

"A generation goes and a generation comes, but the earth remains forever."
(Eccl 1:4 HCSB)

J ust as the book of Ecclesiastes describes, generations have come and gone in Southern Baptist life. The Southern Baptist Convention is the largest Baptist denomination in the United States and the world. Composed of more than 15 million church members and nearly fifty thousand congregations and missions in all fifty states of the United States, the Southern Baptist Convention is the largest Protestant denomination in the country. Southern Baptists maintain a visible presence among large segments of the South and in other aspects of the country. But Southern Baptists did not begin this way. As a matter of fact, Baptists did not begin this way.

BAPTIST BEGINNINGS

Baptists began in the early seventeenth century.[1] John Smyth and Thomas Helwys, who sought asylum in the Netherlands, led one of the earliest groups of Baptists. Three decades later a second Baptist movement began on English soil, this time arising from a single Separatist congregation in London. Both General and Particular Baptists began during the early decades of the seventeenth century. Both groups emphasized religious freedom. Both were confessional, with Particular Baptists pointing to the London Confessions while the Standard Confession of 1660 influenced General Baptists, along with the Orthodox Creed of 1678, which Leon McBeth described as "the most complete of all the General Baptist confessions."[2] The Orthodox Creed focused on how much Baptists were

---

[1] See Anthony L. Chute, Nathan A. Finn, and Michael A.G. Haykin, *The Baptist Story: From English Sect to Global Movement* (Nashville: B&H Academic, 2015), 11–38.
[2] Leon McBeth, *The Baptist Heritage* (Nashville: Broadman, 1987), 66–69.

like other Christians, affirming how much they agreed with the Apostles' Creed, the Athanasian Creed, and the Nicene Creed.[3] Each group manifested strengths and weaknesses. The errant thinking among General Baptists tended more toward Socinianism and Arianism. The Particulars, unfortunately, got off track by moving toward an antimissionary mind-set. Dan Taylor rescued the gospel for General Baptists, and Andrew Fuller did the same for the Particulars. Both groups came together around the missionary movement led by William Carey, and both groups rallied to support the development of the Foreign Missionary Society.[4]

Baptists in America had a similar process beginning in Rhode Island in the 1630s. These Baptists, with their statements on religious freedom, paved the way in other states. By 1730–1740 there were eight congregations and about 400 Baptists in this country. Following the First Great Awakening, things began to change rapidly. In 1707 the first Baptist association was established in this country in Philadelphia. In 1751 the first Baptist association developed in the South in Charleston, followed by the Sandy Creek Association in 1755. These three key associations reflected regional and methodological differences, which points to the reality that there was no single early tradition.[5]

In 1812 Adoniram Judson and Luther Rice began the missionary movement among American Baptists, and the Triennial Convention was launched in 1814 with Richard Furman, the great pastor of First Baptist Church of Charleston, South Carolina, serving as its first president. Many Baptist groups during the first half of the nineteenth century adopted the 1833 New Hampshire Confession. Concerns were raised about Free Will Baptists in the 1830s as a variety of Baptists gathered together within the Triennial Baptist movement, including northern business and mercantile leaders, frontier ranchers in the West, and farmers and planters in the South. They each represented different perspectives as they gathered around the gospel.[6]

Differences developed over the understanding of what it meant to be Baptist, including differences regarding the societal model of doing missions, regarding where money would be invested once it was raised for the starting of new churches, and regarding whether missionaries who happened to be slave owners could be appointed as home or foreign missionaries. In 1844 these differences became obvious to all, and those in the South who wanted a convention model, who wanted money to go the South for the funding of new church starts, and who

---

[3]   Ibid.

[4]   David S. Dockery, *Southern Baptist Consensus and Renewal* (Nashville: B&H, 2008), 38–39; Timothy George, *Faithful Witness* (Birmingham: New Hope, 1991).

[5]   See Bill J. Leonard, *Baptists in America*, Columbia Contemporary American Religion Series (New York: Columbia University Press, 2005), 83–87.

[6]   William R. Estep, *Whole Gospel for the Whole World* (Nashville: B&H, 1994), 49–76.

wanted the freedom to appoint slaveholders found all of their ideas rejected by those outside the South.

SOUTHERN BAPTIST BEGINNINGS

In 1845 the Southern Baptist Convention technically began with the consultative charter approved as they gathered in Augusta, Georgia, a charter that was approved officially in Richmond the next year. W. B. Johnson was elected as its first president, a Foreign Mission Board was established in Richmond, Virginia, as well as a Home Mission Board in Marion, Alabama. These Baptists gathered around one overarching purpose: "One sacred effort for the propagation of the gospel."[7] A convention model was adopted, something important and distinctive from Northern Baptists with boards elected to manage the different entities that would come into place. There were nine state conventions at this time that preceded the establishment of the national convention. The initial meeting in 1845 included representatives from 165 churches with 293 messengers.[8]

Southern Methodists had already separated from their northern group, while Presbyterians in the South would do so soon. In light of these trends, it is important to understand that the beginning of Southern Baptist history did not take place in a vacuum. The story of Southern Baptists in many ways has always been the story of the expanding work of missions, the advancement of the gospel, and the multiplication of churches. The American Baptist Tract Society continued to function as the publishing house for both groups, North and South, until the founding of the Sunday School Board near the end of the century.

The state conventions still dominated what took place in Baptist life through the nineteenth century, largely because of distance, travel, and communication. During this time in 1859, The Southern Baptist Theological Seminary was birthed with the founding faculty of Basil Manley Jr., John Broadus, and William Williams, all led by President James Boyce.[9] R. B. C. Howell had been attempting to establish a seminary in Nashville at the same time but was sidetracked continuously by the landmark challenges of J. R. Graves.

The Civil War threatened everything. In 1870, following the Civil War, some tried to rejoin the Northern and Southern Baptists, but to no avail. There was no

---

[7] The preamble of the original constitution of the SBC described its purpose as "eliciting, combining, and directing the energies of the whole denomination in one sacred effort, for the propagation of the gospel." The words are both historically significant and powerful for contemporary Baptists. See Jesse C. Fletcher, *The Southern Baptist Convention: A Sesquicentennial History* (Nashville: B&H, 1994), 46–52; also McBeth, *The Baptist Heritage*, 381–91.

[8] The number (293 messengers) comes from Robert A. Baker, *The Southern Baptist Convention and Its People, 1607–1972* (Nashville: Broadman, 1972), 165–69, 446; Fletcher, *The Southern Baptist Convention*, 395 notes that there were 236 messengers.

[9] See Gregory A. Wills, *Southern Baptist Theological Seminary, 1859–2009* (New York: Oxford University Press, 2009).

longer an issue dealing with slavery, but the South primarily opposed the proposal because of the funding for new church starts in the South and because of the convention model of governance. They said to their brothers in the North, like Paul and Barnabas, it is best if we go our separate ways, with the North adopting a societal model and the South adopting a convention model.

James B. Taylor was appointed to lead the Foreign Mission Board, while I. B. Tichenor became the official leader to guide the Home Mission Board to Atlanta and to its new day. The Sunday School Board was launched in 1891 after a consensus was reached between J. M. Frost and J. B. Gambrell. J. M. Frost became the first leader in 1891, and less than a decade later the important work, *Baptist Why and Why Not*, was published.[10] Southwestern Seminary was birthed in 1908 out of the religion department of Baylor University. Founded in Waco in 1908, the seminary moved to Fort Worth in 1910, with B. H. Carroll serving as the first president until his death in 1914.[11]

GENERATIONAL DEVELOPMENTS

These were important early developments among the initial generation of Southern Baptists. This first generation could be divided into two parts: (1) From 1845 to 1875, moving toward development, including the birth and infancy of the Southern Baptist Convention. (2) From 1875 to 1910, moving toward stability, with the end of this generation marked by the death of B. H. Carroll. During this time the SBC adopted its charter, began to grow, and established the Foreign Mission Board and the Home Mission Board. Southern Seminary went through controversies with C. H. Toy and William Whitsett, the Sunday School Board began to publish, Southwestern Seminary was founded, and the Committee to Study Cooperation was put together in 1900. In the early years of the twentieth century, multiple staffs were starting to be formed in some of the larger churches, staffs that included associate pastors as well as ministers of music and ministers of education. This generation was led by W. B. Johnson, R. B. C. Howell, James P. Boyce, John Broadus, Basil Manly Sr., Basil Manly Jr., I. T. Tichenor, J. M. Frost, J. B. Gambrell, B. H. Carroll, J. R. Graves, and J. M. Pendleton.

From 1910 to 1950, the development of the next generation in Southern Baptist life began to move toward cooperation after initially moving toward development, then secondarily moving toward stability. Southern Baptists witnessed the establishment of the Executive Committee in 1917. The following year, the Baptist Bible Institute, which became New Orleans Baptist Seminary, was birthed. When Southern Baptists gathered in 1925 in Memphis, Tennessee, a hallmark

---

[10] J. M. Frost, *Baptist Why and Why Not* (Nashville: The Sunday School Board of the Southern Baptist Convention, 1900).

[11] Chute, Finn, and Haykin, *The Baptist Story*, 163–84.

convention witnessed the adoption of the Cooperative Program, recommended by a committee led by M. E. Dodd, as well as the adoption of The Baptist Faith and Message as the first official confessional statement of the Southern Baptist Convention.[12]

In the background of that first confessional statement were the issues surrounding the theory of evolution that was beginning to develop and be taught at schools such as Baylor, Wake Forest, Mercer, and Furman. The Poteat brothers, leading Wake Forest and Furman, were to Baptist liberalism what the Manly family had been to Baptist orthodoxy. Behind the 1925 confession was the need to address a framework of confessional orthodoxy, which helped Southern Baptists understand that Darwinism was off limits.

At the same time in the North, Baptists were deeply involved in the fundamentalist-modernist controversy. W. B. Riley led Baptist fundamentalists while Shailer Matthews and Walter Rauchenbush led liberal Baptists. All of these things were swirling around Southern Baptists in 1925 when they came together to adopt their first confessional statement. Also, at Southern Seminary W. O. Carver, one of the first professors who did not study with the founders, began teaching world religions in 1896. He taught at Southern for four decades until 1943, emphasizing his ecumenical perspective, theological progressivism, and incipient universalism.

During the middle of this generation, Southern Baptists saw the deaths of several giants: E. Y. Mullins in 1928, A. T. Robertson in 1934, George Truett in 1944, L. R. Scarborough in 1945, and W. T. Conner, Southern Baptist's last shaping theologian, in 1952.[13]

GROWTH AND EXPANSION OF SOUTHERN BAPTISTS

From 1950 to 1980, Southern Baptists could be characterized by moving toward expansion and efficiency. Underneath this primary characteristic could be found a desire among many leaders to be more like the mainline Protestant denominations. The expansionist mind-set provided motivation for the "Million More in '54" campaign, as well with the move to establish seminaries outside the South: Golden Gate (in California) in 1945 and Midwestern (in Missouri) in 1958. Southeastern was started in North Carolina in 1951 on the former Wake Forest College campus. The Southern Baptist Convention at this time was becoming not just a regional convention but began taking the initial steps to becoming a national denomination, surpassing Methodists as the largest Protestant denomination during this period.

---

[12] See an expanded survey in Baker, *The Southern Baptist*, 403–5; Dockery, *Southern Baptist Consensus and Renewal*, 4; Fletcher, *The Southern Baptist Convention*, 140–46.

[13] See Gregory A. Wills, "Southern Baptist Identity: A Historical Perspective," in *Southern Baptist Identity: An Evangelical Denomination Faces the Future*, ed. David S. Dockery (Wheaton, IL: Crossway, 2009), 65–88.

Following the Civil War, Northern Baptists continued to work in the South, but the Southern Baptist Convention did not move beyond the South until the decade following World War II, largely to establish churches for misplaced Southerners. The 1963 Baptist Faith and Message was adopted to address the crisis that developed around the issue of biblical authority, which had become a public matter with the publication of *The Message of Genesis* by Ralph Elliott.[14]

In 1969 the publication of the Broadman Commentary created another controversy, once again over the legitimacy of the historical-critical method to interpret the book of Genesis. The president of the Southern Baptist Convention in 1969 was W. A. Criswell. While in that role, he wrote a book titled *Why I Preach the Bible Is Literally True*, which was published by Broadman Press with an editorial statement at the beginning saying that this book did not represent the opinions of the publisher.[15] R. G. Lee, W. A. Criswell, H. H. Hobbs, Duke McCall, James Sullivan, Robert Naylor, Arthur Rutledge, and Baker James Cauthon were all household names, along with a name that shaped Southern Baptists both within the Convention and outside as well: Billy Graham.

In 1956 Southern Baptists demonstrated their commitment not only to expansion but to efficiency by inviting Booz Allen Hamilton, the highly touted efficiency managers, to help the convention understand how they could do things more effectively and more efficiently. The SBC had become a programmatic and pragmatic convention, exemplified by the appointment of new presidents at Southwestern and at Southern Seminary at this time who were not theologians; this had never been the case before. President Fuller at Southern Seminary and President Williams at Southwestern Theological Seminary typified the pragmatic, programmatic mind-set of this day.

During the 1960s and 1970s, the consensus that had developed during the 1950s began to break down on many fronts. The consensus was challenged by a series of controversies. During this time there were several notable and obvious strengths, particularly denominational programming and the common worship styles; worship was almost the same from city to city, town to town. During this time, form and freedom merged, along with a strong organizational effectiveness. The challenges came in the areas of biblical authority, the understanding of Baptist heritage, and the meaning of Baptist identity and distinctives.

Worship styles seemed to change with the publication of new hymnals: the *Broadman Hymnal* (1940), the first *Baptist Hymnal* (1956), and the second *Baptist Hymnal* (1975). There is much to be learned from understanding what was going

---

[14] Ralph H. Elliott, *The Message of Genesis* (Nashville: Broadman, 1961).

[15] For a more detailed discussion, see David S. Dockery, "The Crisis of Scripture in Southern Baptist Life: Reflections on the Past, Looking to the Future," *Southern Baptist Journal of Theology* 9 (2005): 36–53.

on with the publication of those hymnals. New Bible translations were coming out almost every year, which also fed into the breakdown of the consensus.[16]

Cultural influences from without also shaped what was going on in the Southern Baptist Convention. With the South emerging from its isolation, American culture was characterized by unrest: the Civil Rights Movement, Vietnam, the sexual revolution, and protests on college campuses. The agricultural society of the old South started to give way to urban and suburban structures. Graduates from the premier seminaries strived to be pastors of county seat First Baptist Churches rather than farmer preachers as in previous generations. Populations grew, but they grew even more diverse, more pluralistic. Employment trends destabilized, interest rates were on the rise, racial tensions soared. The Old South values seemed to be visibly disturbed during this time. All along there remained an undercurrent among some Southern Baptist leaders, a desire to be more like the mainline, which challenged Baptists' identity and theological commitments.[17]

A new generation began in the 1980s, one characterized by public controversy, which, however, led to renewed commitments to biblical authority. The controversy also included calls for denominational restructuring. The restructuring had begun even before the controversy of 1979, with the redefinition of the Cooperative Program. The controversy over Scripture, with challenges coming from leaders like Adrian Rogers, Jimmy Draper, and large-church pastors, changed the convention and included the following turning points:

- 1985, the Convention in Dallas with 45,000 messengers;
- 1986, the Glorieta Statement, in which the six Southern Baptist seminaries said to the Convention that they recognized that their faculties were imbalanced and did not represent Southern Baptists at large;
- 1988, the appointments of Richard Land as president of the ERLC (at that time called Christian Life Commission) and Lewis Drummond as the president of Southeastern Seminary;
- 1991, the publication of the New American Commentary, a commentary series committed to the inerrancy of the Bible;
- 1992, the Doctrine Study of the Southern Baptist Convention, focusing on the nature of Scripture; and
- 1992–93—key changes in the presidencies at Southeastern Seminary (Paige Patterson) and Southern Seminary (Albert Mohler).

Restructuring for a new century began to take place in the middle of the 1990s. The Baptist Faith and Message was revised in 2000. Many Southern

---

[16] See David S. Dockery, "A Call for Renewal, Consensus, and Cooperation," in *Building Bridges,* compiled by David S. Dockery and Timothy George (Nashville: Convention Press, 2007), 13–36.

[17] See David S. Dockery, "Southern Baptists in the Twenty-First Century," in *Southern Baptist Identity,* 13–21.

Baptists hoped the recovery of biblical authority and the message of the gospel had been solidified.[18] During this time there also was a first step to begin to address an issue that had haunted Southern Baptists since its beginning in 1845—race. In 1995 Southern Baptists applauded Richard Land for leading the convention to adopt a resolution on racial reconciliation. This generation, characterized by controversy, in many ways ended with the death of Adrian Rogers in 2005.

PREPARING FOR THE FUTURE

From 2005 until now, Southern Baptists have wrestled with changes brought about by a new generation. This generation could be characterized as moving toward recovery or the reenvisioning of the denomination. Certainly there have been ongoing controversies over the last decade: Landmarkism, the doctrine of Scripture, the meaning of the gospel, rural versus urban, styles of worship and ministry, an educated ministry versus the role of the bivocational pastor. Models and heroes were starting to develop for a generation of pastors, models who seemingly for the first time were people from outside the Southern Baptist Convention. For so many people the heroes had been Richard Furman, George Truett, W. A. Criswell, R. G. Lee, and Herschel Hobbs. Now the heroes were John McArthur, James Boice, Tim Keller, Chuck Swindoll, John Piper, and others from the broader evangelical world. Changes brought about by these different approaches cannot be underestimated.[19]

TOWARD A MULTIETHNIC AND NATIONAL CONVENTION

As the SBC moved into the 21st century, the millennials simultaneously began to move into leadership roles in the churches. Southern Baptists are now a multiethnic denomination with 10,000 congregations whose membership is primarily African-American, Hispanic-American, or Asian-American. The diversity of our nation has begun to be reflected in Southern Baptist life. American evangelicals across the country began to ask questions about their future and turned to Southern Baptists for help even as Southern Baptists had turned in their direction some twenty years earlier. Now Southern Baptists are not as parochial, as regional, as isolated, or as segregated as they had been in the previous generation. Questions began to be raised regarding the understanding of what denominations do, not only among Southern Baptists but also among denominations across the American spectrum. As denominations in this country began to decline, a shift

---

[18] See Nancy T. Ammerman, *Baptist Battles* (New Brunswick, NJ: Rutgers University Press, 1990); Richard D. Land, "The Southern Baptist Convention, 1979–1993: What Happened and Why?," in *Baptist History and Heritage* 28 (1993): 9–11; Bill J. Leonard, *God's Last and Only Hope: The Fragmentation of the Southern Baptist Convention* (Grand Rapids: Eerdmans, 1990).

[19] Dockery, *Southern Baptist Consensus and Renewal,* 16–57.

toward new and more diverse networks began to develop. A true generational shift was taking place.[20]

Southern Baptists in the South until 1950 were primarily located there because of the territorial agreements they had with American Baptists. But as those agreements began to dissipate, things began to change. Baptists were primarily, and still remain, agents of the gospel and advocates for the regenerate church to the South, to the country, and to the world, with evangelism and missions prioritizing their work from the beginning.

TWELVE MARKERS OF IDENTITY AND CONSENSUS

We now find ourselves faced with new questions with a new generation moving toward maturity. With each generation, even with the significant changes through the years from 1845–2015, there has been significant continuity. At least twelve things remain that this generation must understand and wrestle with as they begin to participate more broadly in Southern Baptist life in the days to come.

1. Convention Model

Southern Baptists are and have been a people committed to a convention model of ministry. The SBC has explored the societal model along the way and has asked similar questions over and over again. Each time the SBC has come back to say that the convention model is the best way to fund and organize the work of the Southern Baptist Convention.[21]

2. Controversies

Southern Baptists have been characterized by controversy and conflict along the way, from the beginning with the Northern Baptists in 1845, with Landmarkism in the nineteenth century, with rural versus urban approaches to ministry (which is really what best characterized the primary differences among the Sandy Creek and Charleston Associations), with the evolution issues of 1925, the organization of the Executive Committee, and the accompanying questions about centralization of work and decision making, with universalism and ecumenism—how will Southern Baptists participate with broader denominations—with the interpretation of higher critical issues with the Broadman Commentary, with Calvinism, with the implications of regenerate church membership, and with ongoing ministry and worship style questions. Controversy has characterized Southern Baptist history.

---

[20] See David S. Dockery, "So Many Denominations: The Rise, Decline, and Future of the Denomination," in *Southern Baptists, Evangelicals, and the Future of Denominationalism*, ed. David S. Dockery with Ray Van Neste and Jerry Tidwell (Nashville: B&H Academic, 2011), 3–34.
[21] Dockery, *Southern Baptist Consensus and Renewal*, 16–58.

3. Cooperation

At the same time, cooperation has characterized who Southern Baptists are, both in the collection and distribution of finances and in the approach to implementing the work. Churches, associations, state conventions, and national conventions have found ways to cooperate together to advance the gospel and to extend the kingdom of God.[22]

4. Colleges and Seminaries

Education has been both important and controversial. Colleges preceded seminaries in SBC life. Early Baptist colleges included Georgetown, Mercer, Wake Forest, Furman, and Mississippi College, with Furman being an important school to help launch Southern Seminary in the same way that Baylor was significant for the launching of Southwestern. The educational piece has been vital to the work of Southern Baptists and must be continued.[23]

5. Commission People

Southern Baptists are a commissioned people, a Great Commission people. From day one the focus was on domestic and foreign missions in order to extend the gospel across the region, across the country, and around the world.[24]

6. Confessional

Southern Baptists are a confessional people. While the SBC did not have a public confessional statement until 1925, in 1845 when Southern Baptists came together as a people, they had been shaped by the 1677 Second London Confession, the 1678 Orthodox Creed, the 1833 New Hampshire Confession, the Philadelphia Association Confession, and the important role of the 1858/1859 Abstract of Principles and its influence on Southern Baptists during the convention's early decades. Southern Baptists are a confessional people, particularly related to the Bible, to the gospel, to regenerate church membership, and to believer's baptism by immersion.[25]

7. Congregationalists

Southern Baptists are congregationalists. Southern Baptists believe in autonomous churches, autonomous entities, and regenerate church membership. There have been some differences from the beginning regarding single bishops or single

---

[22] Ibid., 45–52.

[23] Ibid., 134–67.

[24] Ibid., 38–45; Justice Anderson, "The Great Century and Beyond (1792–1910)," in *Missiology: An Introduction to the Foundations, History, and Strategies of World Missions*, rev. ed., ed. John Mark Terry, Ebbie Smith, and Justice Anderson (Nashville: B&H Academic, 2015), 209–10.

[25] Dockery, *Southern Baptist Consensus and Renewal*, 168–200.

pastors versus plural elders; nevertheless, there has been an agreement regarding the autonomy of local churches, the necessity of regenerate church membership, and congregational polity as identifiable matters that have shaped Southern Baptist life and ministry.[26]

8. Communion

Communion has always been important for understanding Southern Baptists. The Lord's Supper is noted over and over again in the book, *Baptist Why and Why Not*, published at the beginning of the twentieth century. Baptists clearly are people who affirm the importance of Communion, unlike the Quakers. They are people who have rejected transubstantiation and consubstantiation. While there has been some variation over the spiritual presence of Christ as opposed to the memorial understanding of the ordinance or whether Communion is to be practiced in an open or closed manner, this ordinance has been significant for defining Southern Baptists.[27]

9. Calvinism

Southern Baptists are not Calvinists; Southern Baptists are Calvinists but never consistent Calvinists. Consistency in this sense refers to the adoption of John Calvin's understanding of the Old Testament law and infant baptism in particular. Southern Baptists have never been consistent Arminians in totally rejecting Calvinism. A modified form of Calvinism has always characterized Southern Baptist soteriology. Even those who affirm the so-called five points of Calvinism are not truly consistent Calvinists. More agreement has been found related to the providence of God rather than the particulars related to God's sovereignty. Calvinism has influenced Southern Baptists whether or not they understand it, particularly regarding the doctrines of the perseverance of the saints and eternal security. Thus, the general understanding of the sinfulness of sin and eternal security have been shaped by Calvinistic doctrines. So while Southern Baptists are not consistent Calvinists and not consistent Arminians, they are modified Calvinists at least in some way. Southern Baptists can neither run away from nor misunderstand the influence of Calvinism throughout their history.[28]

10. Chiliasts or Millennialists

Southern Baptists are not millennialists, never having affirmed premillennialism, amillennialism, or postmillennialism as an essential doctrine in Southern

---

[26] See Jonathan Leeman, *Don't Fire Your Church Members: The Case for Congregationalism* (Nashville: B&H Academic, 2015).

[27] David S. Dockery, "Church, Worship, and the Lord's Supper," in *The Mission of Today's Church*, ed. Stan Norman (Nashville: B&H Academic, 2006), 43–50.

[28] Dockery, *Southern Baptist Consensus and Renewal*, 58–98.

Baptist life. Today Southern Baptists are primarily premillennialists. During the twentieth century the SBC was influenced by megachurch pastors who adopted dispensational pretribulation, premillennialism following the influence of W. A. Criswell. Also the influence of the *Scofield Reference Bible* among laypeople and Baptist pastors cannot be underestimated for movements toward premillennialism. Yet, historically, Southern Baptists have been more amillennial than anything. Postmillennialism was most popular in the nineteenth century, amillennialism predominantly in the middle of the twentieth century, and premillennialism characterizes most Southern Baptists today. Contemporary Southern Baptists involved in theological education are probably more historic premillennialist. A look at the New American Commentary interpretation of Matthew 24–25 in Mark 13 and 1 Thessalonians 4–5 shows that both follow historic premillennial interpretation.[29] The volumes on Daniel and Revelation, however, follow a pretribulation model.[30] So even the New American Commentary writers lack consistency regarding millennialism. Southern Baptists characteristically are not Chiliasts.

11. Culture

Southern Baptists have never adopted a Roman Catholic understanding of the church above culture, nor have they often confused church and state matters. Baptists have always understood the differences between church and state. Neither, even in the most moderate or liberal forms, has the Southern Baptist Convention moved to adopting a position of the culture speaking as a voice to the church, as that articulated by Harvey Cox in 1965 in his well-known work, *The Secular City*.[31] Southern Baptists have dealt with culture primarily in two different ways: either as a church separate from culture or as the church engaging culture. At times the convention has been more one than the other. Influenced largely over the past thirty years by Carl F. H. Henry, Francis Schaefer, and Chuck Colson, Southern Baptists have adopted a model of engaging culture. But as the culture has changed, that call for God's people to be "aliens and strangers" separate from the culture has become something to which many are now prepared to hear afresh. If one looks at the three Baptist Faith and Message statements (1925, 1963, 2000)

---

[29] Craig L. Blomberg, *Matthew: An Exegetical and Theological Exposition of Holy Scripture,* New American Commentary (Nashville: Holman Reference, 1992), 359–69; James A. Brooks, *Mark: An Exegetical and Theological Exposition of Holy Scripture,* New American Commentary (Nashville: Holman Reference, 1991), 208–18; D. Michael Martin, *1, 2 Thessalonians: An Exegetical and Theological Exposition of Holy Scripture,* New American Commentary (Nashville: Holman Reference, 1995), 140–69.

[30] Stephen Miller, *Daniel: An Exegetical and Theological Exposition of Holy Scripture, New American Commentary* (Nashville: B&H Reference, 1994), 305–23; Paige Patterson, *Revelation: An Exegetical and Theological Exposition of Holy Scripture,* New American Commentary (Nashville: Holman Reference, 2012), 127–33, 340–58.

[31] Harvey Cox, *The Secular City: Secularization and Urbanization in Theological Perspective* (New York: Macmillan, 1965).

one can follow the differences in how Southern Baptists have addressed the issues of culture in the final items in each of those confessional statements.[32]

12. Compassion

Southern Baptists are a compassionate people. The work of relief agencies over the last twenty years has raised that commitment to a level for the whole world to see the compassion of Southern Baptists, but all along the benevolence aspect of Southern Baptist ministries and ministry to the poor, the least, and the forgotten, has been exemplary for those who were paying attention.

These twelve markers point to a shared consensus of identity. At the least, they clarify the limits to the options among Southern Baptists as they have been expanded and affirmed for generations to come. These twelve areas have remained rather constant through the years and cannot be ignored without raising questions about the heart of Southern Baptist identity.

POINTERS FOR THE NEXT GENERATION

In conclusion, what should be said to the next generation? Six areas provide pointers for the years to come.

1. International and Global

Southern Baptists must come to grips with where they find themselves in a global world and must serve the global church in a new way, becoming more connected and involved internationally than ever before.

2. Interagency Collaboration

No longer can the SBC duplicate ministry. No longer can one group do the same thing at the state, association, and the national level. There must be interagency collaboration, which is a step beyond cooperation. New approaches must be developed in that regard.

3. Interconnected

Finding ways for Southern Baptists to hold hands with other believers who are committed to the Great Commandment and the Great Commission will be necessary. Southern Baptists can no longer be parochial to advance the gospel in a broader way, yet they must remain convictional about those primary Baptist matters. Southern Baptists must become interconnected with other believers, denominations, and networks.

---

[32] See Douglas K. Blount and Joseph D. Woodell, eds., *The Baptist Faith and Message 2000: Critical Issues in America's Largest Protestant Denomination* (Lanham, MD: Rowman & Littlefield, 2007).

4. Intercultural

Southern Baptists can no longer be insular. The Convention must be intentional in how it thinks about engaging the culture in an intercultural and multi-ethnic way.

5. Interracial

Southern Baptists have to recognize that the most longstanding and most persistent stain and embarrassment on their history since 1845 has been the issue of segregation and racism. The statement on racial reconciliation in 1995 was an important start. The election of Fred Luter as president was another important symbol, but more must be done. Progress has been made, but there is still a long way to go. Not just among African-Americans, but also among Asian-Americans, Hispanic-Americans, and Native Americans. Yes, there are 10,000 churches whose membership primarily consists of ethnic minorities across Southern Baptist life today. This progress is to be celebrated, but more work will be needed throughout the life of the Convention.

6. Intergenerational

Differences can certainly be identified and recognized among the generations. There are differences between the millennial generation and other generations, but most Americans and most Southern Baptists do not find their primary identity in generational identity. Believers must find their identity ultimately and primarily in Christ. And second, they must locate their identity within the denominational markers of conviction. Still there will be a need to respect differences in style, priorities, and emphases. Differences regarding how millennials think about and process matters will need to be clarified, but everyone must recognize that primary identity is found in Christ.

CONCLUSION

Over time, from 1845 to 1870, the founding generation, characterized by development, came to an end with the death of W. B. Johnson. From 1870 to 1900, the generation characterized by stability, came to an end with the deaths of James Boyce and John Broadus. From 1900 to 1950, the generation characterized by cooperation, ended with the death of W. T. Conner. From 1950 to 1980, a generation characterized by efficiency and expansion along with some movement to the mainline, came to an end with the death of Baker James Cauthen. From 1980 to 2005, a generation characterized by controversy and recovery, came to an end with the death of Adrian Rogers. The Southern Baptist Convention today stands at a pivotal moment in need of reenvisioning for the days ahead.

In conclusion, as a blessed future for the SBC is reenvisioned, leaders can no longer be naïve to the multifaceted changes and multilevel challenges all around: technological, economic, educational, cultural, and global. Denominational matters do not take place in a vacuum. The SBC will need to be both confessional and convictional and at the same time bring about a fresh spirit calling for Southern Baptists to reemphasize compassion and cooperation in order to build bridges toward collaborative and shared efforts to advance the gospel. Southern Baptists will need to understand the value of the tradition that has both informed and shaped who they are, even as they recognize the need to think more strategically and intentionally about being intergenerational, intercultural, and international in a transcontinental way in the approach to church, ministry, missions, theological education, and denominational life.

A new spirit of trust, mutual respect, and humility to serve together where there are differences on secondary and tertiary matters must continue to develop. New opportunities for partnerships and collaboration will be needed to pull the SBC out of its inward-focused insularity, particularly serving together in trans-denominational ways in the areas of social action, cultural engagement, the all-important matters of religious freedom, and similar matters related to the public square.

Southern Baptists need to trust God to bring a fresh wind of his Spirit, to bring renewal to confessional convictions, and to revitalize the churches while relating to one another in love and humility. Prayers are offered not only for renewed confessional convictions but for a genuine demonstration of beliefs and orthopraxy that can be seen before a watching world, a world particularly in the Western Hemisphere that seemingly stands on the verge of giving up on the Christian faith, moving toward what Charles Taylor calls a thoroughly "secular age."[33] We pray that the shared and collaborative efforts of churches and Southern Baptist entities will bring forth fruit, and will strengthen partnerships, alliances, and networks for the extension of God's kingdom and the advancement of the gospel across the country and around the world for the eternal glory of our great God.

---

[33] Charles Taylor, *A Secular Age* (Cambridge, MA: Belknap/Harvard University Press, 2007).

More than Fifteen Million Southern Baptists? Recovering Regenerate Church Membership

John Mark Yeats

The old joke takes various forms, but it runs something like this: "The SBC has more than 15 million members, but even the FBI couldn't find half of them if they tried." For a convention of churches that historically anchored its understanding of membership in the discipleship and ongoing growth of the believer, this old bit frames an indictment of carelessness at best and outright spiritual abuse at worst. Either way, it does not look good.

The actual numbers from the Annual Church Profile do not help the case much. Consider the following data:[1]

- The overall number of baptisms continues to drop from highs in 400,000s per year during 1997–2000[2] to just over 300,000 in 2014—a key marker for Baptist churches and those joining their ranks.
- Over the last fifteen years, the SBC total church membership dropped almost a full percent to 15,499,173.
- We have yet to see an increase in overall members since 2006.

As the Southern Baptist Convention, we long upheld the ideal of a regenerate church membership as a biblical concept. Lest we are confused, this is not membership in the means that one joins a country club, American Express, or Costco.

---

[1] The following data is based on numbers reported to the Southern Baptist Convention annually by the executive committee. See The Executive Committee of the Southern Baptist Convention, *Southern Baptist Convention Annual* (Nashville, TN: Southern Baptist Convention, 2009-2014). These are available online through the work of the Southern Baptist Historical Library and Archives at http://www.sbhla.org/sbc_annuals.

[2] 419,342 in 1999 and 414,657 in 2000 according to Executive Committee, *Southern Baptist Convention Annual*, 2001, p. 108. For the 2014 number, see Executive Committee, *Southern Baptist Convention Annual*, 2015, p. 134.

There is no *quid pro quo* or consumeristic value equation when we contemplate membership in the body of Christ, for that only cheapens the idea. Instead, membership is an extension of the grace of God poured out for the life of all believers for the purpose of expanding the kingdom of God. In trusting Christ, we become part of the body of Christ.

The New Testament and the early church echo this sentiment. The reformers challenged abuses in this area, but the point remained: the body of Christ is comprised of those who are regenerated believers. For Baptists our claim has been and remains that this inward regeneration is best demonstrated through the public rite of believer's baptism. This is why we claim a "believer's church." Every member publicly makes a clear profession of faith verbally and through participating in the outward sign in order to be considered a member.

Yet we have a real problem. If there are more than 15,000,000 members in the SBC, where are they? As an association of churches, can we actually claim these numbers with a straight face? What are we to do with inaccurate corporate numbers? As with any undertaking that deals with Baptists, we will begin with the Scriptures first and build a case for a scriptural understanding of membership. From that point we will look at practical realities facing congregations and the Southern Baptist Convention as an association of churches relating to the idea of church membership.

MEMBERSHIP: A SETTLED ISSUE

Baptist ecclesiology continually stresses the importance of a formal membership based upon the clear teaching of Scripture. While true that *membership* as a formal term is not found in the text, the concept is clearly presented and used from the earliest inception of the church. In Acts 2:42 and following, we see the earliest church gathering, worshiping, serving, sharing, and evangelizing. Those who participated were numbered among the believers. Paul, addressing the churches in Corinth and Ephesus, uses the term *melos*—"member"—to refer to Christians and their connection to the body of Christ. In 1 Corinthians 5:1–13 Paul recommends full discipline and removal from the body of an unrepentant congregant. In 2 Timothy 4:9–16 Paul commends some and anathematizes others. This is consistent with Romans 16:1–16 as well. In 1 Timothy 5:1–16 there is a practical suggestion to tend to a list of widows, and the deacons of Acts 6:1–7 took care of the body of Christ.

Here a clear picture begins to emerge. From its earliest stages the Christian church saw itself as individual members connected to something much bigger than themselves. They were joined together under the lordship of Jesus Christ (the head) into the body of Christ. They were members—part of the whole. And, more excitedly, this is part of the clear picture of the gospel at work in the church no matter if the metaphor turns to "family" or "building" or any of the other visual images that the apostles used. There is a place of belonging for each believer through the work of Christ!

The world had no place for the followers of Jesus. They were "strangers," "aliens," or "pilgrims" who did not have a place here in this world (Heb 11:13–16; John 17:16; 1 Pet 2:11). Jesus warned that his followers were in the world but not of it (John 15:19). Paul, encouraging the church in Corinth, reminded them that as believers they were to come out from the world and be separate while grounding this positional relationship in his fatherly presence (2 Cor 6:14–18).

Consequently, the existence of Christians shifts in priority. Since we are no longer of this world but part of the family of God, as sons and daughters of the King, we are conscripted as ambassadors of the gospel (2 Cor 5:20). Our orders come from Christ himself to enter the world with the message of the hope and truth found in our Savior (Matt 28:19–20). Corporately, we become brothers and sisters in Christ, and our love for one another demonstrates the truth of the gospel since, according to Jesus, "By this all people will know that you are My disciples" (John 13:35 HCSB).

As part of this overwhelming grace, the individuals who comprise the church ought to take seriously the calling we possess and participate fully in the body of Christ. There are no "free range" Christians. As we demonstrated earlier, in the New Testament we can readily observe defined lists of who was "in" or "out" of the membership of the body of Christ for the purpose of care, discipleship, and even church discipline. From those participating lists, leaders were chosen, pastors shepherded, deacons served, and members disciplined.

Individuals needing care, such as the poor, widows, and orphans, benefited from the financial resources of the body of Christ (1 John 3:17–18; James 1:27, 2:2–6; 1 Tim 5:3; Gal 2:10; Rom 15:26). While the church did reach out beyond the doors of the congregation evangelistically, early indications were that resource sharing happened internally within the body first. The deacons oversaw such distribution, ensuring that every need was met appropriately within the body. In Acts 6 the appointment of deacons connected directly to this need when the Gentile converts "complained against the Hebraic Jews because their widows were being overlooked in the daily distribution of food" (Acts 6:1 NIV). With the apostles' ministry spent proclaiming the good news, overseeing whose needs should be addressed went beyond their call. When the apostles proposed a practical solution by appointing deacons, the congregation as a whole rejoiced (Acts 6:5). Most importantly, according to Acts 6:7 (HCSB), as a direct corollary of addressing the needs of its community, "preaching about God flourished, the number of the disciples in Jerusalem multiplied greatly."

These same deacons also practiced a discernment role in understanding who should be excluded from needs-based ministry. Note that Paul addresses the church in Thessaloniki with a challenge, "If anyone isn't willing to work, he should not eat" (2 Thess 3:10 HCSB).

The whole church, though, was to "expel the wicked person" who persisted in sin (1 Cor 5:12–13 NIV). Even Jesus in dealing with unrepentant members of the community encouraged the entire church to treat those persons as if they were outside the community. The apostle John argued in his first epistle that even Antichrists would come from *inside the church*.

BOUNDED-SET VERSUS CENTER-SET COMMUNITY

All of this leads to a conclusion of a bounded-set understanding of church membership. The borders of the early church were not porous. You either submitted your life to the lordship of Jesus Christ, or you rebelled against him. In 2 Corinthians 6:14–16, the boundary is so clear we are asked what one group has to do with the other. Further, Paul warns the Corinthian church, "Do not be mismatched with unbelievers" (2 Cor 6:14 HCSB).

During the fashionable season of the so-called emerging church, scholars like Alan Hirsch and Michael Frost joined Phyllis Tickle, Brian McClaren, Tony Jones, and others in arguing for a shift in evangelicalism to center-set understandings of Christian belief.[3]

Drawing from missiologists like Paul Hiebert[4] who warned against erecting artificial boundaries that were unnecessarily prohibitive from those outside of the faith from following Christ, the argument ran as follows: if Jesus is the center, the measurement of following Christ is simply directional. Those facing toward Christ and moving toward him are followers, those facing away or moving away from Christ are not.

On some levels this is helpful, especially when understanding the nature of discipleship. If Jesus is the center, then we should be, as Scripture encourages, fixing "our eyes on Jesus, the source and perfecter of our faith."[5] Believers are moving ever closer to the Savior as the work of sanctification through the power of the Holy Spirit takes place in their lives. Hiebert argued that ultimate worldview shifts only happened through ongoing discipleship and obedience on the part of a new believer over an extended period of time in a healthy faith community.[6] Once a person enters the faith through trust in Christ (bounded set), life becomes a

---

[3] See Alan Hirsch and Michael Frost, *The Shaping of Things to Come* (Grand Rapids: Baker, 2013); Brian McClaren, *A New Kind of Christian* (San Francisco: Jossey Bass, 2008); Tony Jones, *The New Christians* (San Francisco: Jossey Bass, 2008); Phyllis Tickle, *The Great Emergence* (Grand Rapids: Baker, 2012).

[4] See Paul Hiebert, *Transforming Worldviews* (Grand Rapids: Baker, 2008) or his much earlier article in the short-lived journal *Gospel in Context*, titled "Conversion, Culture, and Cognitive Categories," *Gospel in Context* 1 (1978): 24–29.

[5] Hebrews 12:1–2 (HCSB).

[6] Hiebert, *Transforming Worldviews*, 310.

process of increasingly moving to Christlikeness through sanctification (center set).

Increasingly, postmodern and emerging church authors teased the reality of center-set discipleship too far by advocating a full relationship to Christianity as that of a center-set only. One simply journeyed with others in faith. According to Phyllis Tickle, "One simply belongs to a gathering of Christians by virtue of a shared humanity and an affinity with the individuals involved in whatever the group as a whole is doing."[7] There were no boundaries one needed to cross; no specific belief commitment was required. People identifying as Christian simply need to make Jesus the center. Thus, ideas such as membership are moot.

Since its inception Christianity consistently articulated an ethic that sounds center set. Christians abide in Christ (John 15). We identify as disciples as we "believe on the Lord Jesus" (Acts 16:31 HCSB). Quite frankly, Christianity is all about Jesus—the "source and perfecter of our faith" (Heb 12:2 HCSB). Churches are consistently refocusing our congregations to the Lord and Savior Jesus Christ as members grow in sanctification. In effect, we are our best when the church, as the bride, prepares for the groom, Jesus.

But contrary to some, the borders are not unguarded.

Christianity clearly functions as a bounded set with thresholds of entry centered on living according to the lordship of Jesus Christ. As already articulated, this creates standards whereby one could be excluded or anathematized. The standards, or boundaries, are clear. Whether communicated by the apostles or Jesus himself, the demarcated boundaries enabled the church to understand those who were "in" or those who were "out."

For example, the church articulated a consistent entry point—faith in Jesus Christ demonstrated publicly through baptism. With baptism came church membership. There was no further chasm to overcome, no higher bar to reach. A person following Christ *was a member of the local church* and was expected to participate in the life of the body. Evangelism is necessarily churchly. New believers incorporate and become part of the body of Christ.

As members, the believers face expectations. A life of following Jesus consequently involves a continued commitment to *orthodoxy* (rightly ordered belief) and *orthopraxy* (rightly ordered practice). Through active participation in the life of the body, each individual grows together as the corporate body grows more and more like Christ. Along with membership comes an ethical standard that individuals *and* the community continue to meet. Individuals in the body of Christ become full participants in the orthodoxy of the church while living out the consequent orthopraxy.

---

[7] Tickle, *The Great Emergence*, 159.

To this end, evangelism methods of the earliest church nearly always involved submitting one's life to Christ and the community of faith. The Western idea of an "independent" or "self-sustaining" Christian did not compute. As a church called to make disciples of all nations, nothing was understood to further disciple-ship like submitting to the headship of Christ through the local body of believers gathering in worship and service. Salvation without incorporation in the visible church missed the scriptural standard. To be a Christian was and is to be part of the local body of believers—the church. To hear pop-star Justin Bieber claim, "You don't need to go to church to be a Christian. If you go to Taco Bell, that doesn't make you a taco,"[8] grossly misses the point of what it is to follow Christ.

If the church is God's plan, we should tread carefully. We should elevate our understanding of membership so that we place the premium on the thing God's Word does. We should recognize that it is impossible for any believer to claim for himself or herself that I "like Jesus, but not the church."[9]

DISCIPLESHIP OF MEMBERS

Part of the design of the church is for the membership to become more and more like Jesus. This forces us into relationships with others not like ourselves whereby we are called to die to ourselves and love one another. In these "one another" passages the depths of following Jesus are revealed in force. Fifty-nine times in the New Testament the community of faith is told to participate in some level of life together through a "one another" instruction.[10] In the second half of the book of Ephesians alone, we are told to:

- ". . . be patient, bearing with one another in love" (Eph 4:2 NIV).
- "Be kind and compassionate to one another . . ." (Eph 4:32 NIV).
- ". . . forgiving each other . . ." (Eph 4:32 NIV).
- ". . . speaking to one another with psalms, hymns, and songs from the Spirit" (Eph 5:19 NIV).
- "Submit to one another out of reverence for Christ" (Eph 5:21 NIV).

In John's Gospel we are admonished to "love one another" no fewer than five times within Jesus's teaching in chapters 13–15.[11] There is something gospel-orienting about walking in life together that disciples and grows us as believers. And we should be honest with "one another." This is hard work. While not a

---

[8] *Rolling Stone*, "Justin Bieber: I want to live like Jesus," featured on Yahoo! Music, September 25, 2015. Accessed September 29, 2015. https://www.yahoo.com/music/justin-bieber-i-want-to-live-like-je-sus-181943041.html.

[9] See Dan Kimball's challenge in *They Like Jesus but Not the Church* (Grand Rapids: Zondervan, 2007).

[10] Carl F. George, *Prepare Your Church for the Future* (Tarrytown: Revell, 1991), 129–31.

[11] Paul picks up this same theme in Romans 12:10, as does Peter in 1 Peter 4:8. John mentions the same phrase an additional six times in his epistles.

formal survey by any sorts, as the church I pastored sought to address its bloated membership rolls, we discovered large numbers of people with significant "one another" issues. They had feelings hurt by people in the church. Some group did not behave in a way the person expected. Individuals said hurtful things. The list went on.

Surprisingly (or not), many of these individuals failed to ever connect with another church. They simply parked themselves in bed or found other things to do on Sunday instead of pursuing the difficult challenge of dealing with complex interpersonal relationships. Let's face it—many of us do not mind a family reunion for a couple of hours every year or so, but do we really want to hang out with crazy Uncle Fred every week?

But this is *precisely* what Jesus is telling us! "By this all people will know that you are My disciples, if you have love for one another" (John 13:35). When you mix individuals from radically different socioeconomic settings, career trajectories, cultural and ethnic backgrounds, you should expect chaos. But with Jesus the circumstance changes. Paul, addressing the ethnically diverse church in Ephesus, reminded them, "For He is our peace, who made both groups one and tore down the dividing wall of hostility . . . so that He might create in Himself one new man from the two, resulting in peace. He did this so that He might reconcile both to God in one body through the cross and put the hostility to death by it" (Eph 2:14–16 HCSB).

Honestly, and in practice, we resent this. We create spiritual ghettos where one person shares considerable affinity ideals with another. We create new consumer categories as we divide the church into neat little marketing niches. Because of numerical growth in attendees, we never deal with the spiritual vacuity this creates. We never contend with different people or with outsiders and social losers. But as a former pastor once reminded me, "Jesus is for losers."

These relationships with fellow members who are not like us create a powerful testimony to the centrality of Jesus Christ with two results. First, we begin to get over ourselves. There is no way you can adhere truthfully to the claims of Christ and continue to pursue selfish ends unchecked. Life in community forces us to check our pride at the door and carry forward. We become like spiritual sandpaper to one another—rubbing off the rough edges. Church membership taken scripturally provides us the venue to do *exactly* what the New Testament asks us to do—love one another. In the realm of a church serious about membership, we begin to see fruit from Jesus's claim that our love demonstrates our identity as Christ followers. As individuals mature, the corporate body is observably more and more like Christ (John 13:35).

Second, legitimate evangelism takes place—every church must have an intentional evangelism strategy to reach the lost. God built into the nature of the church itself one of the most powerful presentations of the gospel—the local church. Do not laugh. As we participate in the fullness of the grace of Jesus Christ and extend that to our brothers and sisters in Christ week in and week out, the world cannot help but understand there is something different about Jesus Christ. How can a single mom on welfare worship together with the CEO of a Fortune 500 company? How can an African-American grandfather mentor an Asian-American to be a godly young man? How can they together do the work of the gospel? In a world fractured by so many ideologies and subcultures, the Church has one foundation—Jesus Christ our Lord.

If the case holds, though, that together, as a body, we show the hope of Christ, we are forced to move to the more difficult component of church membership—the subject of church discipline.

CHURCH DISCIPLINE

Within the nature of church discipline, the bounded set is truly revealed. Should one person (or a community) seek to violate the orthodoxy of the church, they experience discipline by the leaders and the church as a whole. The goal? Restoration. By pleading with their brother or sister, the aim is to bring members back into full fellowship with the body if repentance occurs and the member submits to orthodoxy. Consider Paul's close to his second letter to Timothy where he expresses frustration at Alexander who "did great harm to me" (2 Tim 4:14 HCSB). We assume this is the same Alexander along with Hymenaeus, whom Paul "delivered . . . to Satan, so that they may be taught not to blaspheme" (1 Tim 1:20 HCSB). Right belief mattered.

But it is not just the case of orthodoxy. With rightly ordered belief came rightly ordered ethics—orthopraxy. If the member of the community rejects the claims of Christ that extend to every area of life, full discipline is applied to members, bringing them back into full relationship with the church. Paul, writing the Corinthian church, castigated their lax practice of church discipline. When a member openly enjoyed an improper sexual relationship, Paul demanded action be taken: "Put away the evil person from among yourselves" (1 Cor 5:13 HCSB).

In Jesus's challenge to his disciples in Matthew 18:15–20, we are given clear instruction that those who fail to reconcile with one another are on dangerous ground. Stressors in interpersonal relationships seemingly elevate situations to full-church adjudication. And, as church members work together, healing and restoration are the desired outcomes.

But this is hard work. No one truly craves church discipline any more than a parent craves disciplining his or her child. No one truly longs to die to our selfish wants and desires either. The author of Hebrews is clear, "No discipline seems enjoyable at the time, but painful. Later on, however, it yields the fruit of peace and righteousness to those who have been trained by it" (Heb 12:11). Our life of "one another" in the kingdom is designed for our good and to demonstrate the truth of the gospel. Despite our cultural climate of being rather averse to any form of correction, we cannot help but see that Scripture is clear that discipline must be a key component in the life of every church.[12]

MORE THAN 15,000,000 REGENERATE MEMBERS?

Having established this scriptural framework for the local church, turn back to the national level. As Baptists we believe in a regenerate church membership. Our confessions even into the seventeenth century place a high value on a regenerate church membership.

> Christ hath likewise given power to His Church to receive in, and cast out, any member that deserves it; and this power is given to every congregation, and not to one particular person, either member or officer, but in relation to the whole body, in reference to their faith and fellowship. (First London Confession 1646, Article 42)

> Paragraph 12. As all believers are bound to join themselves to particular church-es, when and where they have opportunity so to do; so all that are admitted unto the privileges of a church, are also under the censures and government thereof, according to the rule of Christ.

> Paragraph 13. No church members, upon any offence taken by them, having performed their duty required of them towards the person they are offended at, ought to disturb any church-order, or absent themselves from the assemblies of the church, or administration of any ordinances, upon the account of such offence at any of their fellow members, but to wait upon Christ, in the further proceeding of the church. (Second London Confession 1689, Article 26)

> 1. All saints that are united to Jesus Christ, their head, by his Spirit, and faith, although they are not made thereby one person with him, have fellowship in his graces, sufferings, death, resurrection, and glory; and, being united to one another in love, they have communion in each others gifts and graces, and are obliged to the performance of such duties, public and private, in an orderly way, as do conduce to their mutual good, both in the inward and outward man.
> 2. Saints by profession are bound to maintain an holy fellowship and commu-nion in the worship of God, and in performing such other spiritual services as tend to their mutual edification; as also in relieving each other in outward things accord-ing to their several abilities, and necessities; which communion, according to the

---

[12] For a more helpful, book length study, see Jonathan Leeman's *The Church and the Surprising Offense of God's Love* (Wheaton, IL: Crossway, 2010).

rule of the gospel, though especially to be exercised by them, in the relation wherein they stand, whether in families, or churches, yet, as God offereth opportunity, is
to be extended to all the household of faith, even all those who in every place call
upon the name of the Lord Jesus; nevertheless their communion one with another
as saints, doth not take away or infringe the title or property which each man hath
in his goods and possessions. (Philadelphia Confession 1742, Chapter 28)

A church of Christ is a congregation of baptized believers, associated by covenant in the faith and fellowship of the gospel; observing the ordinances of Christ,
governed by his laws, and exercising the gifts, rights, and privileges invested in
them by his word, and seeking to extend the gospel to the ends of the earth. Its
Scriptural officers are bishops, or elders, and deacons. (Baptist Faith and Message
1925, Article 12)

A New Testament church of the Lord Jesus Christ is an autonomous local
congregation of baptized believers, associated by covenant in the faith and fellowship of the gospel; observing the two ordinances of Christ, governed by His
laws, exercising the gifts, rights, and privileges invested in them by His Word,
and seeking to extend the gospel to the ends of the earth. Each congregation
operates under the Lordship of Christ through democratic processes. In such
a congregation each member is responsible and accountable to Christ as Lord.
Its scriptural officers are pastors and deacons. While both men and women are
gifted for service in the church, the office of pastor is limited to men as qualified
by Scripture. (Baptist Faith and Message 2000, Article 6)

The New Testament speaks also of the church as the body of Christ, which
includes all of the redeemed of all the ages, believers from every tribe, and tongue,
and people, and nation.

We have stated publicly over and again that we believe the church is comprised of baptized believers gathered in local congregations. Yet the irony should
not be lost on us as a confessional people. More than fifteen million members?
Consider John Hammett's powerful claim on this point:

Today, a denomination like the Southern Baptist convention maintains the theology of regenerate church membership in its official statements, but in reality its
churches show little evidence of regeneration in the behavior of their members. It
is widely known that divorce and moral problems are as common among church
members as non-church members. Even the very modest index of attendance at
Sunday morning worship shows close to two-thirds of Southern Baptist church
members missing on any given Sunday morning. Regenerate church membership

cannot be seriously maintained as characterizing most Baptist churches in North America Today.[13]

Russell Moore similarly claimed, "Being Baptist means a regenerate church membership. If church membership is a declaration of the church of a credible profession of faith, then the persistence on our church rolls of so many who do not attend or openly reject the faith is not just a scandal to the gospel—it is anti-evangelism."[14]

To address the issue several motions went forward at both the state and national convention levels to address our denominational bloat and to confront this scriptural challenge our local churches are facing. Resolutions were proposed in 2006 and 2007 on the issue of regenerate church membership. Yet in response to the notion that our churches should carefully reconsider the notion of regenerate church membership in 2006, the committee chair at the national convention remarked that if churches cleaned their rolls, they would lose their greatest prospects for evangelism! We are missing the point.

The 2008 resolution proposed at the national convention held in Indianapolis suggested a helpful way forward that builds on the scriptural foundations articulated here as well as building on the historical framework of our Baptist forebears.

> WHEREAS, The ideal of a regenerate church membership has long been and remains a cherished Baptist principle, with Article VI of the Baptist Faith and Message describing the church as a "local congregation of baptized believers"; and
>
> WHEREAS, A New Testament church is composed only of those who have been born again by the Holy Spirit through the preaching of the Word, becoming disciples of Jesus Christ, the local church's only Lord, by grace through faith (John 3:5; Ephesians 2:8–9), which church practices believers' only baptism by immersion (Matthew 28:16–20), and the Lord's supper (Matthew 26:26–30); and
>
> WHEREAS, Local associations, state conventions, and the Southern Baptist Convention compile statistics reported by the churches to make decisions for the future; and
>
> WHEREAS, The 2007 Southern Baptist Convention annual Church Profiles indicate that there are 16,266,920 members in Southern Baptist churches; and
>
> WHEREAS, Those same profiles indicate that only 6,148,868 of those members attend a primary worship service of their church in a typical week; and
>
> WHEREAS, The Scriptures admonish us to exercise church discipline as we seek to restore any professed brother or sister in Christ who has strayed from the truth and is in sin (Matthew 18:15–35; Galatians 6:1); and now, therefore, be it

---

[13] John Hammett, "Regenerate Church Membership," in *Restoring Integrity in Baptist Churches*, ed. Jason G. Duesing, Thomas White, and Malcolm B. Yarnell III (Grand Rapids: Kregel, 2008), 27.

[14] Russell Moore, "Learning from 19th Century Baptists" in *Southern Baptist Identity: An Evangelical Denomination Faces the Future*, ed. David S. Dockery (Wheaton, IL: Crossway, 2009), 110.

RESOLVED, That the messengers to the Southern Baptist Convention meeting in Indianapolis, Indiana, June 10–11, 2008, urge churches to maintain a regenerate membership by acknowledging the necessity of spiritual regeneration and Christ's lordship for all members; and be it further

RESOLVED, That we humbly urge our churches to maintain accurate membership rolls for the purpose of fostering ministry and accountability among all members of the congregation; and be it further

RESOLVED, That we urge the churches of the Southern Baptist Convention to repent of the failure among us to live up to our professed commitment to regenerate church membership and any failure to obey Jesus Christ in the practice of lovingly correcting wayward church members (Matthew 18:15–18); and be it further

RESOLVED, That we humbly encourage denominational servants to support and encourage churches that seek to recover and implement our Savior's teachings on church discipline, even if such efforts result in the reduction in the number of members that are reported in those churches, and be it finally

RESOLVED, That we humbly urge the churches of the Southern Baptist Convention and their pastors to implement a plan to minister to, counsel, and restore wayward church members based upon the commands and principles given in Scripture (Matthew 18:15–35; 2 Thessalonians 3:6–15; Galatians 6:1; James 5:19–20).

So the problem is solved. Not really.

If you have been around the SBC for any length of time, this resolution was simply that. A resolution. It simply reflected the tenor of the 2008 gathering of SBC churches that met in Indianapolis. As our churches are autonomous, it had no actual bearing on the individual churches but rather expressed the will of those present. In fact, had the motion been fully implemented, we might have expected a greater reduction in the number of individual members reported by our churches, but the following year (2009) only saw a reduction of 0.42 percent, and 2010 only declined an additional 0.15 percent. This is hardly a course correction.[15]

SOLUTIONS AND A WAY FORWARD

So what is to be done? So far we have seen the scriptural argument for local church membership. We have noted the ongoing and consistent advancement of the idea of regenerate church membership in Baptist life. We have even looked at a helpful response to the situation through the 2008 resolution at the national SBC meeting.

As the point of our conversation at this gathering is to look at solutions for the twenty-first century, I would like to turn and examine a few suggestions.

---

[15] Executive Committee, *Southern Baptist Convention Annual*, 2010, p. 138; Executive Committee, *Southern Baptist Convention Annual*, 2009, p. 110; Executive Committee, *Southern Baptist Convention Annual*, 2011, p. 124.

Solutions to the situation:

1. Instruction about membership. If one is preaching the whole council of God, this is, and should be, an inevitable component. The typical practice of older SBC churches of on-the-spot approval of individuals for membership based on a simple confession that one is a follower of Christ is ripe for abuse and, in fact, has been abused. In generations prior the normative experience of most Baptist congregations was that members were outnumbered by attendees every Sunday. Now in many established congregations the number of members far outnumbers regular attendees. If regenerate church membership meets the standards we have articulated here, it is impossible for churches to run in this manner. This instruction must be held forth from the pulpit as we preach the whole council of God. As we encounter the "one anothers" or any of the metaphorical images that apply to the body of Christ, we must press in about the nature of church membership. We cannot let this pass, especially in an era that shies away from commitments to anything long-term. The nature of regenerate church membership flies in the face of our consumer culture, and therefore maintaining any level of meaningful membership will fly in the face of cultural expectations at every turn. It is worth the fight, but we must engage always. The price is too high.

2. Repent for our sin of chasing numbers. The motivation of meeting worldly criteria of success has led to careless practices where pragmatism trumps biblical standards. We even judge one another based on the number of members or individuals we serve. Let this not be! Let us shepherd the sheep God brings us and trust him for the increase!

3. Membership classes. A membership class is the most important change many churches can implement immediately for maximum impact. Gospel, confession, constitution. Potential members should provide a clear testimony of salvation given and an interview with a pastor/elder or membership committee as an essential if we are to provide biblical accountability and appropriate church discipline. How else are we able to rightly administer the ordinances given to the church?

a. In these classes we must articulate what we believe. The confession of faith is essential. Many churches discover that focusing on theology enables them to see individuals come to faith in Christ during that meeting.

b. Individuals need to be growing in faith and should be connected to the expectations of all members. This at a minimum should require an understanding of regularly participating in community worship, serve in the body, grow through ongoing study and share the gospel.

4. Church confession. The church confession should be promoted clearly and a part of the central culture of the congregation. Deviations from the clear faith statement/confession should be roadblocks to membership. If a member chooses to deviate from aspects of the confession, our role is to hold that member accountable. Recent approaches to this have churches reciting their confession (or some part of it) every week to remind one another of the "This we believe . . ." elements. Other congregations like The Village Church in Dallas require members to resign the church confession annually or be removed from the rolls of the congregation.

5. *Clean the rolls.* This could be the most challenging aspect of the entire process. As this happens, a few of things begin to happen:

 a. You realize how important a good church database system is to help manage your people's spiritual growth!

 b. You realize how sloppy membership methods of the past have led to low expectations about membership, authority, and accountability.

 c. That same sloppiness meant there are many on your rolls who do not know Christ. Tell them about Jesus. Then clean the roll.

 d. Your numbers shrink back to a manageable amount. In the case of a church I pastored, our membership rolls shrunk by more than 500 in one meeting.

Can you imagine what would happen if 45,000 SBC congregations cleaned their rolls and became honest about who actually were members? What if corporately we reduced our rolls to the point where we accurately reflected who we are? We would see ourselves move away from chasing power in politics or culture. We would see ourselves honestly projecting who is in our midst. Our regenerate membership would best present the gospel as we lived the life we are called to live.

Returning to our opening joke, we realize the joke is actually on us. The thing that God called precious and beautiful, the organism painted in Scripture as the bride of Christ has morphed into a monster because we are often unwilling to follow the standards God set out for us. Brothers and sisters, this should not be. We must return to the biblical standards given to us and follow Christ in upholding regenerate church membership.

A Denomination Always for the Church: Ecclesiological Distinctives as a Basis for Confessional Cooperation

Jason G. Duesing

FOR THE CHURCH AS A MEANS TO THE END

" ' I am glad that you are here with me,' said Frodo. 'Here at the end of all things, Sam.'"[1] I never expected to get an ecclesiology and eschatology lesson from the concluding chapters of Tolkien's *The Lord of the Rings*, but I did. The hero and his faithful companion, comprising the remnant of a fellowship that set out on a journey to destroy evil and see the return of their king, lay exhausted and helpless, surrounded by an erupting mountain of volcanic proportions with no cause for hope of rescue. Yet in that moment they had the peace and security that only victorious soldiers must know when they, though dying, have saved countrymen or even countries. What was their source of hope? Knowledge that evil was ultimately defeated though the world self-destructed around them and hope in the truth for which they persevered. That and remaining fellowship led them to express gladness and joy there "at the end of all things." Of course, as the story goes, they fell asleep before they were swept up on eagles' wings and awakened to find restored fellowship and the return of the king. I never expected to see the connection between the joy found in fellowship giving hope at the end of the world—I never saw the right connection between ecclesiology and eschatology—but there it was, even in *The Lord of the Rings*.

---

[1] J. R. R. Tolkien, *The Lord of the Rings*, 50th anniversary edition (New York: Houghton Mifflin Harcourt, 2004), 994.

In Tolkien's story there is great hope and joy for those of us laboring as Christians in a self-destructing world, and thankfully that is a mere reflection of the shining light of truth of these themes found in the Bible. In 1 Peter 4:7 the apostle Peter explains that "the end of all things is near," and by that he means that he and his readers were living in the last days before the return of Jesus. Since that time until our own, humanity has been living at the verge of the end of the world, but that is not a cause for despair or hand-wringing. Peter's point was focused rather on how one is to live at the end of all things, and he spends the next few verses underscoring this for believers. Peter explains that while a Christian should have his eyes fixed and his hope set on the soon and certain return of Jesus, he should be using his spiritual gifts, whether they be serving or speaking, for the glory of God. What, then, is the source of our hope, and on what task are we to have our minds and hearts set? Until the end—whether one eats, drinks, preaches, trains, waters, reaps, types, writes, shares, or disciples—he should be doing these things as the biblically prescribed means for carrying out the Great Commission to the glory of God. Such it is, too, with the work of cooperating churches—until the end churches are to cooperate, not as the end but the biblical means to the end. The focus of the Southern Baptist Convention in the twenty-first century should always be for the church. The local churches comprise the headquarters of this denomination, and thus the convention and its entities should serve the churches. The ecclesiological distinctives of the SBC serve as the basis for Baptist churches to cooperate, yet this focus is merely a means to the end. So, for a convention of cooperating churches striving and seeking to fulfill the Great Commission, the prescribed plan for the accomplishing of that task is for that denomination to remain always for the church. In short, our desire to be "for the church" is a desire for increased cooperative ministry for the sake of global evangelism and to see the knowledge of the glory of God among all peoples as the waters cover the sea (Hab 2:14).

Therefore, given that the days are few and the light of the present culture is dimming, I hope to argue for the need for ecclesiological distinctives as a basis for confessional cooperation. That is, for cooperating Southern Baptist churches seeking to strengthen and start other churches as the means to the end of fulfilling the Great Commission and glorifying God, what is the ecclesiological baseline for them to do so? To accomplish this, I will (1) introduce what I call *ecclesiological triage* as a term to help clarify how we should think about ecclesiological distinctives, (2) seek to answer the question, "What is a true church?" and (3) discuss how confessions of faith help accomplish this task.

ECCLESIOLOGICAL TRIAGE FOR NEW TESTAMENT CHURCHES

In the nineteenth century leading Southern Baptist theologian J. L. Dagg wrote this with regard to the relationship of ecclesiology to other doctrines:

Church order and the ceremonials of religion, are less important than a new heart; and in the view of some, any laborious investigation of questions respecting them may appear to be needless and unprofitable. But we know, from the Holy Scriptures, that Christ gave commands on these subjects, and we cannot refuse to obey. Love prompts our obedience; and love prompts also the search which may be necessary to ascertain his will. Let us, therefore, prosecute the investigation which are before us, with a fervent prayer, that the Holy Spirit, who guides into all truth, may assist us to learn the will of him whom we supremely love and adore.[2]

Along these lines, as one reads and studies the Bible, there is a growing realization that some doctrines are more significant than others—not in terms of truthfulness or ultimate value but in terms of priority. In 2005 R. Albert Mohler Jr. provided a word of great clarity to his reading audience with his article, "A Call for Theological Triage and Christian Maturity."[3] In this article, he explains:

A trip to the local hospital Emergency Room some years ago alerted me to an intellectual tool that is most helpful in fulfilling our theological responsibility. In recent years, emergency medical personnel have practiced a discipline known as triage—a process that allows trained personnel to make a quick evaluation of relative medical urgency. Given the chaos of an Emergency Room reception area, someone must be armed with the medical expertise to make an immediate determination of medical priority. Which patients should be rushed into surgery? Which patients can wait for a less urgent examination? Medical personnel cannot flinch from asking these questions, and from taking responsibility to give the patients with the most critical needs top priority in terms of treatment.

. . .

A discipline of theological triage would require Christians to determine a scale of theological urgency that would correspond to the medical world's framework for medical priority. With this in mind, I would suggest three different levels of theological urgency, each corresponding to a set of issues and theological priorities found in current doctrinal debates.

Mohler then unveils a method for organizing doctrines in three levels: first order (fundamental truths of the Christian faith), second order (areas where believing Christians may disagree, but with division, e.g., ecclesiology), and third-order doctrines (areas where believing Christians may disagree yet remain in fellowship,

---

[2] J. L. Dagg, *Manual of Church Order* (Charleston, SC: Southern Baptist Publication Society, 1858), 12.
[3] R. Albert Mohler Jr. "A Call for Theological Triage and Christian Maturity," *Albert Mohler* (blog), July 12, 2005, http://www.albertmohler.com/2005/07/12/a-call-for-theological-triage-and-christian-maturity.

e.g., eschatology).[4] This idea of theological triage has proven helpful for navigating seasons of theological foment and fellowship.

To consider this further against the backdrop of my purpose in this chapter of establishing ecclesiological distinctives as the basis for confessional cooperation, I will look to another earlier president of Southern Seminary.[5] John Broadus, in the late nineteenth century, focused on the Great Commission in his sermon, entitled "The Duty of Baptists to Teach Their Distinctive Views," to explain that the commands of Christ given to the disciples consisted of what he termed both "the internal and the external elements of Christian piety."[6] The internal elements, Broadus explains, are more crucial to the Christian faith as they relate to individuals and their relationship to their Creator. However, Broadus clarifies that any primacy given to the internal elements does not mean the external elements have little value or lack importance. Broadus reasons that if Christ and his apostles gave commands relating to external elements such as the "constitution and government" of churches, then it "cannot be healthy if they are disregarded."[7]

In fact, both internal and external elements are intrinsic in the prerequisite command of Matthew 28:19. First, Jesus exhorts the disciples to "go, therefore, and make disciples of all nations" (HCSB). This mandate speaks of the ultimately internal act of Holy Spirit regeneration that produces a fruit-bearing disciple. As Broadus states, the internal aspect of these commands does take priority. When one of the criminals crucified alongside Jesus asked in faith, "Jesus, remember me when You come into Your kingdom," Jesus replied, "I assure you: Today you will be with Me in paradise" (Luke 23:42–43 HCSB). In this exchange Jesus's affirmation came in response to the outward expression of the internal work in the heart of the criminal. Due to the nature of the circumstances, discussion of Jesus's external commands related to baptism or church order were not as important as the criminal's life after death. This is not to say such commands have no importance but rather, simply, that they are less important than the internal commands which address the question, "What must I do to inherit eternal life?" (Luke 10:25 HCSB).

When Paul writes his magisterial chapter on the resurrection in 1 Corinthians 15, he reminds the believers that what he delivered to them "first" was the gospel,

---

[4] For a similar discussion of "major" and "minor" doctrines, see Wayne Grudem, *Systematic Theology: An Introduction to Bible Doctrine* (Grand Rapids: Zondervan, 1994), 29–30.

[5] The remainder of this section is adapted from Jason G. Duesing, "Introduction: The Duty of Baptists to Teach Their Distinctive Views," in *Upon This Rock: The Baptist Understanding of the Church*, ed. Jason G. Duesing, Thomas White, and Malcolm B. Yarnell III (Nashville: B&H Academic, 2010), 3–9.

[6] John A. Broadus, *The Duty of Baptists to Teach Their Distinctive Views* (Philadelphia: American Baptist Publication Society, 1881), 1. The edition referenced in this chapter follows Madison Grace's transcription published in 2006 by the Center for Theological Research, Southwestern Baptist Theological Seminary, available at http://www.baptisttheology.org/documents/DutyBaptisttoTeachtheir ViewsBroadus.pdf.

[7] Ibid.

namely that "Christ died for our sins according to the Scriptures, that He was buried, that He was raised on the third day according to the Scriptures" (1 Cor 15:3–4). Paul clearly wrote to them about many other vital items of an external nature for the local church, but the first instructions he relayed to the Corinthians were of an internal and more important nature. The priority of the internal teachings of Christianity appear in Paul's letter to the Galatians as well. His expressed concern for believers who were deserting the faith did not revolve around their quibbling over the external teachings related to local church order. Rather, Paul intervenes as a result of the believers entertaining a "different gospel," that is a different teaching of an internal nature than the one Jesus provided (Gal 1). For those altering the internal message, Paul renders them "accursed" (Gk. *anathema*), a term he does not employ, for example, when speaking of divisions within the church at Corinth over external matters related to church leaders and baptism (1 Cor 1:10–17). The internal commands of the New Testament that speak of the reconciliation of lost and rebellious men and women to a holy and wise God through only faith expressed in the work of God's Son bearing the punishment on behalf of humanity are clearly the first commands the churches should carry forth in obedience to Matthew 28:20.

Second, in Matthew 28:19 Jesus instructs the disciples to baptize the new disciples in the name of the Father and of the Son and of the Holy Spirit. Here the command to baptize marks an external component in the commission. The external commands are not as important, as they do not directly convey the power to make one "wise for salvation" (2 Tim 3:15 NIV; see also Rom 1:16). However, the external commands are vital for healthy Christian living, preserving the internal message for future generations, and therefore should not be discarded. When Peter "lifted up his voice" (Acts 2:14 ESV) and addressed the mocking and perplexed crowd who did not know how to make sense of the arrival of the Holy Spirit in Acts 2, he proclaimed "God has made this Jesus, whom you crucified, both Lord and Messiah" (Acts 2:36 HCSB). In response to Peter's wielding multiple Old Testament texts as a sharp, two-edged sword, the crowd was "cut to the heart" (Gk. *katenugēsan*) and asked, "What shall we do?" (Acts 2:37 NIV). Peter responded first with the primary internal command, "repent," signaling the need for both confession of sin and faith expressed in belief. Peter's entrance into his proclamation ministry follows the example of Jesus himself, who began his public ministry saying, "The time is fulfilled, and the kingdom of God has come near. Repent and believe in the good news!" (Mark 1:15 HCSB). Peter continues, however, and quickly articulates the external command for the hearers to "be baptized" (Acts 2:38), thus practicing the entire commission of Jesus, with both internal and externals in view. As with Matthew 28:19–20, the order prescribed by Peter, first internal then external, shows the importance of one over the other, but it does not negate the essential function of both types of commands. To have eternal life, the soon-to-be disciple must repent and believe (internal). To function as an obedient disciple, professing his faith in the context of a local church community, the new disciple must be baptized (external).

The order and connection between the two commands appears also in the encounter the deacon, Philip, has with the Ethiopian court official in Acts 8. After following the instructions of an angel of the Lord to go to "the road that goes down from Jerusalem to Gaza" (v. 25 HCSB), Philip discovers the Ethiopian reading aloud Isaiah 53 and asks, "Do you understand what you're reading?" (v. 30 HCSB). From the top of his chariot, the Ethiopian responds, "How can I, unless someone guides me?" (v. 31 HCSB) and invites Philip to sit with him. As they travel together, Philip proceeds to explain from the Scripture that Jesus is the sheep that "was led to . . . the slaughter" in Isaiah 53:7 (NIV), and the account in Acts relates that Philip, "beginning from that Scripture" (Acts 8:35 HCSB), told the Ethiopian of the internal message regarding eternal life through faith in Jesus Christ. However, Philip appears also to have communicated some of the external commands as well, for when the Ethiopian's chariot came near a body of water, he said, "Look, there's water! What would keep me from being baptized?" (v. 36 HCSB). How would the Ethiopian have known of his need for baptism after he confessed his faith in Jesus if Philip had not already taught him of this external command? The baptism of the Ethiopian reinforces the notion that the external commands given in the New Testament, while not primary, are nonetheless important and should be incorporated properly into any presentation of the "good news about Jesus."

Throughout the New Testament, the local church functions as a repository not only to receive and transmit the internal message of the gospel to the current generation but also to preserve that message for future generations. As a result, the external commands given for the purposes of ordering and governing the church are essential for this task, even though they are not as important as the internal message. When Paul writes to Timothy to instruct him in "how people ought to act in God's household," Paul describes the local church as the "pillar and foundation of truth" (1 Tim 3:15 HCSB). The idea of the local church functioning as a pillar (Gk. *stulos*) and a foundation (Gk. *hedraiōma*) creates a picture of an intentionally designed (i.e., ordered) structure that, through its strength, has been prepared both to uphold (i.e., present or proclaim) an object as well as protect (i.e., preserve) an object. Jesus's promise in Matthew 16:18 (HCSB) that "the forces of Hades will not overpower" the church reinforces the idea that the local church has been given as an indestructible fortress of strength held together by Jesus Christ himself (Col 1:17).

As a result, Jesus and his apostles have given commands of an external nature that must be taught and implemented. But for what end? The object given to the local church to uphold and protect is the "truth." The truth is the message of eternal life—the substance of the internal commands of Christ (1 Tim 2:4; 2 Tim 2:25). The New Testament teaches that this truth was, and is, to be handed over or delivered from one generation to the next through the local church. Luke speaks of this at the beginning of his Gospel when writing to assure Theophilus of the certainty of the things he had been taught. Luke states that he has written an "orderly account" of the things that "those who from the beginning were eyewitnesses and ministers of the word" had "delivered" (Gk. *paredosan*) to Luke and the other apostles (Luke 1:1–4 ESV). Likewise, Paul instructs Timothy and the Ephesian Church to "guard the good deposit" (2 Tim 1:14 ESV; Gk. *paratheken*), a reference to the entire message of the gospel he had taught and given to them. In a broad sense the purpose of all of Paul's letters is to deliver the truth not only to his immediate recipients but also to all who will read his letters and implement the commands in local churches (Col 4:16). Jude reinforces the notion that the truth is the object the local church exists to proclaim and protect. In Jude 3, he explains that "the faith," or the gospel message of eternal life, has been delivered (Gk. *paradotheise*) to the saints. That is to say, the internal command of salvation through Jesus Christ has been handed down to Christians who live out the Christian life in local churches. Jude states that this delivering was done "once for all" (Gk. *hapax*), referencing the complete and final nature of the message rather than communicating that the message had no further need of transmission. Therefore, the local church, the "pillar and foundation of truth," exists to "guard the good deposit" and "deliver" it to future generations. The New Testament commands that speak of the truth are primary or, in Mohler's triage analogy, first order. However, the external commands that speak clearly to the order, practice, and health of the local church, while secondary, should not receive treatment as unessential. Instead, the local church also has a duty to carry forth and teach these commands in obedience to Matthew 28:20.

Following Broadus's help in articulating the relationship of ecclesiology to core doctrines and Mohler's idea of theological triage, I would like to propose that within the confines of ecclesiological work—starting churches, replanting churches, serving in churches—there is a need for a further layer of triage. This "ecclesiological triage" is a similar filtering of doctrines based on urgency or priority—not directly for saving faith—but for the establishment of true and healthy churches. As I will show, the long-standing Protestant and Baptist practice of churches using confessions of faith is a helpful way to accomplish this, but first I would like to establish common ground around specific ecclesiological distinctives. This idea of identifying key marks of the church also is nothing new, but seeing them as a means toward ecclesiological triage for New Testament churches can be a helpful way to answer the question, "What is a true church?"

WHAT IS A TRUE CHURCH?

Nearly sixty years ago, Southern Baptists scholars and pastors gathered on the campus of The Southern Baptist Theological Seminary to study the doctrine of the church in a symposium much like the one from which the current volume was developed. Many of the papers read were later compiled by Southern's president, Duke McCall, and published in 1958 under the title, *What Is the Church?* McCall noted that there was some difficulty, however, in getting these scholars to agree on what is the church and thus some who questioned whether such papers of differing opinions should be published. He said:

> There was unanimity at only one point, namely, that Baptists need to take their bearings on the important doctrine of the church. Within the Southern Baptist Convention more than half a century has passed since the last serious, general discussion of the church. Unfortunately that discussion became so involved in personalities that sight of the real issues was lost. May that not happen again.[8]

McCall here was, of course, referring to the ecclesiological discussions surrounding Landmarkism in the mid to late nineteenth century—a movement with its faults to be sure—but a movement much maligned and misunderstood by McCall's gathering of mid-twentieth-century Southern Baptist scholars. I mention this to say that the effort toward identifying key points of ecclesiology has long been something groups and churches like ours have wrestled with, but I hope that in these days, end times or not, we are in a better position to arrive at agreement and unanimity on ecclesiological distinctives for the sake of confessional cooperation. This is not because we are better than our theologically moderate denominational relatives, but rather because we seek to build churches on a much firmer and more confident foundation thanks to what happened in the Southern Baptist Convention in the decades to follow McCall's gathering.

There Is Such a Thing as the Universal Church

First, in a brief review of the Landmark discussion of the late 1800s, I want to affirm to the contrary that there is such a thing as the universal, or invisible, church and use a snapshot of Baptist history to make that case. The Landmarkers, driven by the admonition in Proverbs 22:28 to reset ancient doctrinal standards, or landmarks, were led by three pastors and teachers residing in Tennessee and Kentucky. As one historian classified, "Pendleton was the prophet, Graves the warrior, and Dayton the sword-bearer" in a movement of ecclesiological significance among Baptists in the nineteenth century called Landmarkism.[9] These three

---

[8]   Duke K. McCall, in *What Is the Church? A Symposium of Baptist Thought*, ed. Duke K. McCall (Nashville: Broadman, 1958), v–vi.

[9]   William W. Barnes, *The Southern Baptist Convention 1845–1953* (Nashville: Broadman, 1954), 103.

formed the great triumvirate that sought to establish local churches upon the original landmarks of a scriptural church, namely Baptist distinctives.[10] At the same time of the Landmark ascendancy, John Leadley Dagg, former president of Mercer University and Southern Baptist leader and theologian, published his *Manual of Church Order*. This volume, devoted specifically to the doctrines of the church, was the second volume in "the first textbook in systematic theology used in The Southern Baptist Theological Seminary."[11]

In the late 1850s Dagg collided with the Landmarkers over the doctrine of the universal church. Landmark views were spreading rapidly with great influence throughout the southwestern United States at the hand of J. R. Graves's popular periodical, *The Tennessee Baptist*. Dagg had recently retired from Mercer and set to work on his systematic theology. Many in the Southern Baptist Convention were concerned with the implications of the Landmark situation, but few Baptists had responded.[12] In the *Manual of Church Order*, Dagg addresses some of the more salient ecclesiological differences facing the people in antebellum America, one of which includes the issues surrounding the church universal. Tom Nettles notes that Dagg's "defense of the church universal is significant in light of the rising power of Landmarkism in Dagg's generation."[13]

J. R. Graves does not have a doctrine of the universal church. When speaking about the references to Paul's persecution of the church, as in Galatians 1:13, Graves believes this is not an indication of a universal church but the local church in Jerusalem.[14] When speaking about those passages in the New Testament that refer to the body of Christ, as in 1 Corinthians 12:13–14, Graves refuses to accept arguments that identify these instances as references to a universal church. In this case he employs his generic-use argument and states that to "understand the 'body of Christ' here to refer to a local church . . . meets all the requirements of the passage . . . but to understand it of a Church Invisible, it meets none of the requirements of the passage."[15] After further explication of his view that these types of passages are to be generically rendered, Graves concludes that there is no passage that affords ground for the idea of a universal church on earth.[16]

While Dagg recognizes that mention of the universal church is significantly less than that of the local church in the New Testament, he believes membership

[10] H. Leon McBeth, *A Sourcebook for Baptist Heritage* (Nashville: Broadman, 1990), 316–27.

[11] Dale Moody, "The Nature of the Church," in *What Is the Church?*, 17.

[12] See Kenneth Vaughn Weatherford, "The Graves-Howell Controversy" (Ph.D. Dissertation, Baylor University, 1991).

[13] Tom J. Nettles, "Preface to the New Edition of Manual of Theology," in J. L. Dagg. *Manual of Church Order* (repr., Harrisonburg: Gano, 1990).

[14] J. R. Graves, *Intercommunion Inconsistent, Unscriptural, and Productive of Evil* (Memphis: Baptist Book House, 1881), 128–39.

[15] J. R. Graves, *John's Baptism: Was It from Moses or Christ? Jewish or Christian?* (Memphis: Southern Baptist Book House, 1891), 78–83.

[16] Graves, *Old Landmarkism*, 32.

in the former is far more important.[17] To assert this belief, however, means that Dagg actually believes there is such an entity taught in Scripture. Here he and the triumvirate part ways. Dagg defines the church universal as "the whole company of those who are saved by Christ."[18] As examined in the Landmark writings, Dagg also provides an interpretation of the passages that refer to Paul's persecuting the church of God (1 Cor 15:9; Gal 1:13; Phil 3:6). Dagg argues for a collective sense of the word "church" in Galatians 1:13. He observes that the objects of Saul's persecution were individuals, not the organized institution of the local church.[19] Therefore, the Landmark generic understanding of the word *church* in these passages would communicate the opposite of what is intended in Dagg's view.[20]

J. L. Dagg reaches his conclusions through a hermeneutic that looks for the simplest reading of the text.[21] Dagg concludes, therefore, that his understanding of the church as universal is found in the New Testament. The church universal includes all local churches, but not in organization, rather in individual members. However, all local churches do not round out the entirety of the universal church, for this term refers to Christians in heaven and on earth, as well as those who are not members of a local church.[22] Thus, in sum, for the purposes of establishing New Testament churches here at the end of all things, it is biblically right to acknowledge that while not the primary emphasis of Scripture, the Bible does affirm the presence of a universal or invisible church. As the Baptist Faith and Message 2000 states, "The New Testament speaks also of the church as the Body of Christ which includes all of the redeemed of all the ages, believers from every tribe, and tongue, and people, and nation."[23]

The Marks of a True Church

Second, for the purpose of arriving at a definition of what is a true, visible church, I want to focus briefly on the marks of a true church. The reformer John

---

[17] Dagg, *Church Order*, 120.

[18] Ibid., 100.

[19] Ibid., 107.

[20] In conjunction with the Landmakers, Dagg (*Church Order*, 110–11) also thought it important to this discussion to investigate the meaning of the phrase, "the body of Christ," as it is often equated in the New Testament with the church. Beginning with Rom 12:4–5, Dagg asserts that "the body of Christ" Paul refers to is not solely the local church at Rome but all individual Christians. Dagg shows why Dayton's argument that Paul is just speaking of the local Roman assembly is faulty in several ways. First, Paul himself was not a member of this church, yet he says in this passage, "We being many are one body in Christ." Second, to understand the text this way "converts the beautiful figure which the Holy Spirit employs to represent the union between Christ and his people, into a monster, having one head and many bodies." Instead, Dagg explains that Paul means to describe the body of Christ as being one body with many members. Further examination of similar passages (1 Cor 12:27; Eph 1:22–23; Heb 3:6) are used by Dagg to bolster his conclusion that the body of Christ referred to in the New Testament is none other than the universal church.

[21] Ibid., 105, 108.

[22] Ibid., 121.

[23] See the Baptist Faith and Message 2000 ecclesiological articles at the conclusion of this chapter.

Calvin said, "Wherever we see the Word of God purely preached and heard, and the sacraments administered according to Christ's institution, there, it is not to be doubted, a church of God exists."[24] This is an oft-used definition that even those ecclesological purists, the Anabaptists, affirmed as well. Theologian Pilgram Marpeck said: "If these three things, the true proclamation of the gospel, correct baptism, and correct communion, are in doubt, there can be no true church of Christ. If one of these parts is missing, it is not possible outwardly to maintain and support a true Christian church."[25] This understanding of the marks of the church, as Mark Dever simply calls, "the right preaching of the Word of God and the right administration of baptism and the Lord's Supper,"[26] is the view adopted by Baptist churches from the time of their formal beginnings in seventeenth-century England, as seen in the First London Confession of 1644 and in the Orthodox Creed of 1679. The Orthodox Creed states, "The marks by which she [the church] is known to be the true spouse of Christ, are these, viz. Where the word of God is rightly preached, and the sacraments truly administered, according to Christ's institution."[27]

At yet another Southern Baptist symposium seeking to define ecclesiological distinctives for Southern Baptist churches, this time at Southwestern Baptist Theological Seminary in 2006, theologian and now university president, Thomas White, sought to provide a definition of a true church as a part of his larger presentation dealing with what makes baptism valid.[28] Following the marks of a church, White further narrowed ecclesiological distinctives into the two categories of "being" (*esse*) and "well-being" (*bene esse*).[29] The being category contains items that one would affirm as being essential to the essence of what is a true church. This is a short list centered around the biblically established marks of the church. The well-being category contains an almost unlimited list of items one would affirm aid the health of churches, but there can be disagreement or failure in these areas, and yet one can still have a true church. This distinction is not new to White, as it is a formula churches have used throughout the history of Christianity, but how he employed it specifically for Baptists churches was

---

[24] John Calvin, *Institutes of the Christian Religion*, 4.1.9.

[25] Pilgram Marpeck, "The Admonition of 1542," in *The Writings of Pilgram Marpeck*, ed. William Klassen and Walter Klassen (Scottdale: Herald, 1978), 292. This is also known as Marpeck's *Vermanung* or *Taufbüchlein*.

[26] Mark Dever, *The Church: The Gospel Made Visible* (Nashville: B&H, 2012), 21.

[27] See Timothy and Denise George, eds., *Baptist Confessions, Covenants, and Catechisms* (Nashville: B&H, 1996).

[28] Later published as Thomas White, "What Makes Baptism Valid?," in *Restoring Integrity in Baptist Churches*, 113.

[29] Malcolm Yarnell suggests a third category of indifference, or *adiaphora*, to give greater emphasis to matters of greater theological weight in the well-being category like mode of baptism. See "Article VI: The Church" in Douglas K. Blount and Joseph D. Woodell, eds., *The Baptist Faith and Message 2000: Critical Issues in America's Largest Protestant Denomination* (Lanham: Rowman & Littlefield, 2007), 68n20.

unique and instructive.[30] In short, building from White's model, I would like to review how the being/well-being formula is a helpful model for the purpose of answering what is a true church as well as establishing appropriate boundaries for ecclesiological triage.

WHAT IS A TRUE CHURCH?

Being (esse)	Well-being (bene esse)
Items essential to a true church	*Items affecting a true church's health*
1. Gospel preached and proclaimed	1. Mode and practice of baptism
2. Baptism	2. Mode and practice of the Lord's Supper
3. Lord's Supper	3. Church officers and leaders
4. Believers intentionally gathered	4. Church discipline
	5. Regenerate church membership
	6. Great Commission focus
	7. Expositional preaching

First, in the being category, I include the gospel preached and proclaimed, the practice of baptism and the Lord's Supper, and the idea of believers intentionally gathered. At the core of a true church is (1) the proclamation of the gospel. If the gospel is wrong or influences or skews the practice of the ordinances, then the church is not a true church (Gal 1:9). The practice of (2) baptism and (3) the Lord's Supper is essential to having a true church as these are the biblically prescribed ordinances given to New Testament churches to proclaim the gospel in their practice (Matt 26:26–30; 28:19–20; Rom 6:3–5; 1 Cor 11:23–29). However, the mode or how they are practiced, as long as such does not compromise the gospel, are areas of well-being. For example, I do not classify as true churches those churches that believe baptism, whether sprinkling or immersing infants or adults, is a requirement for salvation or means of grace. This is not a license to render such a verdict on entire denominations or traditions, but rather, church to church within all traditions, if their practice of baptism communicates or proclaims another gospel, then they cannot be true churches. On the other hand, for churches that disagree about whether baptism is for infants or professing believers, there is room for mutual acknowledgment that both are true churches as long as the understanding of baptism does not underpin the proclamation of the gospel. Clearly, one of the churches is in error, but this is the kind

---

[30] See Gregg Allison, *Sojourners and Strangers: The Doctrine of the Church*, Foundations of Evangelical Theology (Wheaton, IL: Crossway, 2012), 263; idem, *Historical Theology* (Grand Rapids: Zondervan, 2011), 151. See also, John Hammett, *Biblical Foundations for Baptist Churches* (Grand Rapids: Kregel, 2005), 62–66.

of error that affects the church's well-being. Finally, (4) for a church to be a true church, those who comprise it must acknowledge and intend to be a church. That is, regardless if one is on the mission field or a college dorm room, there are no accidental churches—church does not "happen," nor do those gathering informally come to realize that they have been a church for some time. Simply, New Testament churches mean to be such, and if a poll was taken of those attending, there should be a clear acknowledgment that what is happening in that gathering is the meeting of a church.

Second, in the well-being category I include issues related to mode and practice of (1) baptism and (2) the Lord's Supper, (3) biblically designated leadership, (4) church discipline, (5) regenerate church membership, (6) Great Commission focus, and even (7) expositional preaching. These are all items drawn from biblical instruction that speak to the health of the congregation rather than the essence of a church. For example, if one were to conclude that a true church has biblical church leadership, then every time a pastor resigned, the church would cease to exist. Rather, while the Bible is clear that local churches should have leaders, their qualifications, and how to care for them, these are not essential for the establishment of a church but are needed for the church to continue to exist and bear healthy fruit.

Therefore, if believers can come to agreement as to what the New Testament prescribes is the definition of a true church, and the use of ecclesiological triage to determine the boundaries for partnering, establishing, or replanting churches, I would, finally, like to make the case that the way churches can move forward in the last days is by the regular use and recovery of confessions of faith.

Most Surely Held Among Us: Confessions of Faith

Each semester in my Baptist history class, a question that usually arises from a perceptive student concerns how we are to understand the relationship between Baptists and their confessions of faith. Much good work is out there by many who have gone before that details what Baptists have believed about the historic creeds of early Christianity as well as later confessions of faith.[31] In my lectures I usually summarize the matter by saying Baptists have typically used confessions of faith, both in local churches and in their assemblies and conventions, as documents both to define and defend.

Define. Baptists have used confessions to define what they believe both for those who want to partner with them and to set boundaries for fellowship, especially in ecclesiological matters. Confessions, in this sense, are merely summary statements of their corporate understanding of the teaching of Scripture on a

---

[31] See Timothy George and Denise George, eds., *Baptist Confessions, Covenants, and Catechisms*, Library of Baptist Classics (Nashville: B&H Academic), 1999; William L. Lumpkin, ed., *Baptist Confessions of Faith* (Valley Forge, PA: Judson, 1959).

given doctrinal issue. Another way to say this is that confessions are used to define the terms by which Baptist churches include or exclude those with whom they will work. As L. Russ Bush and Tom Nettles noted:

> Confessions of faith have been used in various ways in Baptist life. . . . [T]he major emphasis of most Baptist confessional statements has been expression rather than repression. Instead of attempting to set Baptists apart from other Christians (or from themselves), several early confessions sought to demonstrate Baptist agreement with mainline Protestant theology.[32]

Defend. Baptists have used confessions to defend what they believe to both friends and foes. Sometimes this has been done to show other believers in like-minded, but different, ecclesial traditions that a significant amount of shared theological common ground exists where perhaps many assumed little existed. Other times confessions have helped a watching world see that the claims of a false accuser simply have no rational basis of truth. Never assumed to be infallible documents, Baptists have felt the freedom to revise their confessions as a specific context or theological crisis might require.

Bush and Nettles said:

> The confessions do, of course, defend Baptist views on the church and on the ordinances. However, the ruling principles in these statements are sola scriptura (Scripture alone) and sola fide (faith alone), points that the writers expected would appeal to other Protestant Christians. Early Baptists did not think exclusively in terms of Baptist distinctives. They affirmed Christian doctrines. They believed that they were being true to Scripture in their view of the ordinances, their view of God, and so forth, and they called on other Christians to join them in their faithfulness.[33]

This twofold understanding of confessions of faith is not an original formulation but rather is used consistently by Baptist churches dating back to the Reformation. The first president of Southern Seminary, James P. Boyce, articulated this concept well in his "Three Changes in Theological Institutions":

> This development of their necessity, leads us naturally to believe that doctrinal confessions were applied to this purpose in the Apostolic Churches. Accordingly, we find that the germ of them as used for a two-fold purpose, the declaration of faith and the testing of its existence in others, seems traceable to the Apostles, and even to Christ Himself. It is remarkable that it has been so frequently overlooked, that upon almost every approach to Him for the performance of a cure, Christ

---

[32] L. Russ Bush and Tom J. Nettles, *Baptists and the Bible*, rev. ed. (Nashville: B&H Academic, 1999), 341.
[33] Ibid.

demanded that public confession of his ability to do so, which involved the confession of His Messiahship and Divine authority, and manifested the individual approaching Him to be one of those who had taught by the Spirit. That was a memorable illustration of the same principle, when, after inquiring the views of others, He made a direct appeal to His own disciples, and said—"But whom say ye that I am?" and when Peter answered "Thou are the Christ, the Son of the living God," in commendation of that declaration, He pronounced him blessed, and taught by His Father in heaven. This commendation was given to an express Confession of Faith. The act of baptism also, enjoined by Christ as the initiative rite of His Church, is an act which involves the very formulary which accompanies it, profession of doctrinal belief. . . . By the Baptists of all ages, creeds have been almost universally used, and invariably in this two-fold way. To some of other denominations, it has seemed that we have been without them, because the principle of liberty of conscience which we have at the same time maintained, has forbidden the laying of civil disabilities upon those who have differed from us. We have appeared to them, therefore, to put them forth only as declarative of our principles.[34]

In addition, I have found helpful the following list of five uses of Baptist confessions by Robert G. Torbet in *A History of the Baptists*:

- To maintain purity of doctrine
- To clarify and validate the Baptist position
- To serve as a guide in counseling churches
- To serve as a basis for fellowship with local churches, associations, or denominations
- To discipline churches and members[35]

Finally, the preamble to the Baptist Faith and Message 2000 says well that this confession of faith "endeavors to state for its time and theological climate those articles of the Christian faith which are most surely held among us" and that "we are not embarrassed to state before the world that these are doctrines we hold precious and essential to the Baptist tradition of faith and practice."[36]

FOR THE CHURCH AT THE END OF ALL THINGS

As I mentioned, I did not expect to find an ecclesiology and eschatology lesson when reading *The Lord of the Rings*, but I am glad I did. For we are living at the end

---

[34] J. P. Boyce, *Three Changes in Theological Institutions* (Greenville: Elford's Book and Job Press, 1856), 40–43. Accessed February 23, 2016. Available from http://digital.library.sbts.edu/handle/10392/8.

[35] Robert G. Torbet, *A History of the Baptists* (King of Prussia, PA: Judson, 1963), 46.

[36] The Baptist Faith and Message 2000. Accessed February 23, 2016. Available from http://www.sbc.net/bfm2000/preamble.asp.

of all things (1 Pet 4:7) and yet have every reason for hopefulness and joy as we look forward to the return of the King. In the meantime, the Bible admonishes us to stay busy in the task of Great Commission gospel advance for the glory of God, and the means by which this is to occur is through local churches. Therefore, we live and exist in fellowships—true churches clearly defined and defended by common confessions of faith—partnering together for the church, not as the end but as the biblically designed means to the end of seeing God's great name proclaimed to the ends of the earth. Until we are all swept up on eagles' wings, may Southern Baptist churches be found faithful establishing ecclesiological distinctives for the basis of confessional cooperation.

THE BAPTIST FAITH AND MESSAGE 2000

Article VI. The Church

A New Testament church of the Lord Jesus Christ is an autonomous local congregation of baptized believers, associated by covenant in the faith and fellowship of the gospel; observing the two ordinances of Christ, governed by His laws, exercising the gifts, rights, and privileges invested in them by His Word, and seeking to extend the gospel to the ends of the earth. Each congregation operates under the Lordship of Christ through democratic processes. In such a congregation each member is responsible and accountable to Christ as Lord. Its scriptural officers are pastors and deacons. While both men and women are gifted for service in the church, the office of pastor is limited to men as qualified by Scripture.

The New Testament speaks also of the church as the Body of Christ which includes all of the redeemed of all the ages, believers from every tribe, and tongue, and people, and nation.

Matthew 16:15–19; 18:15–20; Acts 2:41–42,47; 5:11–14; 6:3–6; 13:1–3; 14:23,27; 15:1–30; 16:5; 20:28; Romans 1:7; 1 Corinthians 1:2; 3:16; 5:4–5; 7:17; 9:13–14; 12; Ephesians 1:22–23; 2:19–22; 3:8–11,21; 5:22–32; Philippians 1:1; Colossians 1:18; 1 Timothy 2:9–14; 3:1–15; 4:14; Hebrews 11:39–40; 1 Peter 5:1–4; Revelation 2–3; 21:2–3.

Article VII. Baptism and the Lord's Supper

Christian baptism is the immersion of a believer in water in the name of the Father, the Son, and the Holy Spirit. It is an act of obedience symbolizing the believer's faith in a crucified, buried, and risen Saviour, the believer's death to sin, the burial of the old life, and the resurrection to walk in newness of life in Christ Jesus. It is a testimony to his faith in the final resurrection of the dead. Being a church ordinance, it is prerequisite to the privileges of church membership and to the Lord's Supper.

The Lord's Supper is a symbolic act of obedience whereby members of the church, through partaking of the bread and the fruit of the vine, memorialize the death of the Redeemer and anticipate His second coming.

Matthew 3:13–17; 26:26–30; 28:19–20; Mark 1:9–11; 14:22–26; Luke 3:21–22; 22:19–20; John 3:23; Acts 2:41–42; 8:35–39; 16:30–33; 20:7; Romans 6:3–5; 1 Corinthians 10:16,21; 11:23–29; Colossians 2:12.

Downgrade: Twenty-First-Century Lessons from Nineteenth-Century Baptists

Christian T. George

O n July 17, 1944, an unmanned *Vergeltungswaffe*, or "Vengeance weapon," was catapulted into the sky from an undisclosed location in Nazi-controlled France. Soaring at 400 miles per hour, this long-range German weapon took only twenty-five minutes to cross the English Channel before descending on the beleaguered British population. Stories of air raids and bomb shelters would surface in the novels of C. S. Lewis, in the speeches of Winston Churchill, and in the newspapers that daily tallied the death toll. Approximately 6,000 Londoners would lose their lives to V-1 attacks like these. And yet the particular bomb that fell in the summer of '44 would claim the lives of none.

At 5:12 a.m. an empty nonconformist chapel situated on a grassy knoll in the heart of West Norwood Cemetery exploded into flames. But the 1,800-pound warhead did more than ignite the sixty-by-thirty-foot building; it also damaged the marble tomb beside it—the tomb that held the remains of Charles Haddon Spurgeon. The blast was so forceful that it dislodged the stone statue of Scripture that had been cemented to its façade, and for the first time since 1892, the coffin of England's most popular preacher lay exposed to the elements.

This was not the first time a Victorian nonconformist chapel had suffered attack at the hands of the Germans. Seven-year-old Spurgeon may not have known that Ludwig Feuerbach's *Das Wesen des Christentums* crossed the Channel in Marian Evans's 1841 English translation. Five years later David Strauss launched his own *Das Leben Jesu*. Its opening words foreshadowed the dawning of the age: "It appeared to the author of the work that it was time to substitute a new mode of considering the life of Jesus, in the place of the antiquated systems of supranaturalism and naturalism."[1]

Indeed a time of transition had arrived. The eyes of evangelicalism, once awakened by the impassioned preaching of George Whitefield and John Wesley, had become soporific slits through which an unfamiliar world burgeoned anew. In 1887 Spurgeon lamented the spiritual health of the century: "The Atonement is scouted, the inspiration of Scripture is derided, the Holy Spirit is degraded into an influence, the punishment of sin is turned into fiction, and the resurrection into a myth. . . . Germany was made unbelieving by her preachers and England is following in her tracks."[2]

The attack on Scripture—fueled by the ascendency of secularization, rationalism, and skepticism—left its mark on the Victorians. Join by English-bred scholars like Frederick Maurice, John Colenso, Charles Gore, Benjamin Jowett, and Thomas Huxley, who each contributed in their own ways to the dislodging and demythologizing of the once-cemented axioms of orthodox Christianity, evangelicalism would soon fall out of fashion. With *Origin of Species* published four years after Spurgeon's transition to London and *Essays and Reviews* mere months before the opening of his Tabernacle, Charles Spurgeon witnessed firsthand the explosion, or implosion, of the mid-Victorian church as she came into the crosshairs of an external and internal crisis—a crisis of *faith* as some have coined it,[3] or, as Timothy Larsen better minted the phenomenon, a crisis of *doubt*.[4]

But the Victorian era was not the only one to experience a midlife crisis. The twentieth century suffered its own theological controversies, including the fundamentalist-modernist dispute in the 1920s and 1930s and the Conservative Resurgence in the 1980s and 1990s. Nevertheless, a straight line can be drawn from our day to Spurgeon's day—from the dawn of the twenty-first century to dusk of the nineteenth. And so, for the purpose of this chapter, I would like to submit three conditions—or diagnoses—that affected the health and vitality of the Victorian church and also three correctives—or antibodies—to help us avoid contracting them.

The first condition is *amnesia*, that is, the forgetfulness of who we are, where we came from, and what we know. In 1813 a coalition of Particular Baptist

---

[1] Marian Evans, *The Life of Jesus Critically Examined*, vol. 1, trans. David Friedrich Strauss (New York: Calvin Blanchard, 1860), 5.

[2] Charles Spurgeon, "Another Word Concerning the Down Grade," handwritten notes from the personal collection of Dr. Jason K. Allen, Midwestern Baptist Theological Seminary, Kansas City, Missouri. Also found in *The Sword and the Trowel*, August 1887.

[3] See Richard J. Helmstadter and Bernard Lightman, eds., *Victorian Faith in Crisis: Essays on Continuity and Change in Nineteenth-Century Religious Belief* (Stanford, CA: Stanford University Press, 1990); Sally Mitchell, *Daily Life in Victorian England* (Westport, CT: Greenwood, 1996), 246.

[4] Timothy Larsen, *Crisis of Doubt: Honest Faith in Nineteenth-Century England* (Oxford: Oxford University Press, 2006).

churches united to form a union of like-minded constituencies in England. In order to accommodate the "New Connexion" of General Baptists two decades later, the Baptist Union revised its constitution in 1832 to extend "brotherly love and union among the Baptist ministers and churches who agree in the *sentiments usually denominated evangelical.*"[5] As Baptists became increasingly embracive of mainstream theological trends, the failure to articulate a more robust confession that affirmed the tenets of orthodox Christianity prompted Spurgeon to action. His withdrawal of membership from the Baptist Union sparked the "Down Grade" controversy and, according to his wife, contributed to the premature end of his life.

Karl Barth was not even two years old when, on October 28, 1887, Spurgeon wrote a letter to Samuel Harris Booth, the general secretary of the Union, stating, "I must withdraw from that Society. I do this with the utmost regret, but I have no choice."[6] To remain in fellowship with the Union was, for Spurgeon, tantamount to theological treason. Three months later the Union Council accepted Spurgeon's resignation and voted to censure him. When the Baptist Assembly met in April 1888 to pass a declaration on the tenets of faith, Spurgeon lamented its lackadaisical posture. Fearing universalism and Unitarianism could metastasize in the absence of a doctrinally defined declaration, Spurgeon and thirty like-minded ministers penned one of their own, affirming as the flagship principle the "Divine inspiration, authority, and sufficiency of the Holy Scriptures."[7] The ink had hardly dried when Spurgeon's declaration was opposed by many of his former supporters and friends, including eighty alumni from the Pastors' College and even his own brother, James. "I cannot tell you by letter what I have endured in the desertion of my own men," Spurgeon wrote to a friend on February 21, 1888. "Good bye, Ellis," he wrote three years later, "you will never see me again, this fight is killing me."[8]

To many mainstream Protestant denominations, Spurgeon appeared *behind his time*—a fossil from a bygone era. Indeed, Spurgeon did cling to the doctrines of the past, doctrines that had been rediscovered by the Protestant Reformers, appropriated by the English Puritans, and advanced by the evangelical awakenings. Spurgeon did long for days behind him. If only London could go back to the days of Benjamin Keach and John Gill, before people used words like plesiosaurus and pterodactyl. If only the earth could be 4,000 years old again and the church could talk less about natural selection and more about *super*natural selection, as the

---

5   Gerald Parsons, ed., *Religion in Victorian Britain: Traditions,* vol. 1 (Manchester UK: Manchester University Press, 1988), 72 (emphasis added).

6   Charles Spurgeon quoted in G. Holden Pike, *The Life and Work of Charles Haddon Spurgeon,* vols.1–6 (London: Cassell and Company Lim. [no date]), 6:287.

7   Lewis A. Drummond, *Spurgeon: Prince of Preachers* (Grand Rapids: Kregel 1992), 706.

8   C. H. Spurgeon, *C. H. Spurgeon's Autobiography: Compiled from His Diary, Letters, and Records, by His Wife, and His Private Secretary,* 4 vols. (London: Passmore and Alabaster, 1897–99), 1:152.

Puritans were fond of doing. While it is anachronistic to say that Spurgeon was *Ultimus Puritanorum* ("the last Puritan"),[9] the point is taken. Spurgeon's lifelong affinity for John Bunyan, Richard Baxter, Richard Sibbes, John Owen, Thomas Manton, and a constellation of lesser-known Elizabethan lights provided as much contour to his theological convictions as it did consternation for the neological and heterodoxical inventions of his age.

Here a corrective to our amnesia may be realized. How do we avoid forgetting who we are? The answer is by remembering *who we were*. How do we avoid forgetting *what we know*? By remembering what we knew. And how do we avoid forgetting where we come from? By remembering *where we have been*. We do this by engaging deeply, meaningfully, and practically in the study of theological history—the story of who God is, what God did, and what God is going to do.

Twentieth-century Harvard professor Harvey Cox wrote: "There are two principle sources to which we must look. They are the early period of our history and the most recent. The first Christian generation and the generation just before us."[10] This view of history flanks both sides of the Southern Baptist tradition. We find this view expressed both on the theological left and the theological right. It is harkened not only in the halls of Harvard but also in the familiar banner cry, "No creed but Christ." But this perspective threatens the church's ability to transmit "the faith that was delivered to the saints once for all" (Jude 1:3 HCSB) and leads to the loss of our theological, genealogical, and denominational DNA.

For Baptists moving into the twenty-first century, it is not enough to know the *then* and the *now*; we must also know the *in-between*. It is not enough to know the history of our local church; we must know the history of what God has accomplished in his church universal. We must know our history because you and I are part of that story. We are the continuing chapter in God's grand narrative of redemption. And on that providential plotline, *we are the past* for Christians yet to be born. Between the ancient and the present, between the distant and the recent, between the Bible and the newspaper, God has been up to something.

And so the church must go back in order to go forward. We must go *back to the future*. Back to the creeds, confessions, and catechisms. Back to the councils and controversies that, through the power of the Holy Spirit, determined the boundaries between orthodoxy and heterodoxy. Back to the martyrs and missionaries, preachers and pastors who not only translated our Bible into English but also wrote commentaries to help us interpret it. In 1855 Spurgeon offered a prophetic corrective to the eventual downgrading of Baptist theology: "I am

---

[9] Ibid., 4:296.
[10] Harvey Cox, *Turning East* (New York: Simon & Schuster, 1977), 157.

persuaded that the use of a good catechism in all our families will be a great safe-guard against the increasing errors of the times."[11]

The confession of faith we as Southern Baptists celebrate draws its distinctives from Scripture. But it does not draw from a Scripture devoid of history. Baptists draw our identity from a particular *interpretation* of Scripture as it was hammered out in the sixteenth and seventeenth centuries. To untie our tradition from its historical moorings will lead to theological drifting, as Spurgeon witnessed. The mistakes of tomorrow can be prevented by remembering the mistakes of the past. And we must do this with boundaries and bridges. Baptists need boundaries to protect us from heresies without, and we need bridges to unite us in orthodoxy within. Such shall safeguard us from the errors of our time and the error of think-ing *our own time is the only time.* If ever we, as a convention, needed safeguarding, it is now—safeguarding from the extremes of hyper-Calvinism and semi-Pela-gianism, intellectualism and fanaticism, creedal*ism* and creedal-*phobia.* Baptists do not need to reinvent the wheel of orthodoxy; we need to spin it in a biblical direction.

If amnesia affected the head of the church, *anemia*—the second condition—affects her heart. Anemia results from a shortage of red blood cells in the blood and inhibits the delivery of oxygen to the rest of the body. The causes of anemia are generally hemorrhaging or a lack of iron in the blood.

Following his stance on the authority of Scripture, the doctrine of the Trinity, and the depravity of humanity, another point that Spurgeon penned in his dec-laration encompassed "the substitutionary sacrifice of the Lord Jesus Christ, by which alone sin is taken away, and sinners are saved."[12] The absence of this doc-trine within the Baptist Union struck at the core of Spurgeon's theological convic-tions. In a letter to the general secretary, Spurgeon observed, "Believers in Christ's atonement are now in declared union with those who make light of it."[13] For Spurgeon, such fellowship threatened to destabilize Baptist identity and, more-over, eviscerate the life force, or to use a Puritan word, *vitality*, of Christianity. "The blood," said Spurgeon in 1858, "stands out in solitary majesty, the only rock of our salvation."[14]

---

[11] Charles Spurgeon, *The Complete Works of Charles Spurgeon*, vol. 65: *A Puritan Catechis*m (n.p.: Delmarva, 2003).

[12] Drummond, *Spurgeon*, 706.

[13] C. H. Spurgeon, *The Down Grade Controversy* (Albany, OR: Ages Library, 1998), 44.

[14] C. H. Spurgeon, *The New Park Street Pulpit: Containing Sermons Preached and Revised by the Rev. C. H. Spurgeon, Minister of the Chapel,* vols. 1–8 (Pasadena, TX: Pilgrim, 2006), 5:29. Hereafter, this work will be referred to as *NPSP.*

In the nineteenth century, "sermon tasting"[15] became as fashionable as the "tasting of the waters."[16] In contrast to the intellectual and sophisticated sermons of his day, Spurgeon "talked English instead of pulpit."[17] In doing so, he offered not only a theology for the head but also a spirituality for the heart. It was not with polished pageantry or embellished eloquence that the twenty-something prodigy arrested the attention of London. On the contrary Spurgeon clothed the gospel in earthy, ordinary attire so that even children could wrap their fingers around the deep things of God. Spurgeon once marveled that he could "secure a crowded audience at dead of night in a deep snow."[18] This was not an exaggeration. Spurgeon's picture-packed vernacular appealed directly to the Victorian heart, and for this reason he marshaled the multitudes. Tourists returned to the United States of America to be greeted by two questions: "'Did you see the Queen?' and 'Did you hear Spurgeon?'"[19] In the summer of 1855, Anglicans muscled a bill through Parliament enabling their clergy to "imitate Spurgeon"[20] by holding services outdoors. Their efforts at drawing large crowds succeeded not even a little. Spurgeon succeeded in capturing the spirit of his age, but he also foresaw a growing threat to that spirituality. While the German quest to uncover the Jesus of history accomplished much in recovering Christ's humanity, in doing so they truncated his divinity. England received from Germany an infant who had been born of a woman but not of a virgin, a criminal who died on a tree but did not rise from the tomb. For Spurgeon the outcome of this neology was obvious: if Christ cannot save, the Spirit cannot cleanse. If justification stands trial, sanctification stands trial. If Christology collapses, pneumatology is bound to follow.

From 2013 to 2014, Southern Baptists were confronted with the reality that the convention was hemorrhaging unprecedented numbers of memberships and baptisms. But we were not alone. The accelerated epidemic was found in every major denomination within the U.S. The questions became, What are we doing wrong? and Why isn't this working?"

Victorian evangelicals asked similar questions when they, too, declined at the end of the nineteenth century. In 1851, only one year after Spurgeon became a Christian, the religious census revealed that approximately 41 percent of the

---

[15] Robert H. Ellison, *The Victorian Pulpit: Spoken and Written Sermons in Nineteenth-Century Britain* (London: Associated University Press, 1998), 44.

[16] The phrase "tasting of the waters" was common in Victorian England. See *Newcastle Journal* (June 22, 1864): 2.

[17] *The Spectator: A Weekly Review of Politics, Literature, Theology, and Art*, vol. 57 (London: John Campbell, 1884), 812.

[18] Iain H. Murray, ed., *Letters of Charles Haddon Spurgeon* (Edinburgh: Banner of Truth, 1992), 56.

[19] A. P. Peabody, "Spurgeon," *North American Review* 86 (1858): 275.

[20] See G. Kitson Clark, *The Making of Victorian England* (London: Routledge, 1962; repr., 1994), 187; Owen Chadwick, *The Victorian Church: An Ecclesiastical History of England*, vol. 1 (New York: Oxford University Press, 1966 and 1970), 525.

total English population attended church on one particular Sunday.[21] According to Owen Chadwick, up until the last fifteen years of the nineteenth century, church attendance matched the rise in population.[22] But in 1885, two years before Spurgeon withdrew from the Baptist Union, a sharp decrease in numbers appeared. Chapels and cathedrals, once brimming with congregants, had begun the process of attenuation—a process that continued through the twentieth century and exists to this day. According to the UK Census taken between 2001 and 2011, "the number of Christians born in Britain fell by 5.3 million—about 10,000 a week."[23] The survey also maintains that if this pattern holds, there will not be a single Christian born in the United Kingdom by the year 2067.

While the loss of memberships and baptisms is symptomatic of spiritual decline, the opposite is not always true. Just because a church is large does not mean it is healthy. It could just mean that is it *swollen*.[24] Reacting to the attractional-ecclesial surge in pragmatism in the last fifteen years of our own century, there is evidence of a renewal movement within the Southern Baptist tradition. On the surface you might recognize them by their "Spurgeon Is My Homeboy" T-shirts. But something deeper is going on. Instead of asking the question, "Will this work?" younger generations of Southern Baptists are returning to the question, "Is this biblical?"

Jesus Christ will eventually cauterize our hemorrhaging. He did this for the bleeding woman in Luke 8, and he will do this for us. Of course, the sickness may get worse before it gets better. Spurgeon once said, "There is no greater mercy that I know of on earth than good health except it be sickness; and that has often been a greater mercy to me than health."[25] Our bleeding will stop, but it will not be healed with the bandages of consumeristic Christianity. Jesus told us to be salt, not sugar. Nor will we be healed by grasping the latest, over-the-counter, twelve steps to "Your Best Church Now" concoction. Jesus said we must lose our life to gain it (Luke 17:33).

Instead, our bleeding will stop when, like the woman in the text, we reach out and take hold of the Man himself—when the Great Physician gives us *his* spirit to confront the spirit of our age and when the pulpit, not the coffee shop, pulls people again to the pews. The health of our churches depends not on clever

---

[21] Lynn Holleen Lees, *Exiles of Erin: Irish Migrants in Victorian London* (Manchester: Manchester University Press, 1979), 181. See also Horace Mann, *Census of Great Britain, 1851: Religious Worship in England and Wales* (London: George Routledge and Co., 1854). The Religious Census of 1851 is not without criticism. See Denis G. Paz, *Popular Anti-Catholicism in Mid-Victorian England* (Stanford, CA: Stanford University Press, 1992), 155.

[22] Chadwick, *The Victorian Church*, 232.

[23] Faith Survey, "UK Christianity." Accessed October 15, 2015. http://faithsurvey.co.uk/uk-christianity.html.

[24] Charles Spurgeon, *Spurgeon Gold*, comp. Ray Comfort (Jacksonville: Bridge-Logos, 2005), 31.

[25] C. H. Spurgeon, *Metropolitan Tabernacle Pulpit: Sermons Preached and Revised by C. H. Spurgeon*, vols. 9–62, 62 volumes (Pasadena, TX: Pilgrim, 1970–2006), 38:270.

inventions but on the lifting up of Christ (John 12:32). We are healed because Christ was harmed. We are saved because Christ was slain. Christ's bleeding disorder heals our bleeding disorder, and the nails that pierced his skin contained enough iron to ward off the anemia that threatens our spirituality.

If amnesia robs our heads and anemia robs our hearts, then the final condition the twenty-first-century church must guard against is one that affects the body—*atrophy*, or the wasting away of muscle tissue often caused by extended periods of immobility.

Spurgeon's conversion is a familiar story. Caught in a snowstorm in January 1850, he stumbled into a Primitive Methodist church in Colchester, England. In the absence of a preacher, a layperson—likely a shoemaker or tailor—ascended the pulpit and preached from Isaiah 45:22 (KJV): "Look unto me, and be ye saved, all the ends of the earth." Spurgeon later said, "I looked until I could almost have looked my eyes away."[26] It was a sermon with an active verb attached to it: "Look!" It was a challenge to *do something*. Spurgeon later said, "When our lives are to be written at last, God grant that they record not only our saying, but also our doings."[27]

The next forty-two years of Spurgeon's ministry would be crammed with active verbs. Spurgeon would *do* a lot. He preached to crowds of 3,000 and 23,000, baptized almost 15,000 members, maintained a weekly attendance of 6,000 people, and spawned sixty-six parachurch ministries, including two orphanages, a book fund, a retirement home, and a theological college. Every week Spurgeon digested six meaty books, preached often three to ten times, and constantly switched hats among pastor, president, editor, author, and evangelist. By 1892 Spurgeon had published more words in the English language than any other Christian in history,[28] a staggering 18 million words,[29] which is more than is found in the famed 1875–89 ninth edition of the *Encyclopedia Britannica*.[30] Spurgeon truly became a *"wunderkind* of mid-Victorian nonconformity"[31] or as Carl F. H. Henry called him "one of evangelical Christianity's immortals."[32]

---

[26] Spurgeon, *Autobiography*, 1:106.

[27] *NPSP* 6:245.

[28] Lewis A. Drummond, "The Secrets of Spurgeon's Preaching: Why Would Thousands Come to Hear Him?," *Christian History and Biography* 29 (1991).

[29] Eric Hayden, *Highlights in the Life of C. H. Spurgeon* (Pasadena, TX: Pilgrim, 1990), 75.

[30] Eric W. Hayden, "Did You Know?," in *Christian History and Biography* 29:2 (1991). In his *Christian History* article, Hayden notes the total number of volumes in the ninth edition of *Encyclopaedia Britannica*. In actuality the ninth edition contains twenty-four volumes with the additional index volume, not twenty-seven volumes as indicated in Hayden's research and John Piper's article "Preaching Through Adversity." See John Piper, "Preaching Through Adversity," *Founder's Journal* 23 (1996). For more information see www.britannica.com/EBchecked/topic/186618/Encyclopaedia-Britannica/2107/Ninth-edition.

[31] German, "wonder child"; Chris Brooks and Andrew Saint, eds., *The Victorian Church: Architecture and Society* (Manchester, England: Manchester University Press, 1995), 89.

[32] Quoted in Drummond, *Spurgeon: Prince of Preachers*, 11.

But what is less known about Spurgeon's conversion story is where he attended church that evening. Instead of returning to the Primitive Methodist church, Spurgeon went to Eld Lane Baptist Church and heard Reverend Robert Langford preach a sermon on Ephesians 1:6, "He hath made us accepted in the beloved" (KJV). In the morning Spurgeon was challenged to *do* something for Christ; in the evening he was assured that Christ had done something for him.

As Southern Baptists we must also learn to live in the space between the active and the passive. Our ministers and our ministries must oscillate between Isaiah and Ephesians, between *doing* and *being*, between engaging and withdrawing.

Three years after Spurgeon withdrew from the Baptist Union and one month before he died, he delivered a brief talk to a few friends at the Hôtel Beau Rivage in Mentone, France. "When our Lord prayed that his church might be one," he said, "his prayer was answered, and his true people are even now, in spirit and in truth, one in him. Their different modes of external worship are as the furrows of a field; the field is none the less one because of the marks of the plough."[33]

Although Spurgeon had been raised as an Independent Congregationalist, educated at an Anglican boarding school, and converted in a Primitive Methodist chapel, he nevertheless adopted and retained a lifelong commitment to the Baptist tradition. His mother once said, "Ah, Charles! I often prayed the Lord to make you a Christian, but I never asked that you might become a Baptist," to which Spurgeon replied, "Ah, mother! The Lord has answered your prayer with His usual bounty, and given you exceeding abundantly above what you asked or thought."[34]

However, during the throes of the Downgrade Controversy, when Spurgeon's own denomination abandoned and censured him, Spurgeon's ecclesiology broadened. Those once-envious Anglicans stood in the trenches with Spurgeon and, along with other evangelicals, awarded Spurgeon such a standing ovation at the Evangelical Alliance that tears streamed down his face. It was, after all, not a Baptist whom Spurgeon entrusted with the pastorate of his Tabernacle in 1891 but instead the American Presbyterian A. T. Pierson. Spurgeon's budding ecumenism requires further analysis, but it offers our churches a corrective to the atrophy that can prevent us from moving forward.

As a dyed-in-the-wool, lifelong member of the Southern Baptist family, I believe I can say this without the outbreak of too much sibling rivalry: Jesus did not come to earth *only* to start the Southern Baptist Convention. Jesus came to found *the church*. I know this goes without saying, but as Southern Baptists move into the next century, perhaps we could say it more loudly. Paul reminded his church in Corinth, "Now you are the body of Christ, and each one of you is a part of it" (1 Cor 12:27 NIV).

---

[33] Charles Spurgeon, *From the Pulpit to the Palm-Branch: A Memorial of C. H. Spurgeon* (London: Passmore & Alabaster, 1902), 26.

[34] Spurgeon, *Autobiography*, 1:69.

The church that Christ established is a multicultural, multiethnic, poly-chromatic expression of the wisdom of God. In Ephesians 3:10, Paul uses the word *polypoikilos*—multicolored, multifaceted. The Septuagint used the root of this word, *poikilon*, in Genesis 37:3 to describe Joseph's coat of many colors. Historically we Southern Baptists have a tendency to split over things like col-or—whether it is the color of carpet or, and far more tragically, the color of skin. But Jesus was not crossing his fingers in John 17:21when he prayed "that all of them may be one, Father, just as you are in me and I am in you" (NIV). Our local churches are part of larger, older caravan of Christians who, as Augustine wrote, travel "forward on pilgrimage amid the persecutions of the world and the consolation of God."[35]

Southern Baptists will likely face moral, ethical, doctrinal, and missional challenges over the course of this new century. And in the trenches of those un-born controversies, we may just find ourselves, as Spurgeon did, standing closer to those outside her tradition than those within it. It is perhaps ironic, given Spurgeon's early, 295-page treatise against the pope, that in 1892 he shared more in common with some of the teachings of Roman Catholics on the subjects of the infallibility of Scripture, the supernatural miracles, the Trinity, and the divinity of Christ than he did with many of his own Baptist brethren who claimed the Scriptures were mixed with error, that Jesus did not physically rise from the dead, that he was not born of a virgin, and that the miracles were mythological inven-tions engendered by an unenlightened and superstitious era.

So what lessons can the nineteenth century teach the twenty-first? The Victorians remind us to keep ourselves on guard against the amnesia of the mind, the anemia of our heart, and the atrophy of the body. They teach us that if we fail in any one of these areas, the whole body will suffer. If we neglect theology, then we have spirituality without *mission* and ecclesiology without *message*. If we ne-glect spirituality, then we have theology without *vitality* and ecclesiology without *doxology*. And if we neglect ecclesiology, then we have theology without *applica-tion* and spirituality without *incarnation*.

At 11:05 p.m. on January 31, 1892, after a long battle with gout, kidney dis-ease, and depression, Spurgeon's suffering came to an end when he fell into a coma and did not recover. A telegraph was sent around the world, spreading the news of his death. "If every crowned head in Europe had died that night," said B.H. Carroll, the founder of Southwestern Baptist Theological Seminary, "the event would not be so momentous as the death of this one man."[36] Throughout England sympathetic letters were sent from William Gladstone, the Prince of Wales, the

---

[35] Augustine, in *A Select Library of the Nicene and Post-Nicene Fathers of the Christian Church*, 14 vols., First Series: *The Early Church Fathers*, (Grand Rapids: Michigan, Eerdmans, 1956), 2:392.

[36] Quoted in Drummond, *Spurgeon: Prince of Preachers*, 751.

chief rabbi, and bishops of the Church of England. More than 100,000 people passed by Spurgeon's coffin during its installation in West Norwood Cemetery.

But just before his death, Spurgeon offered a farewell prophecy: "I am quite willing to be eaten by dogs for the next fifty years, but the more distant future shall vindicate me."[37] Over a century has passed since Spurgeon uttered those words. Yet today, perhaps more than ever, evangelicals continue to glean wisdom from the words and witness of the Prince of Preachers. Like Abel, who "even though he is head, he still speaks through his faith" (Heb 11:4 HCSB), Charles Spurgeon still has something to say. From the grave he speaks clearly and loudly about the battles worth fighting and the hills worth dying on.

Today if you go to West Norwood Cemetery and climb the grassy knoll leading to Spurgeon's tomb, you will notice cracks in the marble—scars still evident from the explosion of 1944. The small, nonconformist chapel behind it was never rebuilt; a crematorium was constructed in its place—a fitting picture, to be sure, of the spiritual climate of twenty-first-century British evangelicalism.

And yet, nineteen years after the Germans launched their Vengeance Weapon, a remarkable endorsement for Spurgeon was sent by publication across the English Channel. It was penned by none other than a German theologian by the name of Helmut Thielicke. In his book *Encounter with Spurgeon*, Thielicke described Spurgeon as the combustion of "oxygen and grace"[38] that towered over the likes of even Friedrich Schleiermacher, Johann Tobias Beck, and Ludwig Hofacker. In Thielicke's words Spurgeon's life

> was not merely a life lived in constant association with Holy Scripture—lest that life be regarded as a burdensome yoke of the law—but rather in every word of actually bringing that life into being by making the ubiquity of the Scriptures a real and living fact. . . . When Spurgeon speaks, it is as if the figures of the patriarchs and prophets and apostles were in the auditorium. . . . The Bible is so close that you hear not only its messages but breath its very atmosphere. [Spurgeon]'s heart is so full of Scripture that it leavens the consciousness, peoples the imagination with its images, and determines the landscape of the soul by its climate.[39]

Seventy-two years have passed since the burning of Spurgeon's tomb, and yet the words of that German theologian still echo into the twenty-first century: "That bush from old London still burns and shows no sign of being consumed."[40]

---

[37] Charles Spurgeon, *An All-Round Ministry: Addresses to Ministers and Students* (repr., 1900; Edinburgh: The Banner of Truth, 2000), 360.
[38] Helmut Thielicke, *Encounter with Spurgeon*, trans. John Doberstein (Minneapolis: Fortress, 1963), 19.
[39] Ibid., 9.
[40] Ibid., 4.

Steel-Toed Birkenstocks and Doctrine-Loving Christians: Southern Baptist Witness and Ethics in the New Sexual Age

Owen D. Strachan

We begin with Oprah. Actually, with Oprah *and* Rob Bell, a potent—even combustible—spiritual combination. In February 2015 Bell and his wife, Kristen, talked about marriage during a Valentine's weekend episode of Winfrey's *Super Soul Sunday* television show:

> "One of the oldest aches in the bones of humanity is loneliness," Bell said. "Loneliness is not good for the world. Whoever you are, gay or straight, it is totally normal, natural and healthy to want someone to go through life with. It's central to our humanity. We want someone to go on the journey with."[1]

That statement prompted a question from Oprah: "When is the church going to get that?" Bell responded with his customary brio:

> We're moments away. I think culture is already there and the church will continue to be even more irrelevant when it quotes letters from 2,000 years ago as their best defense, when you have in front of you flesh-and-blood people who are your brothers and sisters and aunts and uncles and co-workers and neighbors and they love each other and just want to go through life with someone.

---

[1] Matt Vande Bunte, "Rob Bell on Gay Marriage: We're 'Moments Away' from Embracing It," *MLive*, February 16, 2015. Accessed February 24, 2016. http://www.mlive.com/living/grand-rapids/index.ssf/2015/02/rob_bell_on_gay_marriage_were.html.

Bell's wife, Kristen, then chimed in: "There are churches who are moving forward and there are churches who are almost regressing and making it more of a battle."

These emotive remarks drew a strong response from the audience. Many cheered them online as well. Bell's prediction represents the viewpoint of a good number of Americans. According to the Pew Forum, 55 percent of all Americans supported gay marriage in 2015.[2] The Supreme Court ruled that gay marriage is constitutional in the summer of 2015, bringing the crushing weight of the law to bear on this vexing cultural question. With data and developments like this, we recognize that Bell voiced the mind-set of a majority of the American people. A large number now see gay marriage, and beyond this an LGBT lifestyle, as a permanent and even virtuous part of the body politic. Such is life, and ministry, in the brave new world of the early twenty-first century.

Christians must reckon with this new reality. Stories of transgender transitions are no longer confined to exotic coastal locales. Colleges and universities are cracking down on evangelical campus groups that dare to require student leaders to affirm biblical sexual ethics. A sexualized culture targets children and encourages men and women to think of themselves as fundamentally sexual beings. Before our eyes this society has morphed. The nature of America is changing and has changed. We must ask the elephant-sized question, then: is Bell right—is the church "moments away" from affirming gay marriage and the broader LGBT revolution? Let us put the question this way: are Southern Baptists about to kiss the steel-toed Birkenstock of the sexual revolution? Many would say we are. They would affirm Bell's prediction. They would nod their head at Kristen Bell's comment—yes, churches that hold to conservative convictions are angry, standing against progress, and combative. In this mind-set the church and its stout biblical doctrine are the problem, not the solution. In this frame of mind, Southern Baptists are the squealing creature caught beneath the wheels of history. You put the car in drive, feel a bump, and then there is nothing to worry about.

I take the exact opposite position. I believe Southern Baptists are not going anywhere. With many conservative allies, we are not flinching in the moment of reckoning. We are not close to affirming gay marriage. We are not scared of the culture and its grandstanding. We have been given a sturdy and time-tested body of doctrine and ethics, and we will not give up this confessional inheritance. But our posture is not preeminently defensive. We believe biblical truth is not only that which will preserve us but that which will free the lost, raise the dead, and lift the redeemed to heaven.

Theology, we recognize, is not the problem. Theology enables us to taste and know the goodness of God in all its manifold wisdom. In what follows I want to

2   Pew Research Center, "Changing Attitudes on Gay Marriage," July 29, 2015. Accessed February 24.2016. http://www.pewforum.org/2015/07/29/graphics-slideshow-changing-attitudes-on-gay-marriage.

examine this claim with special reference to gender and sexuality by considering the standing evangelical and Southern Baptist conversation on these issues and tracing the Bible's presentation of these issues. In sum, I hope to offer a way forward for confessional Christians in a contested culture.

A BRIEF HISTORY OF EVANGELICAL THINKING ON SEXUALITY

Al Mohler and Carl F. H. Henry were walking on the campus of The Southern Baptist Theological Seminary. It was a lovely day in Louisville, Kentucky, and Mohler was making the most of his opportunity to pick the brain of the greatest evangelical theologian of the post-World War II era. It was 1984, and Mohler found himself surprised by the studied lack of interest in Henry on Southern's campus. Mohler's fellow doctoral students and professors made little effort to engage the titanic theologian when Henry made a visit to the campus, and Mohler was especially stunned when Henry was not even allowed to say a word of greeting when he sat in on a theology class at SBTS.[3] The class discussed three well-known theologians—all of whom Henry had either debated or conversed with in preceding weeks!

Forget contributing—Henry could have taught the course without a moment for preparation. He had recently published his magisterial six-volume set, *God, Revelation, and Authority*, a body of work that represented the most serious engagement with epistemology and biblical authority by an evangelical since the days when B. B. Warfield stalked the campus of Old Princeton.[4] Henry's six volumes were dense, often brilliant, occasionally quixotic, and surprisingly devotional in places. The text spoke to the character of the man, for Henry was *sui generis*, one of a kind. Though he possessed incredible gifts, Henry had not made a career in theology for his own sake. He sought to be faithful to Scripture, and he pursued the text's takeaways without fear of cultural reprisal.

This was true on the issue of gender and women's ordination. In this period Mohler hewed to the line common to SBTS and most every high-flown seminary. He was an "egalitarian" and thus believed that women could serve as pastors. This came up in conversation with Henry, with Mohler making the case for his

---

[3] Matthew Hall and Owen Strachan, *Essential Evangelicalism: The Enduring Influence of Carl F. H. Henry* (Carol Stream, IL: Crossway, 2015), 29–31.

[4] Carl F. H. Henry, *God, Revelation, and Authority*, 6 vols. (Waco, TX: Word, 1976–1983), hereafter *GRA*. The six volumes in order of publication: Henry, *God, Revelation, and Authority, Vol. 1: God Who Speaks and Shows, Preliminary Considerations* (Wheaton, IL: Crossway, 1999 [Word, 1976]); idem, *God, Revelation, and Authority, Vol. 2: God Who Speaks and Shows—Fifteen Theses, Part One* (Wheaton, IL: Crossway, 1999 [Word, 1976]); idem, *God, Revelation, and Authority, Vol. 3: God Who Speaks and Shows, Fifteen Theses, Part Two* (Wheaton, IL: Crossway, 1999 [Word, 1979]); idem, *God, Revelation, and Authority, Vol. 4: God Who Speaks and Shows, Fifteen Theses, Part Three* (Wheaton, IL: Crossway, 1999 [Word, 1979]); idem, *God, Revelation, and Authority, Vol. 5: God Who Stands and Stays, Part One* (Wheaton, IL: Crossway, 1999 [Word, 1982]); idem, *God, Revelation, and Authority, Vol. 6: God Who Stands and Stays, Part Two* (Wheaton, IL: Crossway, 1999 [Word, 1983]).

position. Henry, a man overflowing with words, had only a few for his young friend in this instance. "One day," he said to Mohler, looking him in the eye, "you'll be embarrassed to have made that argument."[5]

Henry was right. Soon after this exchange, Mohler embraced what would soon be called "complementarianism," the view that men alone are called to be pastors of the local church and heads of the home. But Mohler's strong defense of egalitarianism made sense in his context. The rise of feminism in the 1960s and its subsequent academic embrace by leading institutions ensured that divinity schools like Harvard, Yale, and Princeton stood against the historic position of the Christian church. The Reformers, Anabaptists, Calvinists, Puritans, Edwardseans, Baptists, Presbyterians, and many others had for four centuries held to what we would call a "complementarian" position. One can find examples of egalitarian theology and practice in evangelical church history—John Wesley, for example, allowed some women to preach in his time, and Aimee Semple Macpherson hit celebrity status in the 1920s—but they are rare and essentially nonexistent among confessional Christian movements that connect ecclesial life to a fulsome body of doctrine codified in a statement of faith.

Evangelicalism had for some time drifted on the issue of gender. The assumed position of many an intellectual evangelical was egalitarian. Among other texts, Fuller Theological Seminary professor Paul Jewett's popular book *Man as Male and Female* helped provide the scholarly ballast for this position in 1975.[6] Jewett, Daniel Hubbard, and Daniel Fuller championed the egalitarian perspective at Fuller, with women gaining eligibility for pastoral programs in 1968.[7] At Gordon-Conwell Theological Seminary, Roger Nicole influenced many students to affirm women's ordination.[8]

Southern Baptists held to conservative biblical doctrine on this issue. The 1963 Baptist Faith and Message did not speak to the office of pastor or to the nature of roles in the family. The SBC was moving into a kind of two-tiered approach to the gender issue. The vast majority of Southern Baptists were complementarian in their theology and practice. In the pew, and among thousands of pastors, biblical teaching carried the day. Not so in the seminaries and colleges. As Gregory Wills has shown, leading Southern Baptist theologians and administrators hankered after the model and theology of the elite divinity schools. They

---

[5] Hall and Strachan, *Essential Evangelicalism*, 32.

[6] Paul King Jewett, *Man as Male and Female: A Study in Sexual Relationships from a Theological Point of View* (Grand Rapids: Eerdmans, 1975).

[7] See Marianne Meye Thompson, "Interview: Fuller, Women, and the Bible," *Fuller Magazine*. Accessed January 18, 2016. http://fullermag.com/fuller-the-bible-and-women.

[8] Nicole was a giant of a theologian and made major contributions to various doctrines: atonement, inerrancy, and baptism among them. His take on gender roles did not always convince his students. See the warm-hearted reflections of Mark Dever, "Reflections on Roger Nicole," *9Marks*, June 11, 2014. Accessed February 24, 2016. http://9marks.org/article/reflections-on-roger-nicole.

yearned to be free of the shackles of confessional conservatism and to have "academic freedom" such that the Scripture would not—in their mind—constrain their conclusions.[9]

This meant that by the 1980s bright young students like Mohler assumed that the egalitarian position alone was tenable for thinking Christians. Most of Mohler's seminary professors paid public homage to the stolid biblicism of lay Christians and small-church pastors but undermined and even derided this confessional instinct in the classroom. The same was true for evangelical life more broadly. Should one attend the annual meeting of the Evangelical Theological Society, one might come away thinking that complementarians were a limited, strange, and unwanted species at the gathering.

Wayne Grudem, a young complementarian theology professor in the 1980s, later reflected on his experience at ETS. In 1985, Grudem published a stemwinder of an article on the use of *kephale*, "head," in Ephesians 5 and other texts.[10] He was invited to give a plenary address at the 1986 meeting of the ETS and did so despite great odds against him: "The theme was 'Manhood and Womanhood in Biblical and Theological Perspectives.' The program chairman (Walter Dunnett) had invited six plenary session speakers. I was the complementarian—that is, the token complementarian." Grudem found himself in a situation so stacked against him it was almost humorous: "The other five were egalitarians (Gilbert Bilezekian, Catherine Kroeger, Walter Liefeld, Aida Spencer, and David Scholer). And the program was set up so that all of the plenary session speakers would respond to the other plenary sessions, so it was a five-to-one situation. Quite exciting!"[11]

Grudem survived the gender Thunderdome and soon linked up with pastor-theologian John Piper (both of them credobaptists by conviction) and others

---

[9] Gregory Wills, *The Southern Baptist Theological Seminary, 1859–2009* (New York: Oxford University Press, 2009).

[10] The article is found in Wayne Grudem, ed., *Biblical Foundations for Manhood and Womanhood* (Wheaton: Crossway, 2002). It is accessible online at http://www.waynegrudem.com/wp-content/uploads/2012/03/kephale-article.pdf. Accessed February 24, 2016

[11] Wayne Grudem, "Personal Reflections on the History of CBMW and the State of the Gender Debate," *Journal for Biblical Manhood and Womanhood* (2009). Accessed February 24, 2016. http://cbmw.org/uncategorized/personal-reflections-on-the-history-of-cbmw-and-the-state-of-the-gender-debate. Years later, in November 2015 at the business meeting of the ETS, members affirmed the following four resolutions (coauthored by Rob Schwarzwalder and me). With others I was heartened by this action on the part of the society.

(1) We affirm that all persons are created in the image and likeness of God and thus possess inherent dignity and worth.

(2) We affirm that marriage is the covenantal union of one man and one woman, for life.

(3) We affirm that Scripture teaches that sexual intimacy is reserved for marriage as defined above. This excludes all other forms of sexual intimacy.

(4) We affirm that God created men and women, imbued with the distinct traits of manhood and womanhood, and that each is an unchangeable gift of God that constitutes personal identity.

For details, see David Roach, "ETS Meeting Addresses 'Marriage and Family,' Baptist Press, November 20, 2015. Accessed February 24, 2016. http://www.bpnews.net/45887/ets-meeting-addresses-marriage-and-family.

to write the Danvers Statement in 1987.[12] Not long after, The Council on Biblical Manhood and Womanhood (CBMW) emerged in 1988 as the outworking of conversations shared by Grudem, Piper, Paige and Dorothy Patterson, and others. Now complementarianism had a voice and a platform. In 1991 Piper and Grudem published the edited volume *Recovering Biblical Manhood and Womanhood*, which featured outstanding scholarly work by figures like Douglas Moo, Tom Schreiner, and D. A. Carson.[13]

The drive to recover complementarianism went hand in hand with the drive to recover inerrancy in the SBC. During the 1980s and 1990s, all six SBC seminaries were recovered by inerrantists. By 1998 the SBC had published a fresh version of the Baptist Faith and Message that included a new article on the family. This article propounded a complementarian position on male headship and female submission while affirming the full equality of men and women:

> The husband and wife are of equal worth before God, since both are created in God's image. The marriage relationship models the way God relates to His people. A husband is to love his wife as Christ loved the church. He has the God-given responsibility to provide for, to protect, and to lead his family. A wife is to submit herself graciously to the servant leadership of her husband even as the church willingly submits to the headship of Christ. She, being in the image of God as is her husband and thus equal to him, has the God-given responsibility to respect her husband and to serve as his helper in managing the household and nurturing the next generation.[14]

The BFM2000, as it is often called, made clear that only men could serve as pastors in the church: "While both men and women are gifted for service in the church, the office of pastor is limited to men as qualified by Scripture." The SBC, as a denomination, now owned in full the complementarian position. The official confession of all churches and organizations that aligned with the SBC was robustly biblical.

THE BIBLICAL PRESENTATION OF GENDER AND SEXUALITY

The preceding material should bolster the convictions of modern Southern Baptists. It is clear that our secular culture has moved away from its original Judeo-Christian framework (one bearing the trappings of Enlightenment thought

---

[12] Find the statement in full at http://cbmw.org/about/danvers-statement. Accessed February 24, 2016.
[13] John Piper and Wayne Grudem, *Recovering Biblical Manhood and Womanhood: A Response to Evangelical Feminism* (Carol Stream, IL: Crossway, 1991).
[14] See The Baptist Faith and Message 2000. Accessed February 24, 2016. http://www.sbc.net/bfm2000/bfm-comparison.asp.

as well).[15] It can feel like the odds are dead set against us and that the pressure we face is too much to bear.

But Southern Baptists—with our confessional friends of other movements and denominations—have faced stiff winds before. The rescue of the SBC and the fresh promotion of inerrancy and complementarianism reveals that something profound changed in the SBC between Mohler's conversation with Henry and the publication of the BFM2000. As the denomination recovered the doctrinal foundation of inerrancy, it owned rigorously complementarian theology as well.

The question for the SBC in our time is not whether it will embrace complementarianism. This matter has been settled. The question before us today is a subtler one: will we affirm a bare-bones presentation of gender and sexuality, or will we see the biblical witness on humanity and sexuality as a blessing and a gift? Put more starkly, will we adopt a minimalist view of complementarity or a maximalist view?

Today, Southern Baptists face pressure to soften their doctrine. In what follows, I will give seven points that show us our understanding of complementarity transcends a mere sorting out of technicalities on a couple tough issues. Complementarity is a way of life. The Bible's teaching on manhood and womanhood, in other words, shapes the patterns and structures of our day-to-day lives.

Complementarity Shows Us What God Wants Humanity to Be

God does not create generic human blobs. He created "male and female" according to Genesis 1:27. The Lord is not threatened by human diversity. He himself loves diversity. He wants men and women to image his glory. Manhood does not owe to John Wayne as a structural archetype; womanhood is not the fever-dream of Martha Stewart. Manhood and womanhood proceed from the mind and design of Almighty God. Each is thus to be received as a gift of God not treated as an accident of biology.

The core of the reality of our humanity is this: God has made us either a man or a woman for his glory. We share a tremendous amount as men and women. We each bear the image of God. But we are *essentially* different. Our differences as designed by God are not a problem or a threat. They are glimpses of God's overspilling superintelligence.

Complementarity Explains the Dynamics of Marriage

The Lord creates the family as the first institution of the created order. The man is alone, which is "not good" in God's eyes (Gen 2:18 HCSB). From this lack the Lord brings plenty: the woman is made from the man's rib, and she is

---

[15] See George Marsden, *The Twilight of the American Enlightenment: The 1950s and the Crisis of Liberal Belief* (New York: Basic, 2014).

his "helper" (Gen 2:18, 22). The man names the woman, indicating his domestic authority (Gen 2:23).

We take from this portrait the responsibility to train boys from their earliest days to be leaders of women. We never know for certain whether our children will be married, but we have a duty to shape our boys as leaders and our girls as those who gladly help men, who welcome masculine leadership as a gift. This does not mean women should never make decisions or assert themselves; Proverbs 31 shows us otherwise. But it does mean those who love the Bible train boys and girls in certain ways to the greater honor and renown of the Lord. Should our children marry, they will find their God-given roles less chafing and more satisfying.

Complementarity Makes Sense of the Fall

When the snake enters the garden, the man is nowhere to be found. The snake speaks to Eve, and the man should have rebuked and attacked the snake given his protective duty and the God-given commission to subdue the earth and the animals (Gen 1:26–27). The woman, we remember, is his own flesh, made from the man's body. But the man allows the snake to deceive his wife, and he takes the forbidden fruit from her, showing us that she is leading and he is passive. This may sound odd to our gender-neutral-trained ears, but the fall is at base a failure to practice biblical complementarity (Gen 3:1–7).

The curse that follows yields profound and ongoing pain between men and women. The woman will seek to usurp her husband, and the man will dominate his wife (Gen 3:16). All the suffering, all the brokenness, all the evil that transpires in postgarden marriages owes to the fall, when men and women lost sight of the intrinsic goodness of their God-given roles.

Complementarity Offers Hope for Sin-Affected Marriages

In Ephesians 5:22–33 the apostle Paul lays out the blueprint by which any and every union of one man and one woman may thrive. The husband must lovingly lead his wife as Christ leads the church, and the wife must lovingly submit to her husband as the church submits to Christ. When these patterns are in place and each spouse seeks to outdo the other by righteous action, the curse is quieted, if not fully overcome. The gospel has taken hold of the marriage, and though the couple will not live perfectly with each other, they may show the world that trusting the gospel and living according to Scripture yields surging hope and happiness in a marriage.

It is great to get marital advice and learn more about each other in practical ways. But we do not need generic maxims to thrive in our marriages. We most need the Christ-church pattern as our emblem, as the image we strive toward as husbands and wives. In the language of Genesis 2:24, men must "hold fast" (ESV) to their wives even as Jesus never lets go of his bride and thus must take the initiative to cultivate their marriages. Modern men have learned the none-too-subtle cues of a feminist culture and feel chagrin and even shame when they lead. But Scripture gives us a better blueprint for our marital flourishing, one in which men act in glad and frequent consultation with their wives to lend great strength to their families.[16]

Complementarity Structures the Nature of Church Leadership

Men are called to be elders and pastors according to Paul's apostolic direction and the order of creation (1 Tim 2:8–15). If someone asks, "What should a church look like? How should it be structured?" gender concerns are front and center. They are not incidental. The Lord desires that men would both hold the office of pastor and take responsibility for the oversight, teaching, and shepherding of the flock. This is a massively important call to men.[17]

Just as we cannot assume that boys without training will magically mature into godly men, we cannot assume that men without shepherding will magically mature into elders. The church has a mandate to train men to be godly and thus to lead the congregation. Too many churches, even Southern Baptist churches, are formally complementarian but functionally egalitarian. The men hold the offices they are supposed to hold, yes, but the balance of leadership in the congregation swings in the direction of committees and programs run by women. This is not the biblical pattern. If elders are really elders according to 1 Timothy 3:1–7 and Titus 1:5–9, then they are not simply titular heads but must serve as on-the-ground shepherds. Their fingerprints are to be all over the church.

Women can and even must serve in countless ways in the life of the body. If women are not teaching other women, for example, then they are disobeying Titus 2:3–5. Complementarian men do not muzzle women. Complementarian men want women to be strong in Christ. We want women to flourish. We know that God's teaching and biblical roles always bring happiness and health. We take the biblical portrait of church leadership with great seriousness, and we recognize that gender is a vital part of it.

Complementarity Helps Us Make Sense of the Chaos of Our Culture

These are strange days. Never before have women been more "liberated" than now. We are thankful for some cultural changes, of course; the instinct of fallen men to dominate women and leave them without agency is evil, and thus we are glad women have much greater flexibility and opportunity in society than in previous generations.

---

[16] For practical help on these matters, see Jonathan Parnell and Owen Strachan, eds., *Designed for Joy: How the Gospel Impacts Men and Women, Identity and Practice* (Carol Stream, IL: Crossway, 2015).

[17] For the definitive scholarly analysis of this text, see Andreas J. Köstenberger and Thomas R. Schreiner, eds., *Women in the Church: An Analysis and Application of 1 Timothy 2:9–15* (Grand Rapids: Baker, 2005).

But our post-Christian culture is not a thriving garden of male-female interaction. It is a wasteland. This is, after all, the age of *50 Shades of Grey*, a book
and movie that encourage women to be used by men sexually as an embodiment
of their sexual license and that goads men on to see women as little more than
bedroom conquests. Elite gender-studies classes built on exotic theories have not
solved all the problems of the sexes; they have exacerbated them, leaving us with
a generation that scoffs at romance and gender roles but thrills to Tinder and
random hookups. "The pill" has actualized and enabled all of this, detaching sex
from marriage and causing many to believe the lie that sex is just a function of the
body and has no consequences for the heart and soul.[18]

Beyond the sexual act, transgender ideology argues that gender is just a "construct," a cultural fiction dreamed up by oppressors. One's body may not consti-
tute one's gender identity. The two may go totally different directions, occasioning
the need for a "transition," a change made famous by the decathlete formerly
known as Bruce Jenner (now Caitlyn Jenner in public record). First gender roles
were attacked; then gender differences were undermined; now even the notion of
fixed sexuality is outmoded. The end result is this: humanity unbounded, with no
limits, no duties, no script for life. The pagan impulse of our modern culture de-
nies "twoness" in favor of a bludgeoning "oneness" that reduces all to sameness.[19]
It goes beyond this and revolts against contingency itself. We become gods, creating new selves, giving our lives our own self-assigned meaning, subject to no one.

Complementarity speaks a better word. Our body is God's kindness to us. It
is formed by him, "woven," (ESV), in the psalmist's words, in the womb, and our
days are numbered—and thus limited—by God (Ps 139:13–16). Because of the
fall, because of abuse, we may not feel like our body is good. We may yearn to reb-
el against the constraints of our sexuality (as in Deut 22:5). But complementarity
grounded in the Bible clarifies and purifies our toxin-invaded worldview. It is good
to be made by God. It is good to be drafted into either manhood or womanhood
as a direct response to our body. It is good to strive toward the fullest realization
of our manhood or womanhood in Christ (see 1 Cor 11:1–14). The authority
of the man is not located in some bygone stereotype; it is the outworking of the
headship of God the Father over the Son (1 Cor 11:3). Complementarity owes
not simply to God's design for humanity but to the roles filled by the Godhead.[20]

Only complementarity equips the church to rescue men and women trapped
in false visions of gender and sexuality. Complementarians know that God has

---

[18] See Mary Eberstadt, *Adam and Eve After the Pill: Paradoxes of the Sexual Revolution* (San Francisco: Ignatius,
2012).

[19] See Peter Jones, *Pagans in the Pews: Protecting Your Family and Community from the Pervasive Influence of the
New Spirituality* (Norwood, MA: Regal, 2001). Far too little attention has been paid to the influence of pagan-
ism on the West.

[20] See Bruce Ware, *Father, Son, and Holy Spirit: Relationship, Roles, and Relevance* (Carol Stream, IL: Crossway,
2005).

made us for his glory and that our bodies are not mere biological facts. Our bodies give us a script for our lives. When we minister the gospel to people caught in myriad sexual perversions, people who reject both bodily norms and gender roles, we are not simply offering them a call to faith but a call to embrace God's good design. The gospel and sexuality cannot be separated; this relationship cannot be minimized. When you are saved, you do not become a generic Christian person. You become a Christian man or a Christian woman. The divine design you may have resisted all your days now becomes a source of profound blessing to you.

Complementarity Helps Us Answer Tough Questions About Everyday Living

It is not always easy to know how exactly to live as a godly man or woman in this world. But the biblical picture of our God-given sex helps us begin to make sense of what confuses us. Women know that they are uniquely called to have a "gentle and quiet spirit" (1 Pet 3:4 HCSB). This means a woman of Christ does not approach men with an overbearing temperament. This teaching informs how women conduct themselves in work settings, ordinary conversations, and everyday life. So too do men know that they are uniquely called to pursue the character of an elder. This means they must treat women well, seeing them as sisters, and thus approaching them "with absolute purity" (1 Tim 5:2 NIV). Men are to reverence women, never abuse or use them. This too informs how men behave in every facet of life. Single men and women will not enter into the direct headship-submission relationship of a married couple. But fundamentally, women can take great pleasure in being women, and men can take great pleasure in being men. One need not be married to experience tremendous delight in one's God-given sex. In fact, single men and women have the opportunity to show the world that there is something better than romance: loving Christ.[21]

It is the culture, after all, and not the church that has defined humanity in terms of sexuality. The church follows a Lord who never shared the marriage bed, never enjoyed inside jokes with a spouse, never tousled the hair of his beloved child. Jesus shows the world that one need not be married or having sex to be whole. The happiest person who ever lived was Jesus, and his example speaks a better word than the culture's.

FACING TOMORROW: THE WAY FORWARD IS GOOD

In this chapter I have attempted to show that the church—and the SBC in particular—has returned to complementarian teaching even as it has embraced inerrancy. Instead of following the directives of a secular culture, the SBC has staked its

---

[21] For more on this essential point, see Rosaria Butterfield, *Openness Unhindered: Further Thoughts of an Unlikely Convert on Sexual Identity and Union with Christ* (Pittsburgh: Crown and Covenant, 2015).

ground on Scripture. We traced how the Scripture speaks to core realities of our lives, showing that the Bible gives vital direction to our daily existence.

We are reminded that the Bible is not only true but good. This is the central fight of our time: to believe in the God-drenched goodness of the Word. Faithful Southern Baptists fought hard to preserve the denomination's trust in the Bible. We emerged from the fire with the Scripture firmly in our hands. But in recent times the goodness of biblical teaching has come under fire. It is not so much the truthfulness of Scripture that is undermined today but the goodness of Scripture that suffers assault. As a result, many believers feel nervous about the times. They worry that they are now seen as not only backwards but antiwoman, antigay, and even antihumanity.

I understand the reason for this concern. In terms of the pushback from our peers, it is fearsome. But we have nothing to fear. If we stand on the Word of God, we may live in fullness of confidence and steadfastness of hope. God is not only *on* the right side of history; God *is* the right side of history. We do not need to soften God's words; we do not need to perform crisis PR work for Almighty God. He does not need to apologize to our unbelieving age for hurting its feelings and dampening its plans for rebellion. He calls us to declare the whole counsel of God and leave it to him to sort out the details.

Southern Baptists have a strong confessional foundation. Previous generations have left the rising pack with a rich doctrinal inheritance and a catalytic legacy of courage. Names like Pressler, Patterson, Mohler, Rogers, Vines, and many others echo in the minds of young Southern Baptists. The charge before us is to remain faithful to this heritage and to continue speaking courageously to our fallen world.

We will be tested in coming days. We will see whether the younger generation's embrace of the gospel has led to a new version of pietism, a form of the faith that reduces it through the language of "gospel centrality" to the merest steps of salvation or whether the gospel-centered movement joyfully owns the full-throated Christian worldview. This worldview issues from the Lion of Judah who roars over his creation, who trembles before no man, and who spoke truth every chance he got. Through the truth salvation came. Theology, in sum, is not causing us problems. The truth has never caused division or pain. Theology, proceeding from the Word of God himself, is saving our soul.

CONCLUSION

In counterpoint to the barbed but anemic words of Rob Bell, we end with the words of Winston Churchill, who once said, in England's greatest hour of need, when the Nazis threatened to overwhelm even the mighty English war machine, "If this long island story of ours is to end at last, let it end only when each one of us lies choking in his own blood upon the ground."[22] Churchill made this pronouncement to his war cabinet, and his words carried the day. England refused to appease Hitler, the RAF ascended the skies, and eventually, Western civilization was saved.

We fight a much greater war. This war is for souls. The hour is dire, and the need for fearlessness is great. Let us resolve here and now that, as in past days, we will not give up the faith. We will not allow the eclipse of gospel witness on our watch. Powered by the majestic engine of God's grace, we will guard the good deposit and promote Christ in all the world.

We will do so no matter the cost. We have given up on image maintenance and brand management. We fear no man. The opponents of God's truth can have their say, but when it comes right down to it, the only thing we are "moments away" from is this: seeing Christ split the clouds, terrible in glory, and call his embattled but persevering church to himself.

---

[22] See Jonathan Rose, *The Literary Churchill: Author, Reader, Actor* (New Haven, CT: Yale University Press, 2014), 303.

SOUTHERN BAPTIST
MINISTRY AND MISSION

Kindling Afresh the Gift of God: Spiritual Renewal, Strategic Reinvention, and the SBC

Ronnie Floyd

I am so encouraged by the purpose of this book project devoted to the Southern Baptist Convention in the twenty-first century, as well as the symposium where these chapters were first presented as plenary addresses and breakout sessions. Usually these conversations are informal. They are usually not public but private. Oftentimes when they occur, they do not build trust but distrust among our family. As we share ideas and grow together, we do not do so with the intent to hurt or destroy but to grow and flourish together in the twenty-first century.

The topic assigned me is one I believe in and am genuinely humbled to address. As the current president of the Southern Baptist Convention, there is some level of risk for me to be open and honest concerning this subject. Yet this is not about me, and in reality it is not even about the Southern Baptist Convention; *it is* about the progress and the advancement of the gospel to the nations through the cooperative work of our churches through the Southern Baptist Convention.

My topic is titled "Kindling Afresh the Gift of God: Spiritual Renewal, Strategic Reinvention, and the SBC." A fire left to itself usually goes out. General William Booth, founder of the Salvation Army, told those who worked with him, "The tendency of fire is to go out; watch the fire on the altar of your heart."[1]

When writing to his protégé Timothy, the apostle Paul, with a sense of urgency knowing that his days on this earth were coming to an end through martyrdom, challenged Timothy to do whatever it takes to ensure he lived and ministered with

---

[1] Earl Creps, *Off-Road Disciplines: Spiritual Adventures of Missional Leaders* (San Francisco: Jossey-Bass, 2006), 181.

the full flame of the Holy Spirit. This is why Paul told Timothy to stir up the gift within him, to keep the Spirit of God blazing through is life and ministry.

In 2 Timothy 1:6–7 (HCSB) Paul writes, "Therefore, I remind you to keep ablaze the gift of God that is in you through the laying on of my hands. For God has not given us a spirit of fearfulness, but one of power, love, and sound judgment." With Nero reigning ruthlessly and violently against Christians, bringing their lives to an end in all kinds of ways, Paul wanted to tell Timothy there was no need to fear but to be filled with God's power, motivated by God's love, and to navigate through the future with sound judgment.

It is *not* God who would motivate any of us to run from the battles against Satan and his demonic forces. Cowardice was not cool for Timothy and is not cool for Christian leaders today. It is *not* God who would invoke in us self-preservation and inflated pride, but *it is* God who calls us to an unconditional, sacrificial love that is willing to give our all to our Savior in these difficult days in the twenty-first century. It is *not* God who leads us to live undisciplined lives personified through slothful living and careless leadership, but *it is* God who roars from the heavens ordering our days, prioritizing our lives, and empowering us with confidence in this hour.

Satan is powerful and spiritual warfare is real. This is why we must kindle and fan into flame the gift of the Holy Spirit living within us, and we must keep it in full flame. If we want the power of the Spirit to be everything through us that he is within us, we must take the initiative personally and intentionally to fan the flame of the Spirit of God.

Paul did not tell Timothy the fire of the Spirit had gone out of his life and ministry. This was not a rebuke but a reminder of the necessity that is laid on Timothy to always prioritize his own spiritual life in his God-assigned ministry. While we know the apostle Paul refers in his writings about the *gifts* of the Spirit, here he is referring to *the gift* of the Holy Spirit. Within the context of this text, we know that the power of the Spirit of God is the only One who can replace fearfulness with fearlessness, selfishness with sacrificial love, and disorder with discipline.

Unquestionably, the Holy Spirit indwells us at salvation. We read in 2 Timothy 1:14 (HCSB), "Guard, through the Holy Spirit who lives in us, that good thing entrusted to you." The Holy Spirit, who is in us, empowers us to experience spiritual renewal that results in a robust explosion of the gospel through us to the nations. When Timothy was set aside with a calling and the council of elders laid their hands on him, affirming him publicly through their prayerful support, he was told not to be neglectful of his spiritual life as a minister of the gospel. Please note the words recorded in 1 Timothy 4:14–16 (HCSB), "Do not neglect the gift that is in you; it was given to you through prophecy, with the laying on of hands by the council of elders. Practice these things; be committed to them, so that your progress may be evident to all. Pay close attention to your life and your teaching;

persevere in these things, for by doing this you will save both yourself and your hearers."

The call here is to prioritize your spiritual life, keeping the Spirit of God within you, blazing with a full flame endlessly. We should not ever neglect our personal spiritual life and development in ministry but always advance, growing in personal holiness that results in spiritual power.

As Southern Baptists, we have two undeniable priorities: (1) Prioritize your spiritual life. We forfeit our leadership when we do not prioritize our personal spiritual life. From God-called ministers all the way to the preschool ministry of our churches, each person should be called to prioritize their spiritual life. (2) Prioritize the power of God in ministry. Far too long the world has seen what we can do; now the world needs to see what God can do. I am not authorizing or endorsing anyone to go chasing after the hands of God. However, I am calling us to seek the face of God, resulting in spiritual renewal. *We must cease being content doing ministry without the power of God.*

The power of God comes when God's people pray and fast, when the Word of God is proclaimed and the gospel is shared, penetrating the darkness of lostness. The power of God comes upon the church when we surrender to him in worship while walking with him in purity both privately and publicly. Each of these is important, and when they occur simultaneously, spiritual renewal and power come, changing the future of everything around us, from life to family to ministry and even to the world itself.

This leads me to a fascinating finding that intrigues me as a follower of Christ and as a Christian leader. When your spiritual life and the power of God are your priorities, structures and systems change. *Listen carefully: structures and systems flow from the work of God; they do not create the work of God.* Genuine change occurs from the inside out, not the outside in. Please remember, Paul told Timothy to pay close attention to the fire of the Holy Spirit in him, challenging him never to neglect his spiritual life.

Additionally, other than Jesus, no one in the New Testament operated his ministry with the power of God more than the apostle Paul. He understood that structure and systems do not create the work of God but flow from the work of God.

Therefore, understand clearly: *Spiritual renewal leads to strategic reinvention.* As Christian leaders in our Southern Baptist Convention, we should not attempt to reduce the supremacy of Christ to our fallen nature by negating the opportunity for God to lead us toward our future together. I am all for brainstorming sessions and ideas written on a whiteboard *if* those in the room with me have a blazing fire of the Spirit within them that is evidenced through them in Christian ministry. Otherwise, pragmatism rules rather than the power of God reigning in an energizing experience about how we can reach the world for Christ together in the future more effectively.

When we humble ourselves, pray, repent from sin, and obey God, we move into a season of spiritual renewal where we experience the manifest presence of God personally and even collectively. This season of spiritual renewal moves us into being changed inwardly, living in obedience to God outwardly, and results in advancing the gospel and God's kingdom locally, statewide, nationally, and globally.

When God renews His people, things change. The way things are done changes. The attitudes change. How does this occur? Let me illustrate this for you:

- Jacob, on his return to Bethel, told his family to rid themselves of their false gods and purify their lives. They buried their false gods, changed their clothes, and met with God at Bethel. During the evening and into the early morning hours, God met with Jacob, changing everything in his life, including changing his name to Israel. His future purpose and path changed. Also, the people he led changed. God's meeting them at Bethel changed everything.[2]

- Moses, on his departure from Egypt leading toward the promised land, experienced the presence, guidance, and miraculous provision of God. The work of God that began in him at the place of the burning bush altered not only the course of his entire life but that of an entire nation.[3]

- King Hezekiah experienced a personal spiritual renewal that led to the re-opening of the temple and its repair. The people followed their leader, got their lives right with God, and celebrated their worship of God again. This prepared them for a miraculous move of God that saved them against the greatest army in the world.[4]

- Josiah, another king, led toward revival and reform when he repented of his sin and sought to obey the Word of the Lord again. Josiah rid the people of false gods, leading them into a time of cleansing and the repairing of the temple. He then reinstituted the reading of the Lord's Word publicly, leading the people into covenant with God to walk with him boldly, resulting in celebrating the Passover again.[5]

- Nehemiah experienced a mighty work of God while fasting and praying then was called back to Jerusalem to rebuild the wall around the city. Even through vicious, ongoing attacks, he kept his eye on the wall, completing his task of rebuilding the wall in fifty-two days. This resulted not only in securing the city again but also in a glorious celebration of the reading of

---

[2] See Genesis 35.
[3] See Exodus 3–5.
[4] See 2 Kings 18–20.
[5] See 2 Kings 22–23.

God's Word, the teaching of Scripture, and worship that changed their future.[6]

- Peter and Paul, both major leaders in the New Testament church, experienced the mighty movement of God within them that changed them dramatically. This work of God in them altered God's work through them, resulting in a mighty church growth movement that took the gospel throughout their world. The development and strengthening of the churches resulted in supernatural movements of evangelism, church planting, and growth in and through the churches.[7]

Again, I believe it is imperative to highlight the truth I stated earlier: *spiritual renewal leads to strategic reinvention.* Structures and systems flow from the work of God; they do not create the work of God. When God moves among his people, the way they carry out the work of God through structures and systems becomes altered.

No one believed this more and portrayed this greater than Jesus Christ himself. When Jesus confronted the legalistic teachings of the Pharisees with his counterdoctrine of grace, they were confounded. They did not know how to respond to words like those recorded in Matthew 9:17 (HCSB), when Jesus said to them, "And no one puts new wine into old wineskins. Otherwise, the skins burst, the wine spills out, and the skins are ruined. But they put new wine into fresh wineskins, and both are preserved."

I openly confess to you that I am one Baptist who is not a scholar on wine and wineskins. Yet I have studied this passage multiple times. Old wineskins become inflexible, brittle, and lose their elasticity. Therefore, Jesus asked why we would take fresh wine and pour it into old wineskins. As the new and fresh wine would ferment, it would break the old wineskins, losing both the new wine, and the old wineskins. Therefore, Jesus told them, anytime there is fresh, new wine, it needs to be placed into new, fresh wineskins. Then the new wineskins could conform to the wine as it ferments with time.

Jesus ushered into this world the age of grace that led to the outpouring of the Holy Spirit. The Pharisees did not receive Jesus's message of grace due to the rigidity of their legalistic religious system. The religious people of the world today, even in our Baptist world, oftentimes do not receive the message of grace and the outpouring of the Holy Spirit.

Oftentimes a pastor can go to a new church, God begins to use him greatly, and God begins working in the church miraculously. When the new wine or this fresh moving of God begins to pour out upon the church, the old wineskins of the church reject this new wine or this new movement of God among them. *They*

---

6 See Nehemiah 1–2.
7 This story takes up the entire book of Acts.

begin to fight for their tradition much more than they would ever fight for the truth.
This new wine or this fresh moving of God is either rejected by them, resulting in
the demise of God's work in the church, or this new wine or fresh moving of God
is received by them because their lives, their ministry, their wineskins were flexible
enough to align with and adjust to what God was doing through the church.

Let's pause for a moment and reconsider our entire subject at this time. As
we watch over the fire in our heart, keeping it ablaze at a full level of intensity,
we will move into seasons of spiritual renewal. This deep work of God occurring
within us will alter our strategies, reinventing them to the glory of God. And yes,
this needs to happen within our Southern Baptist Convention in the way we carry
out our work together.

America and the entire globe are experiencing revolutionary change. It is
changing the way we think and do all of our business on this earth. *Incremental
change is usually not acceptable any longer, but revolutionary change is expected and
embraced.*

Our Southern Baptist Convention is facing many challenges relating to our
future together. Unquestionably, we are facing monumental spiritual challenges.
Yet, when God renews his people, everything changes. *Spiritual renewal leads to
strategic reinvention.* The Spirit of God is not intimidated by this revolutionary age
of technology, for even this technological revolution can be submissive and serve
the fresh work of God's Spirit among his people. In the backdrop of this technological revolution and with a powerful move of God among his people, Southern
Baptists are facing unprecedented pressure to conform structures and systems to
serve this fresh work of God in this day.

As we cry out to God for fresh power and a new moving of his Spirit, we
should also pray that we will become like fresh wineskins that can conform to
what God is doing. If we hold onto our old structures and systems, more concerned about preserving them than seeing them conform to what God is doing
today, we may lose both the work of God and our present generation of Baptists.
The stakes are high, and we better land with God and refuse to fight against what
he is seemingly doing among us.

In 1845 we were founded with a great purpose and vision to reach the world
for Christ. As we have grown in our organization, we have also grown in our complexity. If this continues, our central focus will become the preservation of our
structures and systems and the budget and the allocation of it to our ministries
rather than keeping our focus on our mission to reach the world. When our goal
is preservation of our tradition and ways rather than propagating the gospel, we
become distracted and create new, competitive ways and projects that challenge
our future together. This results in losing our identity and our reason for being.

Eventually this leads to people and leaders leaving us, taking their support and vision to other places and ministries.[8]

Since I have been asked to address this challenging subject, I hope you understand I have been highly involved in our convention since 1988, when I began ten years of service on the Executive committee of the Southern Baptist Convention. I served as chairman for two years. I have also served as a trustee of GuideStone Financial Resources. Additionally, I was also privileged to serve as the president of the Southern Baptist Pastors' Conference. Most notably for our discussion today, I have served on both restructuring committees that Southern Baptists have had in the last twenty years. I served as chairman of the most recent one, the Great Commission Resurgence Task Force, which I believe handed to a new generation of Baptists an exciting vision they are embracing in church planting nationally and going to the nations globally. As a side note: Dr. Albert Mohler and I have the privilege of being the only two people who have served on both restructuring committees Southern Baptist have had in the past twenty years.

In 2014 I was elected president of the Southern Baptist Convention then reelected for a second term in 2015. I am beginning the sixteenth month of my two years as president. Additionally, I have graduated from two Southern Baptist institutions, earning three degrees. I have pastored Southern Baptist churches for the past thirty-nine years, and as of October 2015 I have served the same church for twenty-nine of these years.

Throughout my tenure as president of the Southern Baptist Convention, I have worked to try to move us forward together. I did not get up years ago and ask God to let me become immersed in Southern Baptist structure, programs, ministries, entities, and future. Yet for some reason God has charted this path in the first half of my life and leadership.

I have been and I am still highly involved in Southern Baptist life. I do not speak as one who does not understand our history or as a newcomer, asking questions that are not truly relevant. I am not one who has been on the sideline, operating with skepticism that leads to criticism. Yet I have never been afraid to challenge what we are doing, why we are doing it, and even the way we may still be doing it. *We do not need to demonize any of our people who ask questions in the right spirit.*

Therefore, as we kindle afresh the gift of God and experience moments of renewal, what should our future together look like? What are some of the difficult questions this generation of Baptists will have to answer together? I will propose more questions than my opinion, even though I probably do have a view on most of them. Most of these questions people have heard already, but some may never have made it to a public arena. I believe it would be negligent of me in dealing

---

[8] P. Cooke, personal communication, September 20, 2015.

with my assigned topic if I chose not to share some of these important questions for this generation of Baptists to consider. Therefore, let me propose a few challenging questions for this generation of Baptists.

Question 1: *When conversing about this subject, is the real question what is best for the entire Southern Baptist Convention and its future together, or is the real question what is best for the advancement of the gospel through our Southern Baptist Convention and its ministries?*

I declare that the way we answer this will frame the mind-set for the way we attack further questions we must answer today. Unashamedly, I believe the real question from which we must answer further issues is: *What is best for the advancement of the gospel through our Southern Baptist Convention and its ministries?* We are a Bible-based, gospel-centered, local-church, Great Commission convention, both historically and presently. We must begin to answer the hard questions about our future together from this perspective.

Question 2: *Do we exist to preserve our present brand, structure, and systems, or do we exist to advance the gospel together regionally, statewide, nationally, and internationally?*

While I do believe initially we would all state we exist to advance the gospel together regionally, statewide, nationally, and internationally, do we make decisions with this foremost in our minds, or do we make decisions with our utmost desire to preserve our present brand, structure, and systems? I wonder what our churches think about our present decision making. How would they evaluate our Southern Baptist Convention presently? Just a reminder to each association, state convention, and Southern Baptist entity, you exist *for the church*, nothing else. The churches do not work for you; you work for the churches.

Question 3: *For the sake of gospel advancement, should the International Mission Board and the North American Mission Board become one mission board, the Global Mission Board of the Southern Baptist Convention?*

This is not a new question at all. Some of us who have been involved in shaping the future have asked this question and tried to answer it honestly. With present matters at hand, this question is being asked more today than ever before. It should be asked and there is nothing wrong with asking it. If this should be done, how? If it should not be done, why?

What has kept us from having just one mission board before? I would suggest three specific things:

1. *The unique roles of each mission board.* While this has been true before, is it still true within the global culture we experience daily and with the reality that ethnicities live everywhere across the world? Is it still true when technology is helping

shape the culture today and can assist us in our mission? Furthermore, with an undeniable global mind-set in America today, is this still the right strategy?

2. The Cooperative Program dollars would be held mostly by one board rather than by two boards. Presently this would mean that 73.20 percent or a proposed allocation in 2014–2015 of $137,616,000 of the entire Southern Baptist portion of the Cooperative Program would be held by one board. Is this really problematic when the board of trustees is responsible to the convention for the fiduciary matters of our entities? Is this really a viable reason this should remain as our strategy? I wonder what our churches think?

3. The timing has never been right. Only God knows the timing. The real question about how to answer the question about the future of our mission boards is this: Which decision will fast-forward the mission of our churches to advance the gospel of Jesus Christ to the ethnicities of the world? This generation of Baptists will have to determine how to answer this question.

Question 4: *Do state conventions and associations have a future in Southern Baptist life?*

Does this structural model still serve us effectively? I propose to you today that if we started with a clean slate in 2015, and our mission was to reach America with the gospel, there would have to be a way to have "boots on the ground" in order to help our churches reach their mission. If we operated from a clean slate today, perhaps it may look somewhat different, but the key reality for the future would be more in their function than in the structure.

For example, I believe state conventions and associations can and do have relevance when these things occur:

1. Clarify their mission. Associations and conventions exist for one purpose alone: to serve our churches in reaching their God-assigned responsibility of going, baptizing, and making disciples of all nations.

2. Simplify their responsibilities. They must do *only* the things that help align with the mission of the churches. Otherwise, they do not need to be doing it. It is not a matter of good versus evil but a matter of what is best versus good. Additionally, state conventions and associations do not need to duplicate and triplicate one another, nor do our national entities. We must find a way to cease duplication and triplication locally, statewide, and nationally.

3. Be agile in their response to the churches. Weighty, needless structure prohibits immediate response to the churches. We need to rid anything in our state conventions, associations, and even our national entities that slows down our responsiveness to our churches.

4. Sustain their work financially. If a ministry cannot sustain itself financially, serious questions have to be asked concerning the ministry. While initial investment of dollars may be necessary in the creation phase of the ministry, perhaps three to five years, beyond that, serious questions should be asked and receive answers. Perhaps the ministry of assisting our churches in going, baptizing, and making disciples of all the nations can be best served by some associations and state conventions merging together for the greater cause of helping our churches more effectively.

There are times when greater personalization is needed, regionalization is realized, and decentralization is imperative for the greater good of assisting our churches in going, baptizing, and making disciples of all nations. Each association, state convention, and even national entity has to address these matters honestly and boldly. Our goal should never be to preserve any of our old wineskins but to exist for our churches so they can advance the gospel in the best way in the world today.

Our polity is not friendly to working together at times because each church, association, state convention, and Southern Baptist entity is autonomous. Therefore, our commitment to cooperating for gospel advancement must be so chiseled into our character and practiced through all of our practices, or our future together will be limited rather than released. I respectfully request that each of us refuse to be held hostage by our present but be freed into a future that is robust with gospel cooperation.

Question 5: *How will we finance our work together in the future in the most effective way?*

Ninety years ago, in 1925, our Cooperative Program was created. Today I do not think our forefathers would fear churches asking serious questions about our financial future and the gospel work we do together. If they had not asked, "What is the best way to finance our work together?" there would be no Cooperative Program today. I have spent a great deal of my time on this in my Baptist life and have really focused on this behind the scenes as president. Just recently I have conducted major conference calls with some of our churches, challenging them to give more through the Cooperative Program. I am about to do a massive conference call with approximately 600 pastors, challenging them to address it with their church now in this present hour. We must focus on seeing our base of giving increase through the Cooperative Program.

I believe there is a more important question to ask today relating to the Cooperative Program: *What do we need to do now relating to the Cooperative Program and the way it works to ensure we enter the year 2025, the Cooperative Program's 100th anniversary, in such a way that it is more viable than ever before in helping us finance the gospel work we do together for the glory of God?*

I would like to suggest these specific actions in answering this question:

1. We need a renewal in teaching biblical stewardship to our people, calling them boldly to 10 percent giving through their church and move forward onto the ramp of generosity.

2. We need our churches to give more sacrificially than ever before through our Cooperative Program annually, beginning as soon as possible, and continuing at least through the year 2020. I do have a strong conviction about this: what God has given to us biblically and missionally, we must refuse to lose financially. This is not about saving the Southern Baptist Convention or the Cooperative Program; it is about understanding the stewardship of the gospel that God has entrusted to our convention of churches. Jesus said in Luke 12:48 (HCSB), "Much will be required of everyone who has been given much. And even more will be expected of the one who has been entrusted with more." It is incumbent upon us to understand the stewardship entrusted to us. Since God has entrusted it to us, he will see us forward.

3. We need our state conventions to consider going 50/50 by the end of the year 2020 or even before. If we did these specific things simultaneously, I submit to you that we would see a mission explosion statewide, nationally, and internationally. As Samuel J. Mills Jr. stated in 1806 to four of his friends in a prayer meeting under a haystack in Massachusetts, "We can do this, if we will!"[9] This became the birthplace of American foreign missions. The field was the world. For me to suggest this to our state conventions is not reducing their value or work at all. It is about getting the gospel to places where the gospel may have never been before across all of America and the world.

4. We need to develop an intentional strategy to enlist other churches in America to join our convention. If they agree with us biblically by adhering to the Baptist Faith and Message 2000, agree with us missiologically in the way we advance the gospel regionally, statewide, nationally, and internationally, and agree with us cooperatively in the way we support our work financially and are willing to join us in this grand task, then we need to open our doors to them. This is no time to fly solo as a church or a leader; therefore, many churches in America have the capacity for us to become their home. I would even suggest that we go online with this strategy, creating a Join the Southern Baptist Convention website and place a link on the websites of each of our state conventions, entities, and our own convention website.

---

[9] *The One Hundredth Anniversary of the Haystack Prayer Meeting Celebrated at the Ninety-Seventh Annual Meeting of the American Board in North Adams, and by the Haystack Centennial Meetings at Williamstown, Mass., October 9-12, 1906* (Boston, MA: American Board of Commissioners for Foreign Missions, 1907), 181.

5. We need each state convention website and our own national convention website to create online giving for our churches. If we exist for helping our churches, we need to provide this option for them in this online world. Since we exist to help the churches, we need to focus on creating options for them to participate with us.

6. We need to consider in the near future a place for affinity groups or networks of churches to participate with us in various ways for the advancement of the gospel. While I believe we will need to answer this question in the near future, I am not knowledgeable enough at this time to state anything relating to it. Perhaps in their study of us doctrinally, missiologically, and cooperatively, they will decide they may desire to be a part of our family. If this occurs, it will be necessary that we are ready to answer this question.

Question 6: *Is there anything new we need to create for today and for the future that will help our churches in their mission of going, baptizing, and making disciples of all the nations?*

Some may say with where things are financially, we cannot do this or even entertain the idea. When a convention or a church asks a question like this and the first question about it becomes, "How much will it cost?" rather than "Whom will it reach?" this does not represent our being healthy or visionary.

We need always to be willing to ask this question because God may want us to use something new to forward his gospel through our churches in a better way. What if we had a compassion arm in our convention that brings all we do presently and all we could do in the future into one entity? I submit to you, if done effectively, it may have the capacity long-term to pay for itself sufficiently. Why? Because Baptists are supporting some of this now through what we are doing already, and they are helping pay for it through others that are non-Baptist ministries. Additionally, it would place our powerful gospel message into this Christless culture that usually appreciates ministries of compassion. It would also positively accentuate our work as Southern Baptists in this Christless culture.

In conclusion, since our Baptist people have given just over $7 billion over the past decade through our Cooperative Program and two mission offerings, and will prayerfully repeat no less than this amount over the future decade, perhaps we need to look at something creatively. While one vein of thought would be, "We need to start with a clean slate knowing we have $7 billion to reach the world for Christ," I would suggest there is an even better way that is more realistic and helpful at this point in our history. Here it is: *Knowing what we know about our past and present, as well as having the resources of churches, people, influence, reach, and dollars, how can we leverage all we have for the purpose of advancing the gospel in an unprecedented manner into places where the gospel has never been before regionally, statewide, nationally, and globally?* This is the question for this generation of Baptists.

In 1956, Dawson Trotman, the founder of The Navigators, gave a talk to pastors on "The Need of the Hour." He wrestled greatly with the Lord over what he should do in this challenge. Should he simply speak to the need for more money, more materials, more people, and more facilities, or was there something else? Trotman said God convinced him that none of these was the real need of the hour. Then God verified to him that the real need of the hour was to believe Isaiah 52:7 (HCSB), "Your God reigns!"[10]

I believe it is important for us to be lean, nimble, and diverse. We need to exalt innovation on the ground and disseminate this innovation as considerations for best practices. But what really propels our innovation?

I submit to you that the Lord propels us. We are called into action because we *believe*. He has already given us all authority in heaven and on earth, and because we *believe* that the Lord desires people from every tribe, language, people, and nation to be in heaven eternally, and because we *believe* that he has declared he will accomplish his purposes, we are called into action.

Because of who he is and what he has declared his purposes to be, we pray frequently, fervently, desperately, and with confidence that he will do it. The need of the hour is to believe *our God reigns!*

Without him nothing durable can be achieved; with him the evangelization of the world is a certainty. *Our God reigns!*

---

[10] Dawson Trotman, "The Need of the Hour," *Discipleship Library.* Accessed February 24, 2016. http://www.discipleshiplibrary.com/pdfs/AA065.pdf, 6.

The Future of the IMB and Our Collaborative Great Commission Work

David Platt

I am amazed when I consider the magnitude of what God in his grace has created in the International Mission Board. To see an organization with over 170 years of mission history in the past is extraordinarily humbling, and then to see more than 50,000 congregations joined together in the present specifically for the spread of the gospel to people who have never heard it is truly breathtaking. Moreover, it practically defies imagination to realize that the International Mission Board exists alongside a North American Mission Board, six of the largest seminaries in the world, a publishing house dedicated to producing gospel-centered, mission-focused resources, an Ethics & Religious Liberty Commission confronting the key cultural issues of our day, and a network of state conventions and regional associations all aimed at serving and supporting local churches on mission. Without question, what God has created not just in the International Mission Board, but altogether in the Southern Baptist Convention, is absolutely remarkable.

So how can the International Mission Board (IMB) steward the trust that God has so clearly given to us and the churches we serve in the future? How can the IMB most wisely collaborate within this remarkable coalition of churches and entities for the ultimate accomplishment of the Great Commission? At the very least, the IMB must focus on four foundational purposes.

EXALTING CHRIST

First and foremost, the IMB exists to exalt Christ. In order for the IMB to be faithful to the collaborative task entrusted to it by Southern Baptist churches it represents, Jesus must be the center of everything the IMB does. According to Matthew 28:20, the Great Commission is Jesus's commission to accomplish, and he has promised his presence toward that end. Jesus's words to his disciples in John 15 remind us that fruit among the nations will only come as a result of faithfully following him.

In order to exalt Christ, then, the IMB must be marked by uncompromising confidence in the Word of God. The Bible must be the authority for everything the IMB is and does. The Bible must serve as the authority for *what* the IMB believes and *how* the IMB operates. In other words, the Bible must drive not only the IMB's theology and ecclesiology but also the IMB's missiology and methodology. God's Word must be the trusted authority around which everything in the IMB revolves.

This is especially important in a day when pragmatic methodology threatens to trump biblical theology at every turn in missions and evangelism in the church. Instead of starting with God's Word in order to determine strategies for mission and evangelism, Christian leaders are prone to start with the world. We ask what kind of methodology is working where, and slowly, sometimes unknowingly, pragmatic observation begins to usurp biblical foundation in the development of mission strategy. What's even more dangerous is when Christian leaders then go to Scripture in order to justify what they observe to be wise methodology. A fundamental difference exists, however, between looking to Scripture for permission to do what we think is best and looking to Scripture for direction according to what God said is best.

The Bible is where the IMB must start in all of our missiology. Leaders and strategists across the IMB must start in God's Word, on our knees, reading, digesting, observing, seeing, learning, and letting the Word drive every facet of our work. The IMB must not argue for missionary methods first and foremost from results. Instead, the IMB must always argue for missionary methods first and foremost from exegesis.

The IMB can do all of this with complete confidence that when we are faithful to God's Word, we will be fruitful in the world. Jesus has promised to bear his fruit (the kind of fruit that will last!) through men and women who abide in him and his Word abides in them. Based on this promise, we can be sure any aim at missional fruitfulness apart from biblical faithfulness will ultimately fail.

As the IMB trusts the Word of Christ, we must follow the plan of Christ. That plan is plainly stated in the Great Commission: make disciples of all the nations. Disciple making is the Christ-commanded, Spirit-empowered duty of every disciple of Jesus to evangelize unbelievers, baptize believers, teach them the Word of Christ, and train them to obey Christ as members of his church who make disciples on mission to all nations. In order to exalt Christ, then, everything the IMB does must remain resolutely focused on this central task.

Disciple making necessarily involves clear and bold proclamation of the gospel in all of its biblical fullness. Many temptations exist in missions today to dumb down and dilute the gospel in order to make it more palatable to people in various religions or with various worldviews. But we do not do God a favor by compromising in any way the message that God has promised to bless for the salvation of the nations. The biblical gospel is the good news that the only true God, the just and gracious Creator of the universe, has looked upon hopelessly sinful men and women and has sent his Son, God in the flesh, to bear his wrath against sin through his substitutionary death on the cross and to show his power over sin and death through his resurrection from the grave so that everyone who turns from their sin and themselves and trusts in Jesus alone as Savior and Lord will be reconciled to God forever. The IMB must never, in any way, compromise on any facet of this foundational message.

In order to ensure that the gospel is clear in missions, IMB missionaries must have a clear understanding of cross-cultural communication and clear convictions regarding contextualization. According to Paul's words in 1 Corinthians 9, we must work hard to remove all obstacles to people hearing and understanding the gospel. At the same time we must be careful never to remove the offense of the gospel. We boldly proclaim the gospel, believing that under the inspiration of the Holy Spirit our message has supernatural power to regenerate hearts and change lives.

Moreover, as IMB missionaries work around the world, we must reflect the life change that is wrought by the gospel. Robert Murray M'Cheyne once said as a pastor, "My people's greatest need is my personal holiness."[1] In a similar way, based on the whole of Scripture and particularly the pattern of God's people we see in the Old Testament, there is a sense in which the nations' greatest need is our personal holiness as Christians in the world. As missionaries go out from churches around the world, the gospel of Christ must be clear from our lips, and the character of Christ must be clear in our lives. As we proclaim the gospel, we must portray the effects of the gospel in goodness and holiness that together resound to God's glory (Matt 5:13–16).

The IMB exists to exalt Christ by trusting his Word, following his plan, proclaiming his gospel, and reflecting his character. When all of these activities are evident in IMB missionaries, then the glory of Christ will be evident to the peoples among whom we work. And this is our primary aim. All those associated with the IMB must want the glory of Christ more than life itself. For everyone associated with the IMB, missions must not be our life. Instead, Christ must be our life, and missions must be the overflow of lives that exist to exalt him.

---

[1] This oft-quoted line by Robert Murray M'Cheyne is cited by Kevin DeYoung, "The Secret to Reaching the Next Generation," in *Don't Call It a Comeback: The Old Faith for a New Day*, ed. Kevin DeYoung (Wheaton, IL: Crossway, 2011), 25.

MOBILIZING CHRISTIANS

As the IMB purposes to exalt Christ among the nations, we must subsequently work to mobilize Christians for the nations. With more than 2.8 billion people in the world who still lack access to the gospel, the IMB cannot settle for anything less than aggressive calls for all Christians to pray passionately, give sacrificially, and go intentionally for the glory of Christ among all peoples.

For far too long, Christians in Southern Baptist churches have seen global mission as a compartmentalized program in the church for a select few people who are called to this purpose. Yet when one looks from cover to cover through Scripture, one realizes that global mission is the purpose for which every one of us has been created. We have all been created, called, and commissioned to be part of making disciples of all nations. This call to mission most assuredly means making disciples right where we live among neighbors, coworkers, and acquaintances in our communities and cities. At the same time, Christians work on mission wherever we live with a continual openness to go on mission wherever God leads.

This is the kind of mind-set that marked the Moravians in mission history. It was said of the Moravians centuries ago that one out of every 92 of them were crossing cultures for the spread of the gospel. Looking out across over 15 million Southern Baptists today, just imagine if that ratio was present among us. Instead of 4,000–5,000 missionaries, we would have well over 100,000 missionaries spreading the gospel around the world.

The key for these Moravians, though, was not a commitment to a sophisticated well-financed mission board. Instead, they were consumed by a mission mind-set. They looked at their lives through the lens of mission, and they were leveraging the opportunities God had given them for work around the world to live in other countries for the spread of the gospel.

If the Moravians were doing this centuries ago, how much more are such opportunities available to Southern Baptists in view of the globalization of today's marketplace? Opportunities abound today for Southern Baptists not only to *leave* their jobs to serve as missionaries in other countries but also to *leverage* their jobs to serve as missionaries among unreached peoples.

So what might happen if this mission mind-set marked not just a few extraordinary people, but everyday, ordinary members across Southern Baptist churches? Envision such members passionate about praying for the nations. Envision men and women rising every morning to take their place on their knees as partners with God in the work he is doing around the world through prayer. Imagine them joining with what God is doing in Central Asia, North Africa, and Eastern Europe in personal time with the Lord on a daily basis and then through corporate time with the church on a weekly basis. What might happen if our churches were marked by Acts 13, Antioch-like pictures of concentrated prayer and fasting for the glory of God among the nations?

Moreover, what might happen if God's heart for the nations was reflected in sacrificial giving among our churches? God has given American Christians unprecedented wealth in the history of the world for a reason: he wants his praise known among all peoples. God gives his people wealth in the world for the sake of his worship throughout the world. May we not, then, waste our wealth on the pleasures, pursuits, and possessions of this world but instead spend our wealth for purpose of God among the peoples of the world.

Finally, what might happen if more people were going to the nations? When I look at the history of the IMB, I praise God for 25,000 missionaries who have served over these last 170 years. However, we need 25,000 now. Such a number necessitates, then, that the IMB think through creative ways for as many God-called missionaries as possible to go the nations, optimizing all the opportunities God has afforded us. Imagine students studying overseas, professionals working overseas, and retirees moving overseas, all doing so intentionally for the spread of the gospel among unreached peoples.

Keep in mind, also, that as Christians are mobilized from Southern Baptist churches to go to the nations through the IMB, the work they do overseas will be deliberately focused on mobilizing more Christians. The work of the missionary involves proclaiming the gospel, making disciples, gathering those disciples together into churches, and then raising up leaders who will shepherd those churches on mission in the world. The missionary task is not fully complete until new churches planted are now joining in the mission. When we look at the world, then, we must not only view unreached people as a harvest field but also as a potential harvest force. For when unreached people are reached, they become an entirely new force now filled with the Spirit and focused on the spread of the gospel to more unreached people.

In the days to come, the IMB must lead the way in mobilizing Christians here and around the world to see the countless doors God has opened wide for the spread of the gospel to the nations through our praying, giving, and going. Indeed, may God bless the IMB in such a way we might be a part of a Moravian-type missions movement in our day that sees tens of thousands of God-exalting, Christ-following, Spirit-led, biblically faithful, people-loving, high-quality missionaries running to the nations for the sake of God's fame.

SERVING THE CHURCH

The local church is God's chosen agent for the accomplishment of the Great Commission. Christ's commission is not going to be completed primarily by individuals, conventions, or even by missions organizations like the IMB, but by local churches that are making disciples and multiplying churches. Therefore, the IMB must be driven by a steadfast desire to serve local churches here and around the world.

This may seem simple, but I am concerned that mission organizations such as the IMB, if not careful, can actually set themselves up to abdicate the responsibility of the local church in the Great Commission. I once read that "the IMB defines its basic strategy—how it accomplishes its task—as sending and supporting missionaries to proclaim the gospel in a way that results in multiplying indigenous Baptist churches."[2] When I read that statement, I could not help but think that though it sounds good, it may not be altogether healthy. For as much as I want to see missionaries sent and supported to proclaim the gospel in this way, sending missionaries is primarily the biblical calling of the church, not a denomination or missions organization. This may sound like semantics, but I believe it is more than that.

We know the Southern Baptist Convention was organized in 1845 for the purpose of "eliciting, combining, and directing churches for the propagation of the gospel."[3] Churches were front and center in that purpose, as they should be. Yet there is an ever-present temptation to put the denomination, or missions organization, in that front and center position. When we do this, we begin to view mission from the top down. We start believing that the denomination, or missions organization, exists to collect funds and find, equip, send, and provide for missionaries. Meanwhile, the church exists mainly to resource mission by producing missionary candidates and sending money to the mission organization. The mission organization's message to the church becomes: "We need you to send people and money in order for us to accomplish this mission."

But biblically there is a better way. That better way takes a bottom-up approach to mission where the local church takes center stage in global missions. George Pentecost said one hundred years ago at a strategic missions conference, "To the pastor belongs the privilege and responsibility of the missionary problem."[4] Pentecost maintained that mission organizations can and should do what they will to facilitate mission, but it is the privilege and responsibility of every pastor of every local church to fan a flame for God's global glory and to lead that church to pray, give, and go accordingly. Now obviously no one church can effectively engage all nations, which necessitates that different churches work together

---

[2] Jerry Rankin, *To the Ends of the Earth: Churches Fulfilling the Great Commission* (Nashville: B&H, 2006), 114–15.

[3] Southern Baptist Convention, "Constitution." Accessed February 24, 2016. http://www.sbc.net/aboutus/legal/constitution.asp.

[4] Quote of George F. Pentecost by David Platt in chapter 3, "Divine Sovereignty: The Fuel of Death-Defying Missions," in *The Underestimated Gospel*, ed. Jonathan Leeman (Nashville: B&H, 2014). This work also contains the same quote spoken by George F. Pentecost at a mission's conference in New York that took place April 21–May 1, 1900.

in collaboration and cooperation. This, then, is where a missions organization like the IMB can and must excel, serving and supporting local churches who are working together for the sake of mission in the world. The IMB does this by pooling together resources from local churches and training and facilitating God-called missionaries sent from those local churches. In all of this, the IMB brings 170 years of history and a global network of relationships to bear on how churches together can best spread the gospel to those who have never heard it.

Some may object, "But what if local churches are not doing mission?" This is a valid question, but the answer is not to have a denominational agency do it for them. The answer is to pour time, energy, and resources into equipping local churches for global mission. Then, when local churches are taking responsibility for global mission, what is needed is not a denominational organization to do mission for them, but a powerful relational network that facilitates and maximizes all they are doing together. In the end mission is ultimately achieved through the avenue God has ordained for its accomplishment: the local church.

A few years ago I found myself sitting around a table with the heads of major mission organizations across North America. We were talking about the importance of the local church when one of the presidents of these organizations made an honest confession. He looked around the table at his colleagues and said: "I believe we have approached the church completely wrong. It's as if we have taken Home Depot's slogan and turned it around, saying to churches, 'We can accomplish this mission, and here's how *you* can help.'" This leader then said, "We've got it totally backward, because we should be saying to the church, '*You* can accomplish this mission, and here's how *we* can help.'"

The IMB must vigorously guard against a "we can do it, you can help" approach to the local church. Instead, the IMB must zealously promote a "you can do it, we can help" approach to the local church. After all, this is the beauty of what God has designed in the IMB. When I looked around that table at all of these other major missions organizations, none of them was tied to local churches like the IMB is. The IMB is strategically positioned in God's sovereign providence to equip over 40,000 churches to send missionaries. So the question the IMB must constantly ask is, "How can we best equip, empower, and enable those 40,000 local churches to make disciples, send missionaries, and multiply other local churches around the world?"

Now I must be clear about what I am *not* saying in this. I am not saying pastors and local churches should neglect local ministry. People in our churches are hurting, their marriages are struggling, their children are rebelling, and they are walking through cancer and tumors and all sorts of other things. We should not neglect local ministry to the body.

Nor should we neglect local mission in our communities or cities. We have been commanded to make disciples, and that command will most naturally and

consistently play out right where we live, in the context of our immediate sur-
roundings. Every church member ought to ask, "With the unique gifts God has
given me and the Spirit of God who lives in me, how can I make disciples today,
right where I live?" In this way, there ought to be church-planting efforts where
we live and across North America. Local mission is necessary.

At the same time, global missions is tragically neglected.

I was near Yemen not long ago. Northern Yemen has approximately eight
million people. Do you know how many believers there are in northern Yemen?
Twenty or thirty. Out of eight million people. That is the populations of Alabama
and Mississippi combined. There are likely more believers in your Sunday school
class or a couple of small groups in your church than there are in all of northern
Yemen. That is a problem. It is a problem because millions of people in the northern part of Yemen have no access to the gospel. They join millions upon millions
of other unreached people in the world who are born, live, and die without ever
even hearing the good news of what God has done for their salvation in Christ.

It is not simply the responsibility of mission organizations to address that
problem. It is ultimately the responsibility of local churches. Specifically, it is the
primary responsibility of pastors to lead local churches to love people in their
church and community toward the end that the name of Christ might be known
and churches might be planted among all peoples. This is what the Spirit of Christ
desires, and so this is what every Christian, every pastor, and every local church in
whom the Spirit dwells desires.

When we read through the book of Acts, we see a clear priority on the role of
the local church in the spread of the gospel across the globe. In Acts 13 we see the
church at Antioch worshipping, fasting, and praying, and in the context of that
local church with its leaders, the Spirit sets apart Paul and Barnabas as missionaries. The church prays over them and sends them out, supporting them as they
go. Twice Paul returns to Antioch to encourage that local church, and then on
his third missionary journey he writes a letter to another local church at Rome to
ask for their support in helping him get to Spain, where Christ had not yet been
named. In this way we see local churches sending, shepherding, and supporting
men and women on global missions.

The IMB exists to partner with more than 50,000 Antiochs across the
Southern Baptist Convention: churches of all sizes worshipping, fasting, and
praying, leading to those churches sending and shepherding missionaries for the
spread of the gospel all over the world. As disciples are made and churches are
multiplied among unreached peoples, the IMB then exists to serve those new
churches with a view toward mission. This leads to the final foundational purpose
of the IMB.

PLAYING OUR PART

The need among the nations is great. Paul knew this when he wrote in Romans of his "obligation" (Rom 1:14) and "ambition" (Rom 15:20–21) to preach the gospel where Christ was not known.

Paul knew that people who have never heard the gospel only have enough knowledge of God to damn them to hell. God has made his character known in creation, and all men and women everywhere have seen God's revelation of himself. Yet all men have rejected God. They have rebelled against him, and as a result they stand condemned before him. Apart from hearing the good news, they have no eternal hope. We need to feel the weight of this reality: at this moment millions of people in thousands of unreached people groups have a knowledge of God that is only sufficient to damn them to hell.

Paul also knew that the grace of God is powerful enough to save people everywhere for heaven. Paul knew that the gospel of Jesus Christ is the greatest news in all the world! But in the words of Carl F. H. Henry, "The gospel is only good news if it gets there on time."[5] There is not a people group on this planet beyond God's power to save. Paul knew that people everywhere will believe the gospel when they hear it. For this reason we are obligated to preach the gospel to the nations.

Paul also knew that the plan of God warrants the sacrifice of his people. He was a servant and slave, set apart and sent out with the gospel into the world. Mission was not only a calling for him; it was a command around which his life revolved. The reason he had breath was to testify to the gospel among the nations. The same is true for us. The proclamation of the gospel to the ends of the earth is not a calling for us to consider; it is a command for us to obey. We breathe for mission.

Ultimately, Paul knew that the Son of God deserves the praise of all peoples. Paul knew the King he served warrants worship from every nation, tribe, and tongue, and he gave himself with all-consuming dedication to making his glory known. We serve the same King, and he is still worthy of the same worship. We want and work for the name of Christ to be heard and hailed among all the peoples of the earth.

Like Paul, then, all those who make up the IMB and work with the IMB must be motivated by a gospel-driven obligation and death-defying ambition to proclaim the gospel among those who have never heard it. Jesus had given Paul, and Jesus has given us, a clear command in the Great Commission to make disciples of "all nations." When Jesus talks about "nations," he uses the word *ethnē* to refer to clans, tribes, and other groups of people united by common languages and cultural characteristics. We have identified more than 11,000 such people groups

---

[5]   See Gregory Alan Thornbury, *Recovering Classic Evangelicalism: Applying the Wisdom and Vision of Carl F. H. Henry* (Wheaton, IL: Crossway, 2013), 175.

in the world. We cannot be sure our definition of people groups squares precisely with what Jesus had in mind when he referred to *ethnē*, but this is our best estimate. And out of those 11,000 people groups in the world, more than 6,000 of them remain unreached by the gospel.

The task that lies before the church of Jesus Christ is clear. We have not just been generally commanded to get the gospel to as many people as possible. Instead, we have been specifically commanded to get the gospel to every people group in the world. This, after all, has been God's plan from the beginning. He blessed Abraham and the people of Israel with the specific purpose of bringing his blessing to all people groups (Gen 12:1–3). He brought his children out of slavery in Egypt and settled them in the promised land for the purpose of his praise among all people groups (Exod 14:4). He sent them into exile and brought them out of exile in order to spread his glory among all people groups (Ezek 36:22–23). Jesus promised that the gospel would be preached to all the people groups (Luke 24:45–49). The story of the church is the story of the spread of the gospel toward every people group (Acts 1:8), and leaders in the early church possessed consuming ambitions "to preach the gospel where Christ was not known" (Rom 15:20 NIV). John puts an exclamation point on God's passion for praise from among all people groups when he records the song resounding from heaven to Jesus in the book of Revelation: "I looked, and there before me was a great multitude that no one could count, from every nation, tribe, people and language, standing before the throne and in front of the Lamb. . . . And they cried out in a loud voice: 'Salvation belongs to our God, who sits on the throne, and to the Lamb'" (Rev 7:9–10 NIV). In the end, just as God planned before time began, every ethnic group will be represented around the throne of Jesus, exalting his name and having received his salvation. In anticipation of that day, John closes the Bible by crying, "Come, Lord Jesus" (Rev 22:20 HCSB).

The great need among the unreached and the global purpose of God in history thus provides the framework for this foundational purpose in the IMB. The IMB exists to exalt Christ by mobilizing Christians and serving churches with a view toward playing our part in getting the gospel to every people group on the planet.

Some in Southern Baptist life have wondered, "With more than 50,000 churches in the Southern Baptist Convention and more than 6,000 people groups in the world, why don't we just get all of our churches to adopt each of these people groups, and we'll take care of reaching them all?" Others have suggested that IMB strategy should revolve around having at least one missionary (or missionary family) focused on every people group in the world. And this might be a sound strategy *if* Southern Baptists were the only Christians on the planet.

But we are not.

In God's sovereignty, he has a global family whom he is leading and guiding for the completion of this commission. What this means is that IMB leaders and missionaries must wisely discern the unique part God is leading us to play in the completion of his commission. In the days to come, the IMB must continually look at the opportunities before us, the resources available to us, and the wisest ways possible to steward those opportunities and resources in obedience to him. Tethered to God's Word and guided by God's Spirit, we must give ourselves to the full missionary task of evangelism, discipleship, church formation, and leadership training among unreached peoples to whom God directs us. As we do this, we must work wisely with churches around the world as our brothers and sisters in Christ play their part in global mission.

Mobilizing Christians and serving churches across the Southern Baptist Convention and around the world, the IMB must work with our eyes fixed on the day when every tribe, tongue, and nation has been reached with the gospel. To be sure, such work will require much risk. Unreached peoples are unreached for a reason. They are hard, difficult, and dangerous to reach. There is a god in this world who has worked for centuries to keep them from being reached, and he is set on distracting, dividing, and destroying everyone who tries to reach them in the future. Ultimately the question facing the IMB and the coalition of churches in the SBC is, "Will we retreat from the mission given to us, or will we risk our lives for it?"

Throughout redemptive history this question has confronted God's people. It was the decision facing the Israelites on a crucial day at Kadesh Barnea. Standing on the brink of the promised land, with the guarantee of God within their grasp, they ran from risk and chose to retreat. Instead of staking their lives on the faithfulness of God, they recoiled in fear. The cost was great, and the Lord left an entire generation to waste away in a wilderness until they died.

Fast-forward a few thousand years, and you come to the people of God standing in a similar moment. We live in a world where half the population is living on less than two dollars a day, and more than a billion people dwell in desperate poverty. Such physical need is only surpassed by spiritual poverty. Billions of people are engrossed in the worship of false gods. Hundreds of millions of them live in hard-to-reach areas of the world that are hostile to Christians—areas of the world where any attempt to make disciples will lead to persecution, imprisonment, or even death.

Though the challenges facing the church are great, the commission Christ has given is clear. Pay the cost to get the gospel to those who have never heard. Go, regardless of risk, trusting in his sovereign authority, depending on his indwelling presence, and experiencing his incomparable joy.

So we stand at our Kadesh Barnea, and we have a choice. We, too, can retreat into a wilderness of wasted opportunity. We as Southern Baptists can rest content in casual, convenient, cozy, comfortable Christian lives while we cling to the safety and security this world offers. We can coast through a cultural landscape marked by materialism, characterized by consumerism, and engulfed in individualism. We can assent to the spirit of this age and choose to spend our lives seeking worldly pleasures, acquiring worldly possessions, and pursuing worldly ambitions . . . and we can do it all under the banner of cultural Christianity.

Or we can decide that Jesus is worth more than this. We can recognize that he has created us, saved us, and called us for a much greater purpose than anything this world could ever offer. As a coalition of tens of thousands of churches with millions of members, we can die to ourselves, our hopes, our dreams, our ambitions, our priorities, and our plans. We can do all of this because we believe the glorious person and global purpose of Christ bring reward that makes any risk more than worth it.

In Matthew 13:44, Jesus tells his disciples, "The kingdom of heaven is like treasure hidden in a field, which a man found and covered up. Then in his joy he goes and sells all that he has and buys that field (ESV)."

This is a picture we must see. Imagine walking in a field and stumbling upon a treasure that is more valuable than anything else you could work for or find in this life. It is more valuable than all you have now or will ever have in the future. You look around and notice that no one else realizes the treasure is here, so you cover it up quickly and walk away, pretending you have not seen anything. You go into town and begin to sell off all your possessions to have enough money to buy that field. The world thinks you are crazy.

"What are you thinking?" your friends and family ask you.

You tell them, "I'm buying that field over there."

They look at you in disbelief. "That's foolish," they say. "Why are you giving away everything you have to buy that field?"

You respond, "I have a hunch," and you smile to yourself as you walk away. You smile because you know that in the end any risk others perceive is nothing compared to the reward you receive. So with joy—with joy!—you sell it all. Why? Because you have found something worth losing everything else for.

This is the picture of Jesus in the gospel. He is something—someone—worth losing everything for. When we really believe this, then risking everything we are and everything we have to know and obey Christ is no longer a matter of sacrifice. It's just common sense. To let go of the pursuits, possessions, pleasures, safety, and security of this world in order to follow Jesus wherever he leads no matter what it costs is not sacrificial as much as it is smart. In the words of Jim Elliot, "He is no fool who gives what he cannot keep to gain what he cannot lose."[6]

---

[6] Elizabeth Elliot, *Shadow of the Almighty: The Life and Testament of Jim Elliot* (San Francisco: HarperSanFrancisco, 1989), 15.

Indeed, our greatest joy is found in God's greatest glory, and Christ is a treasure worth losing and letting go of everything for. His worship among the nations is worth the sacrifice of our lives. So may we in the International Mission Board become in the days ahead, in even greater ways than ever before, an army of men and women who are fearless in the face of risk because we realize that in Christ even death is a reward. And may the legacy of the Southern Baptist Convention be a line of pastors, missionaries, church leaders, and church members collaborating together to play our part in the ultimate completion of his Great Commission.

Every Church on a Mission: The North American Mission Board in the Twenty-First Century

Kevin Ezell

INTRODUCTION

We live in tumultuous times in North America. Since I became president of the North American Mission Board in 2010, the moral climate has certainly shifted in the United States. Gay marriage is now the law of the land. The atrocious activities of Planned Parenthood have been brought to light. Assisted suicide is now legal in a few states. Mass shootings blanket the news. Racial tensions in some parts of the country are at an all-time high. The public assembly rights of Christian churches have been tested in places such as New York City.

"Can the gospel thrive in such a climate?" is a question I would imagine is on the minds of many. Will the church be able to make a comeback when the odds seem to be stacked against it? What, if any, will be the role of a denomination like the Southern Baptist Convention in that comeback?

Many quarters of the church in North America have responded to the cultural crisis by going into survival mode. Many have taken a defensive position—hunkering down in their churches hoping the immorality of the culture does not creep in. This circling of the wagons approach has led to an "us versus them" mentality when it comes to interacting with our communities, and many Christians feel as if the "them" is winning. However, I believe the church is in a great spot. Yes, Christians may be a little down, but the church is certainly not out. The difficulties the church faces can be its greatest asset as we move forward.

It is no secret to anyone who knows me well that I am an avid—almost fanatical—supporter of the University of Kentucky basketball team. Anyone who is around me for a little while will hear me gloat over the Wildcats' record eight national championships. However, in the late 1980s the program was on the ropes. They were mired in a recruiting scandal that left the team in trouble. The sanctions from the NCAA hampered their ability to recruit players and win games. Several dismal seasons resulted. But those down years did not last forever. Since then the program has come roaring back. Since 1996 Kentucky has won three national championships and been to several more Final Fours. It has had countless players make it to the NBA, and two of the coaches during this period have been inducted into the Hall of Fame. Kentucky may have been down for a little while, but it was never out.

The church is never out. We may have a perception that things are going badly for the bride of Jesus, but that is not the reality. I believe we are living in really good days. I have personally seen strong signs of life in the Southern Baptist Convention. The last several months have seen hundreds of churches engaging in church planting. We have seen hundreds of individuals deployed as short- and long-term missionaries. In August of 2015 we saw the largest missional gathering of Southern Baptists in a long time (or maybe ever) when more than 13,500 people registered for the Send North America Conference in Nashville, Tennessee.

As we move forward in the twenty-first century, we see it as our job to come alongside pastors and church leaders to equip churches for mission in the ever-changing context the U.S. and Canada. We have proven equipping and training programs that will help churches of any size and demographic. Being on mission is not a big-church endeavor, but it is an every-church endeavor.

EVERY CHURCH ON MISSION

My first church voted me in seven to zero. I was a new seminary student in Fort Worth. This church needed a pastor, and I needed a job! As I reflect back on those days, they are some of my favorite in ministry. The church embraced the idea of evangelism, and over time they came alive in their mission to their community, North America, and the world. These people sacrificed their time and resources so that the gospel could go forward. No one embodied the missionary spirit of this church more than Linny Fenton. Miss Linny was a lady of below-average financial means. However, she had a deep faith and a strong desire to see people come to faith around the world. I will never forget how Miss Linny sacrificially gave so that our church could be on mission.

The church is not intended to be on the sidelines but front and center in the mission of God to the world. In order to be all God wants for us in North America, every church must be involved. A healthy church is on mission corporately, meaning the church has vision as a unified body to advance the gospel. The church is also on mission as a group of individuals, meaning that the church is specifically calling out and equipping every believer in the congregation to be on mission. I am thankful so many are already connected to a mission field, but we need many more in order to complete the task.

The Church on Mission Corporately

In Acts 1:8 Jesus charges his disciples that they "will receive power when the Holy Spirit has come upon [them], and [they] will be [his] witnesses in Jerusalem and in all Judea and Samaria, and to the end of the earth" (ESV). Mission is the church's essence. When the church was commissioned, it was sent corporately to fulfill God's mission. The church does not simply have mission as one of its objectives; the church is *always* to be on mission. Mission strategist David Bosch says, "Mission is not 'a fringe activity' of a strongly established church, a pious cause that [may] be attended to when the home fires [are] first brightly burning. . . . Missionary activity is not so much the work of the Church as simply the Church at work."[1]

When the church is on mission, it is putting the kingdom of God on display for the world. When Jesus taught his followers to pray, he taught them to pray that the will of God would be accomplished "on earth as it is in heaven." The church is to be a model of Jesus's will for earth. Not that we in some way believe we can usher in his kingdom, but while we are waiting for his return, we are living out, as best as we can, what that perfect kingdom will be. The great missionary Lesslie Newbigin said of this reality:

> The local congregation is to be a sign of the kingdom in its particular place. The question which has to be put to every local congregation is the question whether it is a credible sign of God's reign in justice and mercy over the whole of life, whether it cares for its neighbors in a way which reflects and springs out God's care for them, whether its common life is recognizable as a foretaste of the blessing in which God intends for the whole human family.[2]

The job of the North American Mission Board is to help entire churches realize their missionary calling. We are prepared to come alongside churches as they seek to model the love, peace, justice, and mercy of God in their communities, North America, and the world. Some may be thinking that their church may not have all of the appropriate characteristics of a church on mission, but every church

---

[1] David Bosch, *Transforming Mission: Paradigm Shifts in Theology of Mission* (Maryknoll, NY: Orbis, 2001), Kindle Location 9376–9390. Some excerpts from this section previously appeared in a paper called "Biblical and Theological Basis for Missions" written by Aaron Coe, August 2012. It has been used here with permission.

[2] Craig Bartholomew, *Where Mortals Dwell: A Christian View of Place for Today* (Grand Rapids: Baker Academic, 2011), 129. Lesslie Newbigin, *Sign of the Kingdom* (Grand Rapids: Eerdmans, 1980), 63–64.

can do something. We've found that when any church simply engages in mission outside of its context, it helps members of that church see the local needs around them more clearly.

EVERY BELIEVER AS A MISSIONARY

My daughter and son-in-law, Anna and David, just moved to Asia as missionaries. They are going to be teaching English to Asian students in a university setting as a platform for sharing the gospel. I am excited about God's call on their lives, but I have mixed feelings about their living in Asia. For years I have preached about missions and have helped mobilize hundreds of people to be on mission. Now that my own daughter is the missionary, it is a whole new reality for me. If I am honest, the thought of them (and our future grandchildren) being so far from home causes me to grieve to a certain degree. However, over time, as I have become somewhat comfortable with their being away, I am reminded that God's missionary call is for every believer. I know that I have to trust Jesus's call on their lives just as I have trusted his call on the lives of the others I have pastored and mobilized.

As I have worked through my own daughter's calling to Asia, I am even more resolved that it is every believer's job to live on mission. God did not call a few elite forces, such as Anna and David, to be on mission, but he has called everyone. When Jesus gave the Great Commission in Matthew 28, his command was to all believers. Making disciples of all nations is an all-hands-on-deck proposition. Every believer has been uniquely wired to live mission. Each has been given gifts and talents to participate in God's mission. Additionally, every believer has been given access to people who do not know Jesus to whom others do not have access. Craig Bartholomew says about the missionary calling of individuals: "From the beginning God's people are to be 'missionary.' They are chosen to be a channel of blessing to others."[3]

What does a life on mission look like? I am sure that question is on the minds of many. I have always thought missionaries are Christian superheroes. Though it is true that there are those whom God especially calls and equips to serve in special cross-cultural mission environments, the vast majority of people living on mission are people living their ordinary lives for the glory of God and the spread of the gospel.

As we seek to help every church be on mission, we are helping equip everyday people in those churches on their individual missions. In the summer of 2015, we hosted the Send North America Conference in Nashville around the theme that every life on mission matters. During the two-day event, we featured stories of

---

[3] Craig Bartholomew and Michael Goheen, *The Drama of Scripture: Finding Our Place in the Biblical Story* (Grand Rapids: Baker Academic, 2004), 55.

six different people who are living on mission. One of those stories was of a mom named Danae. Danae and her husband live in the Denver area. They have four kids, full-time jobs outside the home, and are active in their church. Most would say they are doing enough. However, Danae wanted to do more. She had a burden for her neighbors, thinking to herself, *If I love spending time with them now, I will surely want to spend time with them for eternity.* That thought encouraged Danae to turn her home into a mission center. They have turned their front yard into a gathering spot for the neighborhood and their living room into a site for a neighborhood Bible study. Over the past couple of years, Danae's home has become the center of the community. Her neighbors seek her out for biblical counsel, and many are turning their hearts toward Jesus.

Danae would tell you that she is not doing anything special. She is simply living out her life by leveraging the gifts and access she has been given. Jeremiah 29 records the story of the Israelite exiles in Babylon. They were forced with the decision to adopt the culture and the practices of their captors, barricade themselves off from their captors, or figure out a way to live on mission as a distinct people. They chose the last option: to live among the people but be different. Their challenge was to reflect the character of God in a climate in which that seemed impossible. Tim Keller sums up their experience and how it applies to modern-day missionaries by saying:

> Christians . . . work for the peace, security, justice, and prosperity of their city and their neighbors, loving them in word and in deed, whether they believe what we do or not. In Jeremiah 29:7, Israel's exiles were called not just to live in the city to which they had been carried off but also to love it and work for its shalom—its economic, social, and spiritual flourishing. The citizens of God's city are the best possible citizens of their earthly cities.[4]

In the simplest terms, people who live on mission in their everyday lives "are the best possible citizens of their earthly cities."[5] Keller goes on to say that when Christians do "their work in an excellent but distinctive manner, that alone will produce a different kind of culture from the one in which we live now."[6] He says further that "developing humane, creative, and excellent business environments out of our understanding of the gospel can be part of this work. The embodiment of joy, hope, and truth in the arts is also part of this work."[7]

I am excited about many of the things we are doing at NAMB these days, but one of the strategies I am most excited about is called Generation Send (Gen

---

[4] Tim Keller, "A New Kind of Urban Christian," *Christianity Today*, May 1, 2006. Accessed February 24, 2016. http://www.christianitytoday.com/ct/2006/may/1.36.html.

[5] Ibid.

[6] Ibid.

[7] Ibid.

Send). Gen Send is designed for college-age young adults to give them a taste of what their life on mission can be. Each Gen Send participant spends six weeks in one of our Send North America feature cities. They work alongside church planters, learning the culture with the aim of creating strategies to share the gospel in that context. I think what excites me most about Gen Send is that participants are learning how to leverage their lives on mission. When their time in our program is over, they have a new perspective on what mission looks like. They are able to take their experiences and incorporate them into their everyday lives. Some of them will return to their Send City to live on mission, some will become church planters, but all of them will leverage whatever career path they are on to help build up the church.

Deep in my heart I believe the only way North America is going to see a major gospel advance is when every church and believer in those churches are on mission. We cannot afford to have anyone on the sidelines.

THE CHURCH IS AN INDESTRUCTIBLE FORCE

Some are probably wondering why I talk so passionately about the local church. I believe in churches because Jesus believed in the church. I want to put my full weight behind what Jesus puts his weight behind. In my mind a church-centered strategy is not just theological and missiological but practical as well. We have limited time and resources in our pursuit of accomplishing the Great Commission. We cannot afford to waste time on unproven and temporary strategies. We strive to invest in the strategies that have the highest likelihood of success. The local church, according to Jesus, is an indestructible force, so we are behind the church!

My oldest son is a sophomore in college right now. As I have counseled him about his future career options, I, as any parent would, have encouraged him to pick a field that has good job security. I do not want him to pick a passing fad but something that has real staying power. If we are honest, we all want to invest our lives in something that will last.

The most indestructible body on the planet is the local church. Since Jesus left the earth and the church was started, it has survived wars and famines. Governments have risen and fallen, but the church has not gone anywhere! Matthew 16:18 tells us that Jesus promised to build his church, and not even the gates of hell would be able to prevail against it. I give my life for something, I think I would put it with what Jesus thinks is important. So, as I lead NAMB, I will always champion the local church.

THE FUTURE: NAMB AND THE SBC

As I think about the future of the Southern Baptist Convention and the North American Mission Board, there are a few things I believe we have to prioritize. If we want the next decade to be better than the past, we have to prioritize what we do. In the paragraphs that follow, I want to lay out a couple of those priorities.

Champion Pastors

Pastors are on the front lines leading their churches. Every day they carry the burden of shepherding God's people. In so many ways, as the pastor goes, so goes the rest of the church. I am committed to helping pastors be healthy and effective leaders because I know we cannot talk about a church being on mission if the pastor of that church is not thriving.

I am thankful for my friend Johnny Hunt. Pastor Johnny has encouraged me for many years. I do not know of a better friend to pastors than him. What I love about Pastor Johnny is that he not only cares for pastors, but he helps them live on mission. For the last several years, he has conducted seminars that help encourage pastors and churches. Some of these seminars have been specifically related to church revitalization. Others have been focused on the health of the pastor. He has helped countless pastors think through their own situations and become better leaders.

Pastor Johnny leads by example. For years his church, First Baptist Church Woodstock, has been a leader in missions. They have sent millions of dollars to missionaries around the world through the Cooperative Program, Annie Armstrong, and Lottie Moon offerings. In addition, they have spent millions of dollars on supporting missionaries directly. They have planted numerous churches around the world. More than ten years ago they sent Vance Pitman to Las Vegas to plant Hope Baptist Church. Hope has now become a leader for church planting in the western United States.

The missionary activity of First Baptist Woodstock did not start unaided. No, it took a catalyst to get this work off the ground, and Brother Johnny was that catalyst. He will be the first to admit that when they started they did not have everything figured out. Along the way they have learned many lessons by making mistakes. However, the fruit of their labors is now numerous.

It is imperative that in the coming decades we care for pastors who then lead the way in catalyzing their churches for mission. In his own way, every pastor is the head of his own mission agency: the local church. Each church has people and financial resources that will accomplish the work of Jesus around the world. However, it will take pastors to lead the way.

I have been committed to using pastors to train other pastors and churches in mission. When I was a pastor, I always learned more from other pastors who were involved in missions than I learned from most denominational employees. This is not meant as a slight toward those employees, but I learned more because I always felt that pastors understood my situation better. They were able to relate to me and help me in ways that only a pastor could.

Over the past five years, I have enlisted several pastors to serve as ambassadors, mobilizers, and trainers for the North American Mission Board. In addition to Brother Johnny, men such as Fred Luter, Ronnie Floyd, Roger Freeman, Vance Pitman, J. D. Greear, and others are helping encourage and equip local churches for mission. This strategy has gained tremendous momentum because these guys are able to relate to their peers in ways others in our Alpharetta building cannot. If we are going to mobilize hundreds more churches for mission, it will be because pastors have led the way!

Plant Churches Where the People Are[8]

My friend and former colleague, Aaron Coe, has done extensive research on the need for and effectiveness of church planting. He found that more than 80 percent of North America's population lives in our largest urban areas. In the United States the urban trend has been ticking upward from the 1790 census onward.[9] In that year 5.1 percent of the population was considered urban.[10] Since that time the urban percentage has gone up every decade toward where it is now at 80.7 percent.[11] The 1920 census showed for the first time the United States as predominantly urban.[12] From 2000 to 2010, the urban areas of the U.S. grew by 12.1 percent.[13] There are now 486 "Urbanized Areas" of 50,000 or more people and 3,087 "Urban Clusters" of 2,500 or more people in the United States.[14] Additionally, in recent years, the traditional urban cores of U.S. cities have been growing at a faster pace than their suburban counterparts.[15]

The following chart shows the rate of congregational adherence for Evangelical Protestants in the top twenty urbanized areas of the United States.[16] Urbanized

---

[8] This section has previously appeared in "Implications for Urban Missiology in the United States from the Life and Work of Jane Jacobs," a Ph.D. prospectus written by Aaron Coe, Southeastern Baptist Theological Seminary, Wake Forest, N.C., September 2015." Used by permission.

[9] United States Census Bureau, "Population 1790–1990." Accessed July 10, 2015. https://www.census.gov/population/www/censusdata/files/table-4.pdf.

[10] Ibid.

[11] Ibid.

[12] Ibid.

[13] United States Census Bureau, "Growth in Urban Population Outpaces Rest of Nation, Census Bureau Report," *Newsroom Archive*. Accessed July 10, 2015. https://www.census.gov/newsroom/releases/archives/2010_census/cb12-50.html.

[14] Ibid.

[15] Hope Yen and Kristen Wyatt, "Cities Grow More than Suburbs, First Time in 100 Years," *Today*. Accessed February 24, 2016. http://www.today.com/id/47992439/ns/today-money/t/cities-grow-more-suburbs-first-time-years/#.Vsh78cdwXw6)

[16] The definition for Protestant evangelical Christians is from the Association of Religious Data Archives. It is as follows: "Evangelical Protestant denominations emphasize a personal relationship with Christ, the inspiration of the Bible and the importance of sharing faith with nonbelievers. Evangelical Protestantism is usually seen as more theologically and socially conservative than Mainline Protestantism, although there is obviously variation between denominations, congregations and individuals within the 'Evangelical' category." Association of Religious Data Archives, "Evangelical Protestant Denominations." Accessed January 1, 2016. http://www.thearda.com/

areas have 50,000 or more people in a particular geographical location.[17] None of the cities that have a population density of 10,000 people per square mile and above has more than a 7 percent evangelical Protestant adherence rate.[18] None of the cities on the chart has a congregational adherence rate of greater than 26 percent.[19] On average, the adherence rate of evangelical Protestants in the largest cities is 11.36 percent.[20] When the cities of Atlanta (22 percent), Dallas (26 percent), and Houston (26 percent) are removed, the average evangelical Protestant adherence rate is 8.96 percent.[21]

Of the evangelical Protestant groups in the United States, the Southern Baptist Convention (SBC) is one of the largest with 16,160,088 adherents.[22] The SBC finds its core constituency, not surprisingly, in the southern portion of the United States. The states of Mississippi, Alabama, Oklahoma, Tennessee, Kentucky, Arkansas, South Carolina, Georgia, North Carolina, and Louisiana are where the SBC is the strongest, with adherence rates of 305.79 to 156.54 congregants per 1,000 people in the population.[23]

In the states where the SBC is the strongest, the total population of these ten states is 53,483,652 million people, with an average density of 115 people per square mile.[24] By comparison, ten of the states that make up the Northeast corridor (Pennsylvania, New York, Maryland, New Jersey, Massachusetts, Maine, Delaware, New Hampshire, Connecticut, and Vermont) have a total population of 61 million people and have a density of 478 people per square mile.[25] The Northeast corridor is four times more densely populated than the South.

---

rcms2010/evangelical.asp. The chart was formulated by collecting evangelical Protestant data from Association of Religious Data Archives, "U.S. Congregational Membership: Metro Reports." Accessed July 10, 2015. http://www.thearda.com/rcms2010/selectMetro.asp. Additionally, information on the largest metropolitan areas was compiled from United States Census Bureau, "Largest Urbanized Areas with Selected Cities and Metro Areas," July 10, 2015. Accessed February 24, 2016. https://www.census.gov/dataviz/visualizations/026/508.php.

[17] United States Census Bureau, "2010 Census on Urban and Rural Classification and Urban Area Criteria." Accessed July 10, 2015. https://www.census.gov/geo/reference/ua/urban-rural-2010.html.

[18] Association of Religious Data Archives, "U.S. Congregational Membership: Metro Reports." Accessed July 10. http://www.thearda.com/rcms2010/selectMetro.asp; United States Census Bureau, "Largest Urbanized Areas with Selected Cites and Metro Areas." Accessed July 10, 2015. https://www.census.gov/dataviz/visualizations/026/508.php.

[19] Ibid.

[20] Ibid.

[21] Ibid.

[22] Association of Religious Data Archives, "Southern Baptist Convention." Accessed July 10, 2015. //www.thearda.com/denoms/d_1087.asp.

[23] Association of Religious Data Archives, "Southern Baptist Convention—Rates of Adherence per 1,000 population (2010)." Accessed August 7, 2015. http://www.thearda.com/mapsReports/maps/ArdaMap.asp?Map1=630&map2=&alpha.

[24] United States Census Bureau, "Community Facts." Accessed August 7, 2015. http://factfinder.census.gov/faces/nav/jsf/pages/index.xhtml###.

[25] Ibid.

City	Population Density per Square Mile	Evangelical Protestant Congregational Adherence
New York City	33,264	4.02 percent
- New York County (Manhattan)	69,468	4 percent
- Kings County (Brooklyn)	35,367	5 percent
- Queens County	20,553	3.7 percent
- Bronx County	32,903	4.2 percent
- Richmond County (Staten Island)	8,030	3.2 percent
San Francisco	17,179	3.7 percent
Boston (Suffolk County)	12,415	7 percent
Philadelphia	11,380	7 percent
Baltimore	1,345	7.7 percent
Denver	3,923	8.7 percent
Los Angeles	2,420	8.2 percent
Chicago (Cook County)	5,495	8.3 percent
San Diego	736	9.7 percent
Detroit (Wayne County)	2,974	10 percent
Seattle (King County)	913	10.5 percent
Miami (Dade County)	1,395	10.8 percent
Washington, D.C.	9,857	12.5 percent
Minneapolis (Hennepin County)	2,082	14 percent
Phoenix (Maricopa County)	415	14 percent
St. Louis	1,967	16.2 percent
Atlanta (Fulton County)	1,748	22 percent
Dallas	2,718	26 percent
Houston (Harris County)	2,402	26 percent

Evangelical Protestants in general, and Southern Baptists in particular, will need to be geographically present in the places where the highest and most densely inhabited portions of the population live. As our tribe of churches think through our future, we have to think through where we plant churches. We have to be willing to go to the hard places, which happen to be the places where the greatest number of people live.

CONCLUSION: THE CHURCH ON THE MOVE

When I look at the history of the church, not only do I see an indestructible force, but I see a body that is hardwired for movement. The church was never designed to be static but to grow and move forward. From its beginning the DNA of the church has been one of advancement.

In Acts 2 the Holy Spirit comes at Pentecost, and the church is birthed with more than 3,000 people responding to Peter's message being saved and baptized (that was a pretty good day at church). By Acts 7 the church was fully functioning and under attack because of its witness in Jerusalem. As a result of the persecution of the church, it was "scattered throughout the land of Judea and Samaria" (Acts 8:1 HCSB), thus establishing the church beyond the boundaries of Jerusalem. In Acts 13 the church is sending its members on mission to other parts of the region. In general terms through the rest of the book of Acts, the church's mission is perpetually accomplished by sending people (Paul and his associates), usually to a metropolitan area, to preach the gospel. The gospel would be preached and people would respond. The respondents would continually meet together, and Paul would move on. After a season of time, Paul would return to that city and appoint elders for the church. This basic process, which has taken on many manifestations, is how the church has extended its mission throughout the centuries.

The church experienced phenomenal growth in its earliest centuries. By the year 350, the Christian church was the dominant cultural force in the world. I find the following graphic by Rodney Stark helpful as it details the growth of the early church.

**Christian Growth Projected at 40 Percent per Decade
(based on a population of 60 million)** [26]

Year	Number of Christians	Percent of Population
AD 40	1,000	.0017
AD 50	1,400	.0023
AD 100	7,530	.0126
AD 150	40,496	.07
AD 200	217,795	.36
AD 250	1,171,356	1.9
AD 300	6,299,832	10.5
AD 350	33,882,008	56.5

What I find fascinating about this chart is that Christianity became a dominant force on the culture not because it desired cultural influence but because it focused on its mission. Because it focused on leading people to Jesus, discipling them, and forming churches, the church grew. Over time they woke up to the reality that they were a massive force.

As I think about the future of the culture in North America, I would be lying if I did not say that some things concern me. At times the odds seem to be stacked against us. However, I am encouraged by what I currently see. I see pastors and churches stepping up to the task to make Jesus known by directing their churches to be on mission. I am also encouraged by the number of individuals living on mission in their everyday lives and as church planters and other types of missionaries. However, what encourages me the most is knowing that what Jesus has done before in the church, he will do again. Our job is not to fight the culture per se, but it is to live on mission with Jesus. When we invest in the building of his church, it will have huge implications on the culture as a whole. I am praying for a day when I wake up and see the church is once again the dominant force in the culture.

---

[26] Rodney Stark, *The Rise of Christianity: How an Obscure, Marginal Jesus Movement Became the Dominant Religious Force in the Western World in a Few Centuries* (New York: Harper One, 1996), 6–7

Training the Next Generation of Pastors, Ministers, and Missionaries: Southern Baptist Theological Education in the Twenty-First Century

Jason K. Allen

A recent major report on North American seminaries argued that, given the tectonic shifts in theological education—and the dramatic pace of change in higher education in general—a seminary's master plan should project no more than a three-year horizon, and institutions should expect to modify the plan after eighteen months.[1]

As we consider theological education in the twenty-first century, we must do so with that counsel in mind and with the humility it necessitates. Theological education in the twenty-first century, if anything, seems unpredictable. However, my argument is straightforward—*we cannot predict the future of theological education, but we can determine it.*

This chapter considers Southern Baptist theological education in three categories: (1) a historical overview; (2) a current assessment; and (3) ten determinations for the future. We should keep in mind two longitudinal tensions that run throughout the SBC's history.

The first tension is between the theological and the programmatic. Throughout Southern Baptist history these two poles, each with their own gravitational pull, have exerted influence over the denomination. The seminaries, like the convention as a whole, have oscillated between them.

---

[1] Anthony Ruger and Chris Meinzer, "Through Toil and Tribulation: Financing Theological Education 2001–2011," *Auburn Studies* (2014): 22.

This is currently the case. From 1979 through the end of the twentieth century, theological concerns dominated our attention, culminating in the Baptist Faith and Message 2000. Both now and in the past decade programmatic concerns—including how best to operate as a convention and how best to fund our collective work—have occupied the denomination's attention.

Similarly, and more specifically, in Southern Baptist theological education another longitudinal tension runs throughout our history—the tension between mission and money.

By mission I mean what a seminary is to be. Why should it exist? Whom does it serve? What should it teach? To whom should it be answerable? Mission determines the ultimate issues of institutional aspirations and accountability. By money I mean who will support the seminaries. How, and to what extent, will the seminaries be supported? And, of course, the two are related. Morally and legally, those who founded and fund the institution should be the sole proprietors over its mission.

These two tensions run throughout Southern Baptist history and have proven to shape its efforts in theological education. They also occur within and shape this chapter.

AN HISTORICAL OVERVIEW

Since the SBC's founding in 1845, the convention's primary—and most unifying—effort has been collaborative missions. That was our reason for existence in 1845, and it remains primary today.[2] Yet even during the SBC's earliest years, theological education was an accompanying concern. Early SBC luminaries such as R. B. C. Howell, W. B. Johnson, Basil Manly Sr., Basil Manly Jr., and most especially James P. Boyce called for a common theological institution in the South.

By the mid to late 1850s, Boyce had arisen as the effort's most prominent and successful leader. Boyce's inaugural faculty address at Furman University in 1856, "Three Changes in Theological Institutions," called for a dramatic reconceptualization of ministry preparation that would produce a clergy abundant in number, well learned, and doctrinally sound. Boyce realized his dream in three short years with the founding of the Southern Baptist Theological Seminary in Greenville, SC, in 1859.[3]

For nearly fifty years Southern Seminary enjoyed sole status within the SBC. Given its uniqueness as our only seminary, as well as its celebrated faculty, it is

---

[2] Regrettably, the Southern churches' desire to appoint slaveholding missionaries precipitated the schism with the Northern churches. Collectively funding and sending missionaries drew the southern churches together to form the Southern Baptist Convention.

[3] For a history of the Southern Baptist Theological Seminary, see Gregory A. Wills, *The Southern Baptist Theological Seminary, 1859–2009* (Oxford: Oxford University Press, 2009).

difficult to overestimate Southern's influence on the denomination during the institution's first half century.

Yet even in the early decades an uneasy relationship existed between SBC churches and their seminary. An intuitive suspicion of higher education in general—common in the nineteenth-century agrarian South—intensified when concerns over higher criticism, Baptist origins, and, into the twentieth century, the Fundamentalist-Modernist Controversy surfaced. By the early decades of the twentieth century, modern biblical criticism had moved from occasional occurrence to more common acceptance by Southern's faculty.

Southern Baptists Move Westward

Nearly fifty years after Southern Seminary's founding, Southwestern Baptist Theological Seminary was birthed. Under B. H. Carroll's leadership, Southwestern Seminary emerged out of Baylor University. Carroll, the pastor of the prominent First Baptist Church of Waco, Texas, was a titanic figure in Texas and Southern Baptist life. Like the rest of the country, Southern Baptists had moved westward, and by the early twentieth century the need for a complementing institution was apparent. Texas Baptists—and their financial and demographic strength—were more than ready to support our second seminary.

During the interwar years, the SBC morphed from a loose collection of churches into a more functioning denomination, as witnessed through the establishment of the Cooperative Program, the adoption of the first convention-wide confessional statement, and the formation of the Executive Committee. This era also saw the more formal engrafting of Southern and Southwestern Seminaries into the SBC, wherein they reaped the benefits of denominational support and came under more direct SBC control.

Under Carroll's leadership and that of his notable successor, Lee Scarborough, Southwestern Seminary's rise was meteoric. So much so that by the 1960s its enrollment rivaled—and then surpassed—that of Southern Seminary. By the latter decades of the twentieth century, it was Southern Baptists' most influential seminary in terms of enrollment, prominence of alumni, and broad popular appeal due to its comparatively conservative faculty.

Postwar Expansion

The postwar era, especially from 1945 to 1960, was a period of dramatic denominational expansion. By now the SBC had congealed into a more structured, operationally mature, and nationally ambitious denomination. SBC annuals from this period reveal a sense of near-unbounded optimism.

During these fifteen years Southern Baptists added four seminaries. New Orleans Seminary, which began as a Bible institute in 1917, was formally converted into Southern Baptists' third seminary in 1946. Over the next decade the denomination would imagine and found three more theological institutions: Golden Gate Seminary (1946), Southeastern Seminary (1950), and Midwestern Seminary (1957).

Intramural theological disputes appeared almost without end in state papers throughout the SBC's first century of existence. Yet widespread theological controversy, which could potentially lead to significant schism within the SBC, occurred only episodically, most especially in the Toy Controversy, Landmarkism, the Whitsitt Controversy, and the Fundamentalist-Modernist Controversy. Nonetheless, by the mid-twentieth century theological liberalism was well entrenched—if not widely perceived—in Southern Baptist seminaries. Higher criticism, the Documentary Hypothesis, naturalistic explanations for Scripture's miraculous events, and a denial of the historical accuracy of the Bible were all commonly held among SBC professors.

During this era seminary leaders tended toward the managerial not the theological. Like the SBC as a whole, in the seminaries programmatic and administrative concerns displaced doctrinal ones. In fact, this is clearly reflected in trustee minutes from the 1950s, where enormous energy is given to the tedious and administratively mundane. All the while, faculty additions occurred with little attention given to theological matters.

Liberalism Metastasizes

These realities, the need for faculty members at the newly launched seminaries, and a faculty controversy at Southern coalesced to spread heterodoxy. Dubbed the Lexington Road Massacre, thirteen professors were dismissed from Southern Seminary in 1958. The establishment of Southeastern and Midwestern Seminaries provided the perfect "work needed/help wanted" scenario, leading these professors to relocate to Wake Forest and Kansas City, thus metastasizing theological liberalism within the SBC.[4]

By the end of the 1950s, a pronounced theological divergence existed just under the surface between Southern Baptist seminaries and the churches they ostensibly served. The dissonance continued to grow in scope, public awareness, and convention-wide concern. This fact can be seen most especially through the Elliott Controversy of the early 1960s, the Broadman Commentary Controversy of the late 1960s, and, as an artifact, the Hollyfield Thesis of 1976.

Denominational Controversy and Institutional Recovery

By 1979, when the Patterson-Pressler coalition formally launched what has come to be known as the Conservative Resurgence by electing Adrian Rogers SBC

---

[4] Ibid, 351–436.

president, an undeniable dissonance between Southern Baptist seminaries and the vast majority of local churches existed.

What began in 1979 took more than two decades to play out fully: electing conservative SBC presidents, appointing conservative trustees, securing conservative seminary presidents, and building conservative faculties. The culmination of the resurgence was the SBC's adoption of the BFM2000. By the second decade of the twenty-first century, theological education in the SBC was in many ways where it started in 1859, with uniformly conservative seminaries serving Southern Baptist churches.

A CURRENT ASSESSMENT

In light of our historical context and position within the broader evangelical world, one can argue Southern Baptists are now enjoying a golden era in theological education. At least eight factors reinforce this claim.

First, SBC seminaries are more theologically conservative than they have been in a century. In each Southern Baptist seminary, the professors uniformly affirm inerrancy. They covenant to teach in accordance with, and not contrary to, the BFM2000—and they in fact do just that. The BFM2000 is by far the most theologically conservative, convention-wide confession ever adopted by the SBC.

Moreover, accompanying this confessional standard is a living, actual commitment to it by trustees, administration, and faculty. What is more, additional statements like the Abstract of Principles, the Danvers Statement on Biblical Manhood and Womanhood, and the Chicago Statement on Biblical Inerrancy provide supplemental confessional clarity in many of our seminaries.

Second, SBC seminaries' faculties are notably accomplished. A faculty can be theologically conservative yet scholastically unaccomplished. Thankfully, this is not the case in the SBC. Southern Baptist professors are a cottage industry of publishing and academic output. They are widely respected throughout, and even beyond, the broader evangelical world. For instance, SBC personalities now account for nearly one-third of presentations at the annual meeting of the Evangelical Theological Society and often provide leadership of the same.

Third, SBC seminaries are larger—in actual and relative numbers—than ever before. Indeed, we are massive, with a total head-count enrollment of more than 18,000 students. In total enrollment each one of the six SBC seminaries ranks in the top ten largest seminaries in North America—of any and all denominations. Even the smaller SBC institutions are some ten times larger than the average ATS-accredited seminary in North America. Our footprint has never been larger.

Fourth, SBC seminaries are producing high-caliber graduates. Twenty years ago, when conservative SBC seminary presidents looked to fill faculty slots, they often had to hire Baptists serving in institutions outside of the SBC. In other words, we had more open professorates than qualified candidates to fill them. Now the opposite is true. Midwestern Seminary, and each of the other five Southern Baptist seminaries, has a waiting list of highly qualified graduates who desire to teach in our institutions.

Fifth, SBC seminaries are complementing institutions. While each SBC seminary operates in alignment with the BFM2000, each institution has its own identity, culture, strengths, and ministry emphases. This variety is good and right and both reflects and serves the unity in essentials, diversity in nonessentials nature of the SBC. In other words, we do not need six identical chefs preparing six identical meals. Similar chefs, yes; identical chefs, not so much.

Sixth, SBC seminaries remain affordable. This is not a newly realized strength. Thanks to Southern Baptists' generosity through the Cooperative Program, affordability has long been a mainstay. What is remarkable is how SBC institutions remain affordable in light of the relative weakening of the Cooperative Program and the escalating costs of higher education. Indeed, most comparable evangelical institutions charge more than twice what SBC seminaries charge Southern Baptist students.

Seventh, the SBC seminaries are more accessible than ever. The advent of online education, modular and hybrid class options, and the near round-the-clock scheduling of residential education means one can literally receive theological education from anywhere on the globe, anytime. Moreover, resources beyond the classroom, like conferences, intensive classes, free publications, and online content, all have forward-deployed theological education.

Eighth, the SBC seminaries are on mission. The conservative redirection of the seminaries brought with it a renewed emphasis on the Great Commission and serving the local church. In the final analysis these priorities should set a seminary's agenda. Thankfully, for Southern Baptist seminaries these are primary, not secondary considerations.

In summary, the SBC seminaries now stand far healthier than most anyone—friend or critic—would have imagined a generation ago. But the laws of inertia do not apply in theological education. The same will not be said a generation from now unless we make ten commitments, and therefore exhibit ten strengths.

TEN DETERMINATIONS FOR THE FUTURE

General Dwight Eisenhower once mused that when it comes to warfare the plan is nothing but planning is everything. That aphorism brushes up against a reality for seminaries as well: the less predictable the future of theological education is, the more we must work to predict it. Or, better yet, the more we must work to determine it. Keeping these ten determinations will help ensure a healthy future for Southern Baptist theological education.

First, we must maintain confessional integrity. At first glance this determination is so predictable as to almost be taken for granted. However, just because maintaining confessional integrity is expected does not make it any less urgent. We should be reminded that we, as Southern Baptists, have yet to prove we can successfully maintain confessional faithfulness in our seminaries for more than one generation.

Confessional integrity is essential to orthodox belief and witness. Scripture is replete with exhortations for believers to steward and preserve the Christian faith. Appeals like "retain the standard of sound words" (2 Tim 1:13 NASB), "contend earnestly for the faith once and for all delivered to the saints" (Jude 3 NASB) and "guard the truth" (2 Tim 1:14 NLT) stand as theological admonitions, apostolic injunctions for believers.

This confessional commitment must include a statement that is as clear and comprehensive as possible; a faculty that keeps it with full integrity; a president who vigilantly guards the integrity of the process; a governing board that provides ongoing oversight and accountability; and, most especially, churches that remain engaged with their institutions. Churches that fail to exercise oversight will likely become victims of the institutions they founded. Dirty faucets always pollute clean basins.

Southern Baptist seminaries are more theologically conservative than they have been in nearly a century, with the BFM2000—the most conservative and comprehensive statement of faith ever adopted by the SBC—serving as the primary instrument of accountability. Theological trust was hard earned but can be lost easily. It leaves town on horseback; it returns on foot. SBC seminaries, and the denomination as a whole, must maintain doctrinal vigilance.

Public agitation will only intensify on the great social issues of the day, with same-sex marriage being the focal point. Accrediting agencies, the federal government, and other belligerents will likely continue to increase pressure on evangelical institutions.

Deeper into the twenty-first century, if acceptance of homosexuality and same-sex marriage gains momentum within SBC churches, the seminaries could find themselves out of theological alignment with the churches—being more conservative than their churches for the first time in the SBC's history.

The issue is not only rejecting sound doctrine; it is neglecting it. We are aware of the former, but the latter is the more probable concern for us in the near term and is always the gateway to the latter. Therefore, we should ask questions like: How many of our churches are, for practical purposes, facilitating disorderly observances of the Lord's Table? How many of our churches understand the importance of baptism, and why it is nonnegotiable for church membership? How many of our churches are consciously striving for a regenerate church membership? How many of our churches have a clear, convictional understanding of the exclusivity of the gospel?

Our charge is faithfulness to our confessional expectations regardless of from where—and from whom—the agitation to compromise may come. Can we maintain transgenerational theological faithfulness? The SBC has yet to prove it can.

Second, we must maintain mission clarity. The mission of Southern Baptist seminaries is clear: to train pastors, missionaries, and ministers for Southern Baptist churches and for the mission field. However, financial challenges tempt institutions toward mission compromise, and seminaries often succumb to that temptation.

In fact, many seminaries structure their curricular offerings like a shopping mall, offering nearly every program imaginable in order to cobble together a sufficient enrollment to pay the bills. In so doing, they compromise their mission and dilute their institutional emphasis. The seminary that focuses on everything focuses on nothing.

Funding challenges have been a primary—if not the primary propeller of mission compromise. Just as plants grow toward light, so institutions bend toward their sources of funding. Herein is an added reason for strong Cooperative Program support—for the most assured way to maintain ownership and influence is to hold the purse strings.

More specifically, Southern Baptist seminaries must make priority number one training pastors—specifically pastors for Southern Baptist churches. The distinguishing marks of the church are the preaching of the Word of God and the right administration of the ordinances. A pastor is indispensable to these tasks. Furthermore, the vast majority of our churches have one, and only one, staff member—the pastor. If our churches cannot look to our seminaries and find pastors, where will they be able to look?

The preaching and teaching of Holy Scripture is the principal responsibility of the Christian minister, and it is the central need of the church. In fact, in order to be biblically qualified to be a Christian minister, one must be "able to teach" (1 Tim 3:2 NIV). Paul repeatedly charged Timothy to a faithful ministry of the Word with exhortations like, "retain the standard of sound words" (2 Tim 1:13 NASB), "guard the precious truth that has been entrusted to you" (v. 14 NLT), "rightly dividing the word of truth" (2 Tim 2:15 ESV), and "preach the word" (2 Tim 4:2). These exhortations, and many others, require a renewed mind—and an informed one. There simply is no place in ministry for sloppy exegesis, shoddy interpretation, or shallow sermons.

Yet we must not merely produce pastors; we must produce pastors for Southern Baptist churches. Therefore, we must continually ask what our churches need? What skills must our graduates possess to minister most optimally within a Southern Baptist context?

Third, we must develop sustainable business models. This is probably the least glamorous aspect of a seminary president's job, but these days it is the most time-consuming. The escalating costs of higher education, a shrinking offering-plate dollar, tapering national demographics, diminishing confidence in the value of higher education, and a weakened Cooperative Program all coalesce to undermine the business model of the past. At the same time, affordability remains a pressing concern for prospective students.

These challenges create a consumeristic and competitive context in theological education. Simply put, institutions are spending more and more money to recruit fewer and fewer students. These dynamics explain why a recent survey of "turnaround institutions" revealed that entrepreneurial leadership is a consistent trait of successful turn-around schools.[5]

Southern Baptist seminaries are not immune to these challenges. Will Southern Baptists renew their collaborative ministry efforts and strengthen their giving through the Cooperative Program, or will giving continue to soften? The recent downsizing and restructuring at the International Mission Board is the most graphic warning of the financial challenges we face.

Will Southern Baptists continue to fund their seminaries at sustainable levels? Surely the SBC did not spend two decades fighting to recover their institutions theologically in order to forfeit them financially. Though some recent CP indicators are encouraging, this is an open question with significant consequences.

These realities should be interpreted as more than an appeal for more money from our churches. It is an appeal for wise stewardship, entrepreneurial leadership, and skillful management from our seminaries. Deeper into the twenty-first century, there will be two types of seminaries, those who find a sustainable business model and those who find themselves out of business.

Fourth, we must be agile and adaptable. Modern delivery systems have up-ended traditional models of higher education. Online, modular, and hybrid delivery formats have all become conduits to distribute theological education. When these delivery models supplement residential education—forward deploying theological education for those who cannot travel to seminary—it is healthy and commendable. Online delivery systems, when rightly purposed, can expand theological education. When done in a way that compromises sound pedagogy, weakens the rigor of ministry preparation, or practices minimalistic standards, it undermines theological education.

Innovation is a wave to be ridden—not a liability to be avoided—for it can greatly extend a seminary's reach. Regardless, the future is here, and it cannot be wished away. Nonetheless, residential education should always be primary and

---

[5] Amy Bragg Carey, "On the Edge: A Study of Small Private Colleges That Have Made a Successful Financial Turnaround," *Christian Higher Education* 13 (2014): 306–16.

preferred. It should be most incentivized by the SBC, the seminaries, and our funding models. This prioritization is in the best interest of the students, the seminaries, the church, and the entire SBC.

Fifth, we must serve Southern Baptist churches. Southern Baptist seminaries exist to serve Southern Baptist churches. As long as Southern Baptist churches exist, they will need prepared ministers. Therefore, the mandate for theological education will persist as long as there is a Southern Baptist Convention.

The most biblical seminary understands it has a right to exist inasmuch as it serves the local church. Out of mission, opportunity, and necessity, now is the time for theological education to be wedded to local churches. The decades ahead should be a season of great partnership between the seminaries and the church. Tragically, in our past this has not always been the case. One of the most depressing glimpses of a seminary not serving the church is recorded in the pages of Clayton Sullivan's depressing memoir, *Called to Preach, Condemned to Survive.*

Sullivan, who attended Southern Seminary in the 1950s and early 60s, bemoans how subtly and incrementally his call to ministry shifted. Seminary, which was intended as a preparatory season of training, became an all-encompassing stage of life with its own sense of momentum, achievement, and finality. He writes:

> By this time, the cart was before the horse. The means had become the end. When I first enrolled in seminary I'd looked upon study as a means by which to prepare to be a preacher. And I'd viewed Southern Seminary as a temporary dwelling place on my way to the pastorate. But to me, an overcooked graduate student, study by now had become an end within itself.[6]

Sullivan continues:

> My seminary professors tended to look upon preachers as hucksters, denominational drumbeaters, or dummies. That's why one of my seminary professors remarked, "The most brilliant Southern Baptist ministers become seminary professors and college teachers. The rest have to go into the pastorate.[7]

On the contrary, we must, in curriculum and culture, be absolutely given to serving the church. After all, our role is not to be church critics but church servants.

Sixth, we must prioritize the master of divinity degree. In the world of theological education, the master of divinity degree has long been the gold standard for ministry preparation, and its sole status is well deserved. In it one finds the complete tool kit for ministry service: Greek and Hebrew, New Testament and

---

[6] Clayton Sullivan, *Called to Preach, Condemned to Survive* (Macon: Mercer University Press, 2003), 81.
[7] Ibid.

Old Testament, theology, church history, preaching, pastoral care and counseling, evangelism, missions, and much, much more.

Yet, in many seminaries the master of divinity degree has fallen on hard times. In recent years shorter and less rigorous master of arts degrees have siphoned off students from the master of divinity degree. The advent of online education accelerated this shift, with accrediting agencies approving the shorter MA degrees nearly a decade before approving the MDiv degree.

The urgency of recovering the MDiv is not rooted in what it offers but in what ministers and churches need. Ours is an exhilarating age in which to live and minister. The unpredictable challenges of a decadent culture, the perennial needs of the church, and the demands of twenty-first-century Christian service all point to the urgency and consequence of the master of divinity degree. In other words, the needs of the church are great, and the church's expectations of their ministers will be greater still.

We do not settle for shabbiness in any other area of life, so why would we settle for it in Christian ministry? When my automobile needs servicing, I do not take it to a backyard mechanic. When I need an accountant, I do not look for someone merely good with a calculator. When I have a sick child, I do not take him to a physician who occasionally dabbles in pediatrics. Let us not subject our churches to such shoddiness either. Sunday morning at 11:00 a.m. is no time for amateur hour.

The sad reality is most church members are pathetically ill informed, but their lack of biblical training is not a permission slip for ministers to exhibit the same. God does not grade ministers on the curve. We are judged by New Testament standards of biblical knowledge and ministerial fitness, not by whether we know the Scriptures marginally better than our ill-informed church members.

Seventh, we must continually make a prima facie case for our existence. Our cultural moment necessitates rigorous ministry preparation. Every generation presents the church with particular challenges, but our generation comes with unique baggage and angularity. It is not that the twenty-first century is more fallen or more secular than previous ones, but it may well be more complex.

Befuddling ethical questions, the often tortuously complex ramifications of sin, and a cultural intelligentsia devoting its best energies to undermining the Christian belief system all present the church with serious challenges. The lost need more than shallow answers from ill-equipped ministers. They need ministers prepared to bring the full complement of Christian truth to bear in a winsome, thoughtful, and compelling way.

Will our churches continue to value theological education? Can we continue to make the case for theological education? The irony is, our churches have great needs—unlike they have ever experienced before—and need our ministers greater still.

Eighth, we must determine to celebrate enrollment in terms of strength, not primarily size. There is a difference between the two. We are Southern Baptists and we like big. However, the future likely will present us with a different scenario. Tapering national demographics and a contracting denomination may bring our seminaries smaller enrollments in the future. After all, we receive no more students than the churches call out and send to us.

There are technical, operational challenges associated with a smaller enrollment, but there are also the psychological ones. We live in a world, and minister within a denomination, where bigger is always better. This is not altogether bad. All along we best judge ourselves by how many pastors (first) and ministers (second) we are producing for Southern Baptist churches. Therefore, we will do well to understand our health in terms of strength of enrollment, not size of enrollment.

Ninth, we must determine to look to churches for accountability and partnership. Simply put, as a seminary president I care more about the issues than I care about the institution I lead. If in the future this seminary gives up the inerrancy of Scripture or forfeits the gospel, I am happy for the buildings to crumble. My hope for the long-term doctrinal soundness of my institution is not rooted in the confidence I have in my successor several times removed; it is rooted in the confidence I have in grassroots Southern Baptists.

Tenth, we must determine to labor for the overall SBC project. The liability of the SBC, as a denomination, is that it gives more to every entity at every level—local, state, and national—than it requires of us to put into it. We can either work together, collectively, faithfully, and earnestly, to strengthen our partnership through the Cooperative Program, or we will one day find ourselves collectively suffering, the likes of which will make the current IMB restructuring look mild. In the long run one cannot have healthy SBC seminaries individually without a healthy SBC corporately.

CONCLUSION

Are Southern Baptists enjoying a golden era in theological education? Absolutely. But present health does not guarantee future health. The twenty-first century demands seminaries be strategic with resources, intentional in serving their constituencies, and unquestionably faithful to the Word of God and the classic disciplines of theological education.

After all, theological education, at its core, is timeless. In many ways theological education in the twenty-first century should resemble theological education in any century—transmitting the classic disciplines to pastors, ministers, and evangelists for the church. If we remain strategic and faithful, keeping these ten determinations for the future, our churches will be strengthened, and our golden era will be extended.

The story goes that as the 1787 Constitutional Convention adjourned in Philadelphia, a woman approached Benjamin Franklin and asked, "Mr. Franklin, what kind of government have you given us?"

"A republic, madam," Franklin replied, "if you can keep it."[8]

Similarly, we might ask, "What have Paul Pressler, Paige Patterson, and Adrian Rogers bequeathed to this generation of Southern Baptists?" The answer is healthy seminaries, but we must determine to keep them.

---

[8] Walter Isaacson, *Benjamin Franklin: An American Life* (New York: Simon & Schuster, 2003), 459.

Every Kindred, Tongue, and Tribe?
Ethnic Diversity in the SBC

Daniel L. Akin and Walter R. Strickland II

A t the 2012 Southern Baptist Convention in New Orleans, messengers narrowly approved the name "Great Commission Baptists" as an alternative or complementary name for our convention. The recommendation inspired spirited debate on the convention floor. Some thought this decision helps describe who Southern Baptists have become and hope to be in the future. Still others felt this was an unnecessary waste of time. For the latter, the name "Southern Baptist Convention" served well in the past and would do the same in the future.

In our estimation the concern was not that we be called Great Commission Baptists but rather that we would we be Great Commission Baptists. As we progress into the twenty-first century, will Southern Baptists bear the marks of a Great Commission people—serving King Jesus faithfully as he reclaims all that rightly belongs to him—or will we sit on the sidelines distracted, divided, and in disobedience? Will we pine for "the good ol' days," or will we plead with God for our best days to be ahead of us? In Romans 15:14–24 Paul puts forth six marks of a Great Commission people. He describes the essence of a Great Commission people (marks 1–4). The fifth mark explores the breadth of God's mission, and the sixth mark emphasizes the breadth of the Great Commission call among God's people. We will explore these six marks and then consider their impact on gospel partnerships in the context of kingdom diversity.

MARKS OF A GREAT COMMISSION PEOPLE

The first mark of a Great Commission people is *keeping focused on the most important things amid many good things* (Rom 15:14–16). Paul was confident the church at Rome was doing a number of good things; he notes that they were (1)"full of goodness," (2) "filled with . . . knowledge", and (3) "able to instruct [or "admonish," NASB] one another" (v. 14 HCSB). These believers embodied what it meant to live good lives informed by good theology. Although their lives and doctrine were consistent (i.e., their beliefs informed their practice), if one got off course, they lovingly corrected one another.

Since Paul knew "the good" is always the greatest enemy of "the best," he took an opportunity to graciously remind the Roman church of their calling to be "minister[s] of Christ Jesus to the Gentiles." The word "Gentiles" (v. 16 HCSB) does not fully capture all Paul is describing in this context. A better translation of the word *ethnē* in this context, also used in Matthew 28:19 (ESV), is "nations." Nations is not a reference to political or national boundaries but to peoples or people groups—persons with a distinct language, culture, and identity.

According to the International Mission Board, there are more than 11,500 distinct people groups in the world today, and more than 6,800 are unreached with the gospel.[1] The IMB reminds us that, of the nearly 7 billion people on planet earth, 3.8 billion do not have adequate access to the gospel.[2] Of even more concern, 1.27 billion have never and will never hear the name of Jesus in their lifetime if things remain as they are.[3] This means that most of these people will be born, live, die, and spend eternity separated from God, in a place called hell, never having heard a clear presentation of the gospel. It pains us to think that there are places in the world where we could walk days, weeks, and months, and we would neither encounter a church or meet a Christian.

Southern Baptists do a number of good things, and we should continue to do most of them, but like Paul, our challenge is to keep focused on the most important thing. The great Baptist theologian Carl F. H. Henry was right, "The Gospel is only good news if it gets there in time."[4] John Keith-Falconer adds, "I have but one candle of life to burn, and I would rather burn out in a land filled with darkness than in a land flooded with light."[5] Our denomination must keep our focus on lands filled with darkness.

The second mark of a Great Commission people is *an awareness that introducing the nations to Jesus is an act of worship to God* (vv. 15–16, 19). Holding missions

---

[1] International Mission Board, "Research Data." Accessed December 9, 2015. http://public.imb.org/globalresearch/Pages/default.aspx_statistics.

[2] International Mission Board, "One Sacred Effort." Accessed December 9, 2015. http://mediamanager.mediasuite.org/files/179/17983/17983-100088.swf.

[3] Staff, "Missions Around the World: A Messenger Exclusive Interview with IMB President Tom Elliff," *Baptist Messenger of Oklahoma*, November 14, 2012. Accessed February 24, 2016. http://www.baptistmessenger.com/missions-around-the-world-a-messenger-exclusive-interview-with-imb-president-tom-elliff.

[4] Marvin J. Newell, ed., *Expect Great Things: Mission Quotes That Inform and Inspire* (Pasadena, CA: William Carey Library, 2013), 157.

[5] Ibid., 202.

and theology together helps us understand missions as a service of worship to our God. Keeping missions and theology together will also help us understand that a proper motivation for doing missions is gratitude, not legalistic guilt. As a result, we believe missions and theology must always be linked together. In fact, the greatest missionary who ever lived was also the greatest theologian who ever lived; his name was Jesus. Furthermore, the greatest Christian theologian who ever lived was also the greatest missionary who ever lived—the apostle Paul. It could be argued that Paul was a great theologian because he was a missionary since you cannot have one without the other. Thus, any theology that does not issue forth in a passion for God and the nations is not Christian theology.

In wonderful Trinitarian language Paul describes his calling to the nations saying, "Because of the grace of God given to me by God [the Father], I am a minister of Christ Jesus [the Son] to the nations serving as a priest of God's good news. I serve as a priest in this act of worship so that the offering of the nations may be acceptable to Christ, an offering made acceptable and sanctified by the Holy Spirit" (vv. 15b–16 ESV). Missions is the fruit of worship initiated by the Triune God and accomplished through his believer priests.

Missionary service is all for God's glory, like the Old Testament priests bringing offerings to God in worship. This is why John Stott says,

> The highest of missionary motives is neither obedience to the Great Commission (important as that is), nor love for sinners who are alienated and perishing (strong as that incentive is), but rather a burning and passionate zeal for the glory of Jesus Christ. . . . Only one imperialism is Christian . . . and that is concern for His Imperial Majesty Jesus Christ, and for the glory of his empire.[6]

The triune God is glorified in our service to the nations because in worship each member of the Godhead is exalted in his role of salvation. Our gracious Father initiates salvation, the Son provides the means, and the Holy Spirit's power accomplishes it (v. 19). Missions is worship, and worship provides a motivation and power that no amount of guilt could provide. John Piper says it best:

> Missions is not the ultimate goal of the church, worship is. Missions exists because worship doesn't. Worship is ultimate, not missions, because God is ultimate, not man. When this age is over, and the countless millions of the redeemed fall on their faces before the throne of God, missions will be no more. It is a temporary necessity, but worship abides forever. Worship, therefore, is the fuel and goal of missions. It's the goal of missions because in missions we simply aim

---

6 John R. W. Stott, *Romans: God's Good News for the World* (Downers Grove, IL: InterVarsity, 1995), 53.

to bring the nations into the white-hot enjoyment of God's glory. . . . Missions begins and ends in worship.[7]

The third mark of a Great Commission people is *being Christ centered and boasting only in Him* (vv. 17–19). Elsewhere Paul declared, "But far be it from me to boast except in the cross of our Lord Jesus Christ, by which the world has been crucified to me, and I to the world" (Gal 6:14 ESV). In Paul's missions manifesto, Romans 15, he makes a nearly identical statement, saying that he can be proud of his toil for God but only because of Christ (v. 17 ESV). Paul only speaks of "what Christ has accomplished through [him] to bring the nations to obedience" (v. 18 ESV). This was accomplished by the power of the Spirit through signs and wonders as the gospel advanced into new territories and enabled them to fulfill the ministry of the gospel of Christ (v. 19). Paul knew that being Christ centered would radically impact how we think, speak, and live, thus implanting the Great Commission germ into our souls.

Henry Martyn was a missionary to India and Persia, and in God's mysterious providence he died at age thirty-one. A prolific writer, Martyn wrote, "The Spirit of Christ is the spirit of missions. The nearer we get to Him, the more intensely missionary we become."[8] Count Nicolaus Ludwig Von Zinzendorf, a great Moravian missionary, adds, "I have but one passion: it is He, it is He alone. The world is the field and the field is the world; and henceforth that country shall be my home where I can be most used in winning souls for Christ."[9]

The fourth mark of a Great Commission people is *never losing sight of the centrality and nature of the gospel* (vv. 16, 19–20). The book of Romans is a gospel book, and its theme is captured in Romans 1:16–17 (ESV), "For I am not ashamed of the gospel, for it is the power of God for salvation to everyone who believes, to the Jew first and also to the Greek. For in it the righteousness of God is revealed from faith for faith, as it is written, 'The righteous shall live by faith.'" Paul articulates the gospel in three distinct ways calling it the "gospel of God" (Rom. 15:16 NIV), "the gospel of Christ" (v. 19 NIV), and simply "the gospel" (v. 20 NIV). Paul knew the power of salvation was not in him or any man. The power of salvation is in the gospel made alive in the lives of sinners by the Spirit of God (vv. 16, 19).

Paul's insistence about the power of the gospel raises the question, "What is the gospel?" Mistakenly, the gospel is assumed to be similar to what Mark Twain said about the church: "The church is good people standing in front of good

---

[7] John Piper, *Let the Nations Be Glad: The Supremacy of God in Missions*, 3rd ed. (Grand Rapids: Baker Academic, 2010), 35–36.

[8] Newell, *Expect Great Things,* 135.

[9] Ibid., 201.

people telling them how to be good."[10] This is tragically wrong, and unfortunately many in our churches define the gospel similarly. For years Billy Graham lamented because he believed that on any given Sunday 50 percent of those attending church were lost because of a faulty understanding of the gospel. Several years ago I had the privilege of spending some time with him, during which I asked if he still believed this. Sadly, he said, "No, I think the number is much higher than that."

The question remains, "What is the gospel?" Some helpful contemporary summaries are:

- A Twitter summary: "The gospel is the good news that King Jesus died and paid the full penalty of sin, rose from the dead, and saves all who repent of sin and trust him."
- A clear contrast: "Every religion in the world can be located under one of two words: *do* or *done*. Christianity is a *done* religion; we are saved by what Christ has *done* for us, not by what we *do* to earn salvation.
- A striking declaration: "The gospel is the good news that God killed his Son so he would not have to kill you" (see Isa 53:10).
- A wonderful promise: "The gospel is the good news that the person who has Jesus plus nothing actually has everything." And, "the person who has everything minus Jesus actually has nothing" (see Mark 8:36).

The first four marks that describe the essence of a Great Commission people lay the foundation for our missiological efforts: (1) keeping our focus on the most important call of taking the gospel to other *ethnēs*; (2) maintaining an awareness that participation in God's mission is worship; (3) maintaining a Christ-centered disposition; and (4) understanding the nature and centrality of the gospel. Upholding these marks leads us to explore the breadth of God's mission.

BREADTH OF THE GREAT COMMISSION TASK

The fifth mark of a Great Commission people is *being consumed with the gospel's reaching those who have never heard the name of Jesus* (vv. 20–24). Paul's plea is found in Christ's final words in Matthew 28:19 (ESV), "Go, therefore, and make disciples of all nations, baptizing them in the name of the Father and of the Son and of the Holy Spirit." It is common for well-meaning believers to say that "the light that shines farthest shines brightest at home," "missions begins with our Jerusalem and then moves to the ends of the earth," or "people are just as lost in Arkansas, Oklahoma, and Louisiana as they are in Algeria, Oman, and Laos." Although these statements are well intended, they reveal a fundamental

---

[10] Quoted in Jerry Rankin and Ed Stetzer, *Spiritual Warfare and Missions: The Battle for God's Glory Among the Nations* (Nashville, TN: B&H, 2010), 216.

misunderstanding of the breadth of God's mission both theologically and missiologically. Missiologically, the issue is not lostness but rather access to the gospel. Theologically, this belief misreads the strategy of the apostle Paul and the methodology laid out in Acts 1:8.

Paul says that he fulfilled his gospel ministry from Jerusalem to Illyricum (modern Albania) (v. 19) and that it is his ambition to preach the gospel where the name of Jesus is unknown (fulfilling the prophecy of Isa 52:15) (v. 20). Then Paul boldly declared his intent to head to Spain, simply passing through Rome on the way stating, "I no longer have any room for work in these regions" (Rom 15:23–24 ESV).

Paul's statement raises the questions, "Are you saying everyone who needs to hear the gospel in these areas has heard?" or "Are you saying all the churches that need to be planted in these areas have been planted?" Paul would certainly respond negatively to both questions. Paul argues that because a gospel witness is already present in these places and there are locations that exist with no gospel witness, he is consumed with getting the good news to the places where the name of Christ is not known. The breadth of God's mission demands Paul's passion to become our passion.

The sixth mark of a Great Commission people emphasizes the breadth of service among God's people in that *each person does his or her part to see the mission completed* (v. 24). Paul insists that every believer is called to leverage his or her resources and talents for God's purposes. Charles Spurgeon said, "Every Christian . . . is either a missionary or an imposter."[11] Wrongly understood, this statement can send us on a spiritual guilt trip, but rightly understood it is liberating. Paul knew that every person will not go to the nations, but every believer is called to do his part to see the gospel advance to the far reaches of the earth. Getting church planters, evangelists, and missionaries to underserved areas and unreached peoples is the responsibility of every Southern Baptist—no exceptions.

Paul's desire was to take the gospel to Spain because they had never heard the name of Jesus, but he needed resources to do so. He called upon the church in Rome to do what William Carey asked of British Baptists in 1792, to "hold the rope."[12] In Romans 15:24 Paul requests financial resources to see his missionary work continue. In recent years cuts to the International Mission Board personnel have forced Southern Baptists to rethink how effectively we are "holding the ropes." At Southeastern Seminary alone, we ended last year with many qualified individuals who applied to give their lives to global missions but whom we could

---

[11] Charles Spurgeon, "A Sermon and a Reminiscence: A Short Sermon by C. H. Spurgeon from the March 1873 Sword and Trowel," *The Spurgeon Archive.* Accessed December 10, 2015. http://www.romans45.org/spurgeon/s_and_t/srmn1873.htm.

[12] Andrew Gunton Fuller, "Memoir," in *The Complete Works of the Rev. Andrew Fuller, with a Memoir of His Life by Andrew Gunton Fuller*, ed. Joseph Belcher (Harrisonburg, VA: Sprinkle, 1988), 1:68.

not resource and send. Here is the simple truth: apart from revival in the church, the pool of people willing to be sent and the pool of people willing to send them is insufficient and shrinking. Participation in God's mission involves sacrificially giving of our financial resources but also of our gifts, talents, and vocational and technical skills to advance the gospel to the *ethnē*.

DEPTH OF GOSPEL PARTNERSHIPS

The breadth of the Great Commission features the proclamation of the gospel to the ends of the earth (fifth mark) and the inclusion of every believer in the task (sixth mark). The depth of the mission is characteristic of the relational ties among believers (of every *ethnē*) in God's mission. The people of God are comprised of several types of diversity, including race, nationality, age, gender, marital status, and stage of life. Depth in the body of Christ implies that God's people should not simply *look* diverse but actually *be* diverse by embodying the Christ-exalting unity and diversity that is indicative of his kingdom.

In the twenty-first century the church has an opportunity to take the lead in the area of racial reconciliation because God grants true unity and that unity is expressed most clearly through his mission. Biblical unity is distinct from secular ideas about producing equality because Scripture assumes diversity within a shared humanity in Christ. It is a unity bound together by blood, namely the blood of Jesus. Out of this unity we participate in God's mission. In essence, genuine unity and diversity are only a possibility within the people of God because only here can we find relational depth that extends beyond superficial commonalities. Again, this unity in diversity is made possible by the blood of Christ that creates "one new humanity" (Eph 2:15 NIV).

The significance of God's people pursuing the Great Commission together is often overlooked. If the gospel is true, then evidence of restoration should be most tangible among the redeemed. The community of faith displays the reconciling spirit of the gospel as an indispensable characteristic and testimony to its power. Missional efforts that demonstrate the diverse tapestry of the kingdom are often effective because the people embody the "one another" mentality required to live one to another across the lines of difference. Those same characteristics are employed to beckon the lost to enter into the people of God. Ultimately, racial reconciliation, especially among Christians from every kindred, tongue, and tribe, is a gospel issue.

Genuine gospel partnerships in God's mission assume a type of equity that is elusive in the broader culture. In fact, it is unfortunately rare in the church as well. Scripture calls believers to assist in maturing one another in the faith in the context of authentic equitable partnerships that develop among God's people. In Romans 15 Paul declared that his "purpose is that the offering of the Gentiles [nations] may be acceptable, sanctified by the Holy Spirit" (v. 16 HCSB). Moreover, Paul desired to make the Gentiles obedient to God's call in both word and deed (v. 18). Similarly, Christ reminds his people to "teach others to observe everything I have command you" (Matt 28:20 ESV). The result of both our Lord's command and Paul's pursuit is that brothers and sisters of every *ethnē* become mature in Christ and become genuine partners in proclaiming the gospel of the kingdom.

BARRIERS TO GENUINE GOSPEL PARTNERSHIPS

From its inception the Southern Baptist Convention has been a missionary people that began to cooperate in an effort to reach the nations with the gospel of Jesus Christ. Like many other strengths, our passionate pursuit of the Great Commission is accompanied by unintended consequences that could hinder genuine gospel partnerships from developing. In a real sense Southern Baptists have, in pursuit of obedience, proclaimed the gospel around the globe and as a result have assumed a position of prominence in gospel partnerships, especially when ministering with minority Christians. Although there have been a number of positive developments to involve minority Southern Baptists, equitable gospel partnerships are not the norm stateside or abroad.

Believers seeking to cultivate genuine gospel partnerships should avoid four impediments that stifle authentic unity. First, Christians must identify other believers not as "projects" but as full partners in ministry. It is doubtful that Southern Baptists intentionally carry this disposition, but the social and economic power the majority culture has retained in American contains an inherent "hero" disposition. This trait creates two classes among God's people: the helper/helped and the privileged/underprivileged. Paul never envisioned anything like this in the church.

The helper/helped dynamic is an unhealthy idea believers may have unconsciously assimilated from an American history rife with the "white good/black deviant" dualism. "Black" in this instance transcends the African-American distinction and extends to all minority peoples in America. A divide that demarcates the perpetual helper and the perpetually helped bears the marks of inherent inequity that the gospel seeks to reverse if not abolish. In this framework the helped remain perpetually voiceless and powerless and are not equitably included in the denomination's pursuit of the Great Commission.

The helper/helped dynamic was not Christ's or Paul's hope for the Gentiles (i.e., the *ethnēs*); rather, they hoped all believers would become mature and able to contribute to the mission of God in a meaningful way as family. This divide among God's people is not only damaging to the helped but also destructive to the helper. Believers who are understood to be the helpers in a gospel partnership are hampered because of an assumption that relationships across the privileged-underprivileged divide are not mutually beneficial. A common symptom of this phenomenon is when affluent Christians take a trip to serve impoverished believers either oceans away or in an urban area and they are astonished upon their return that the "least" had blessed them so powerfully when their intent was to serve them.

It is not wrong for economically privileged Christians to think that underprivileged believers can benefit from the gifts God has given them to steward (Acts 4:32), but it is unbiblical to think those that are helping cannot gain anything from their brothers and sisters who are helped. The apostle Paul affirmed the vulnerable members of the body by saying:

> And the eye cannot say to the hand, "I have no need of you"; or again the head to the feet, "I have no need of you." On the contrary, it is much truer that the members of the body which seem to be weaker are necessary; and those members of the body which we deem less honorable, on these we bestow more abundant honor. (1 Cor 12:21–23 NASB)

The formal study of theology and missiology often reflects a belief that minority Christians are incapable of contributing to the Great Commission efforts of the dominant culture of believers. For example, one can attain a laudable theological education without having read a book or article by a minority scholar. Said differently, among Southern Baptists a dominant-culture Christian can be considered well versed in theology and missiology without having read the works of a person of color. The inverse, however, is unthinkable.

In the spirit of "iron sharpening iron" (Prov 27:17), believers are able to benefit from one another's insights and perspectives as one Spirit-filled body. Providentially, the most acute sharpening occurs along the lines of difference. In Baptist life we have rightly cherished the fruit of diversity with older mentoring younger (Titus 2:1–8) and in marriage as man and woman are satisfied when joined together (Eph 5:22–33). However, Southern Baptists have largely neglected the opportunity of being sharpened across the lines of race or class.

The admonition for dominant-culture Christians is not to elevate the voices of minority Christians to the neglect of the majority but to purge a long-standing bias deeply rooted in our nation's history. In addition, minority Christians in America must not neglect the insights of dominant-culture believers in God's mission just because they are not consistently heard in the collective kingdom effort. God's mission calls the people of God to embody the strengths of the entire body of Christ and leverage its strength toward a unified goal. When writing to the church in Corinth, the apostle Paul expressed the diversity of God's people while maintaining its single purpose using the illustration of the human body:

> For the body is not one member, but many. If the foot says, "Because I am not a hand, I am not a part of the body," it is not for this reason any the less a part of the body. And if the ear says, "Because I am not an eye, I am not a part of the body," it is not for this reason any the less a part of the body. If the whole body were an eye, where would the hearing be? If the whole were hearing, where would the sense of smell be? But now God has placed the members, each one of them, in the body, just as He desired. If they were all one member, where would the body be? But now there are many members, but one body. (1 Cor. 12:14–20 NASB)

A second impediment to cultivating genuine gospel partnerships is tokenism. As a preface, there is a difference between tokenism and the first of an unrepresented group entering a community of believers in hope for more to come. Tokenism is the recruitment of a symbolic minority to give the *appearance* of racial equality and acceptance. Thus, if a single person or one family within your fellowship constitutes a minority, take heart—you are not automatically guilty of tokenism. In order to steer clear of this trap, we offer three manifestations of tokenism found in both majority and minority-majority contexts.

One manifestation of tokenism is the acceptance of specific types of outsiders while rejecting the whole. The "acceptable" among others are those who closely resemble the dominant demographic of a group. This tendency exists because it requires less of the dominant group to accept and accommodate a newcomer. As fallen humans we all have innate biases and preferences we tend toward, but they are only a problem when we normalize our preferences and they become the basis of appropriateness. Another expression of tokenism is giving an underrepresented person a leadership position without the ability to express his or her cultural perspective and affect genuine change. Said differently, this would be giving someone a seat at the table while giving him no influence at the table. A leader can also be a token if he is invited to develop a program alongside the existing structures to accommodate the minority without disrupting the status quo. Each of these scenarios thwarts genuine diversity in exchange for hollow unity.

A final symptom of tokenism is a willingness to invite other cultures in until it requires accommodation and change from the dominant group. In a homogeneous local body, it is easy to believe everyone with good taste has similar preferences because it is true of the group. The assumption becomes that since there are so many like us, there is no need to change. It is similar to inviting someone to live in your home but doing nothing to accommodate him. Welcoming new people into the family of God is reminiscent of welcoming a child home for the first time: there is evidence of the newcomer integrated throughout the entire house. A special place is made for the baby to sleep, at mealtimes the child is given appropriate food, and there are age-appropriate toys for playtime. While the home does not cease being what it was before the child arrived, there is evidence of the child's arrival in every facet of home life because the child is genuinely welcomed into the family. Fostering depth within the people of God requires the same holistic integration as bringing a new family member into the home.

Another impediment to genuine gospel partnerships is relegating minority believers to caucuses within a denomination. In the 1960s caucuses were generated within denominations to support churches and their members who felt alienated within predominantly white denominations. Southern Baptists eventually followed suit. Ethnicity-specific fellowships have served a strategic purpose within denominational life and continue to do so at present. Caucuses provide a space to engage the unique challenges of an underrepresented demographic, generate fellowship among the few who share similar life and church experiences, and offer a safe place to have constructive conversations about denominational policies, practices, and structures.

While these groups are valuable, they must not become the sole location where multicultural leadership is expected within denominational life. Diverse leadership throughout Southern Baptist life is the primary means of ensuring that the ideas and needs of all the constituents, recognized as God's people, undertake the delicate balance of caring for those within the family of God in the pursuit of the Great Commission. Another danger is that minority constituents might allow interaction within a caucus to become the totality of their convention involvement. Although it is a path of less resistance, involvement exclusively in caucus-related activities strips the whole body of being able to live out the "one anothers" of the New Testament and mutes the testimony of Christ's reconciling power among all peoples.

In the end the gospel is about relationships: God the Father orchestrated the redemption of all that was lost in the fall through his Son, Jesus Christ. The cross of Christ brought about the possibility of a restored relationship with God to humanity and reconciled relationships with our brothers and sisters. As a result, God's people must relate to one another rightly to demonstrate the power of the gospel. In our relationships with one another, God's people ought to be a picture of the coming kingdom where every kindred, tongue, and tribe are represented (Revelation 5; 7). The often-used illustration of a melting pot does not fully capture the multifaceted wonder of the kingdom. While it symbolizes the idea of becoming one, it muzzles the wonder of uniqueness, and all distinctions are potentially lost. Others have employed the imagery of a salad bowl to represent the unity and diversity of the kingdom. The tendency with the salad illustration is, despite the integrity of the constituent pieces remaining intact, it too easily drenches the salad in ranch dressing so that everything tastes the same.

Derick Hicks of Wake Forest Divinity School delivered an excellent lecture on the campus of Southeastern Seminary in the fall of 2014 titled "Christian Community as a Complex Brew." Dr. Hicks explained how the complex brew of gumbo should mirror the people of God. He explained that gumbo is not a tidy dish but is an assortment of flavors and colors that oddly come together and create a glorious taste. Unlike the melting pot, gumbo represents the colorful expressions of given communities and does not disguise the robustness of the elements. Gumbo is not only profound unto itself; Hicks stressed that it must be shared because in its essence the dish exudes a posture of fellowship and cooperation.

Hicks shared, "You can't make gumbo without sharing it with a whole lot of folks."[13] When people come together over gumbo, ideas are swapped, traditions uncovered and created, songs are sung, and friendship bonds are formed. In a real sense, when the people of God display deep relational bonds, they simultaneously embrace and transcend the different tribes that comprise God's people. The depth of these bonds assumes a Christlike disposition that bleeds an ethos that naturally pursues and welcomes the lost into the fold.

Genuine gospel partnerships not only have depth; they also affirm the biblical testimony that the gospel has the power that can synchronously unite believers to Christ and to one another (Ephesians 2). Such partnerships also assist in the practice of gospel ministry because blind spots are eliminated when people of a variety of backgrounds are on the same mission together. Genuine gospel partnerships are also theologically illuminating, as diverse voices of the redeemed sing the song of redemption to the ends of the earth. Such unity is a profound mystery to a watching world, and that is the best type of attractional ministry.

In an article for Life Action ministries, Tom Elliff, former president of the IMB, expressed the dire need for God to send revival in order to "get the job done." He said:

> So what is the answer? It's for God's people to respond to the Great Commission. It is here that we find the utter necessity of revival. During periods of revival, there is a resurgence of interest in missions, and willingness to commit a lifetime to mission service. Every great missions movement in Christian history was born out of some type of spiritual awakening among believers.
>
> Today, we see evidence that God is stirring hearts. A new generation has interest in going to the ends of the earth, giving their lives to reach the most remote corners of the world. *But the sad fact that is so distressing to me is that there are now far more people who are willing to go than there are resources being made available to send them.* God must stir not only those willing to go, but also the hearts of those who will help them go financially, as well as the hearts of moms and dads who will let them go, and the passions of people who will pray for those who are going. . . . Only the Holy Spirit can stir up the supply needed in our churches to meet these great needs. . . .

---

[13] Derek Hicks, "Christian Community as a Complex Brew" (lecture, Southeastern Baptist Theological Seminary chapel, Wake Forest, NC, November 4, 2014.)

What a tragedy it would be if we lost our opportunity to play a significant role in God's plan to save! How tragic to forfeit such vast opportunity because of our unwillingness to surrender to the lordship of Christ.[14]

These are sobering words we all must consider. All of us! Each of us together!

CONCLUSION

Just before former SBC president Adrian Rogers died, he shared a concern that Southern Baptists had become distracted and even divisive over petty and nonimportant issues. When asked what the problem was, as he saw it, he used a striking analogy we must never forget. He said that during the Conservative Resurgence those who believed the Bible is the infallible and inerrant Word of God were on the battlefield shoulder to shoulder fighting a common enemy. After winning the battle, inerrantists retreated to the barracks and are no longer shoulder to shoulder but face-to-face. Since we are used to fighting, but are no longer fighting the enemy, we are fighting one another. We have turned our brothers and sisters into our enemies in the midst of our missional calling.

He went on to say that what Southern Baptists need to do is get out of the barracks and back on the battlefield where the real enemies are, the real enemies of sin, Satan, death, and hell. Dr. Rogers was right: our real enemies are not Calvinists or traditionalists, those with different worship styles or dress codes, those who prefer the name "Southern Baptist" or "Great Commission Baptists." No, our real enemies are sin, Satan, death, and hell. Southern Baptists as a diverse family from every tribe, tongue, people, and nation must be Great Commission Baptists taking the battlefield under the bloodstained banner of a crucified and resurrected King whose marching orders are clear and whose promise to be with us as we go is certain. Once more we must declare war on the evil, Satanic empire whose doom is certain, answering the call to arms of the Captain of our salvation.

The Great Commission is not an option to be considered. It is a "war-time gospel command" to be obeyed. By his grace and for his glory alone, Southern Baptists must be an obedient people. Our prayer is that Southern Baptists will be Great Commission Baptists demonstrating the proper breadth and depth of the call until the day we see coming from heaven a rider on a white horse! Then and only then will we know our mission is over.

---

[14] Tom Elliff, "Getting the Job Done," *Life Action*, November 10, 2015. Accessed February 24, 2016. http://lifeaction.org/getting-the-job-done. Emphasis is his.

Preach the Word! Biblical Preaching and Congregational Renewal

Tony Merida

B art Ehrman serves as a religious studies professor at UNC Chapel Hill. Although he teaches the New Testament, he does not believe it is actually God's Word. In fact, as a professing agnostic, Ehrman is known for debating evangelicals about the inspiration of Scripture. Every semester he begins one of his courses with a class exercise.[1] He begins, "How many of you believe the Bible is the inspired Word of God?" According to Professor Ehrman, the majority of students at UNC raise their hands. Then he asks, "How many of you have read [and he will select a popular novel] . . . *The Hunger Games* by Suzanne Collins?" Usually every hand goes up across the room, with only a few exceptions. Ehrman follows with a third question, "How many of you have read the entire Bible?" And virtually no one raises his hand. Then comes Ehrman's punch. He inquires, "Now I can understand why you would read Collins's book. It's entertaining. But, *if you really believed God wrote a book, then wouldn't you want to read it?*"

Ehrman exposes a major problem. He highlights how those raised in a culturally Christian setting have some major inconsistencies with what they *say* and with what they *do*.

We show what we believe about the Bible by how we use the Bible—not merely by what we *say* about the Bible. When it comes to preaching, we show what we believe about the Bible by how we use the Bible in *the pulpit*. A high view of the Bible should lead to substantive, biblical preaching. Paul moves from the doctrine of the inspiration of Scripture in 2 Timothy 3:16–17 (ESV) to the

---

[1] I have heard Ehrman use this illustration in public debates. I have also had seminary students tell me about being in Ehrman's class and participating in this exercise personally.

command to preach it in 2 Timothy 4:1. It is a natural transition. If God wrote a book, then should you not want to preach it?

Strangely, many preachers today affirm the inspiration of Scripture, waving it in the air, claiming that the Bible is "infallible, inerrant, inspired" (and other "I" words!), but for whatever reason, they fail to deliver Word-driven, Bible-saturated, expositional messages. What's more, others in the Christian community downplay the importance of weekly, Bible-saturated, pastoral preaching altogether. They seem to have adopted the culture's negative view of preaching.

PASTOR, DO NOT PREACH

Modern-day people have an increasingly negative vibe when hearing or talking about "preaching." Madonna used to sing "Papa Don't Preach," and today many are now saying, "Pastor, do not preach." Church inviter cards say things like, "Come to our worship service. Our pastor won't *preach* to you." The pastor is viewed as a speaker, a storyteller, or an advice giver, but not a preacher.

This spirit reflects a larger desire to keep Christianity from being so "strange" in the eyes of culture. But it will not work. Christianity is strange. Look at how Paul was viewed in the book of Acts (e.g., Acts 26). Look at how Paul talked about preaching in 1 Corinthians 2:1–5. It is a strange method, a strange message, and a strange man delivering the message.

An additional reason for this negative vibe concerns the definition of preaching itself. People associate preaching with yelling, agitating others, ranting, or shouting moral "dos and do nots." But furious moralizing is not preaching, and personal ranting is not preaching. One can rant about anything. One can yell and throw a fit about anything. What makes preaching "preaching" is the gospel *message*. Preaching is bound up with the announcement of the good news. Preaching is explaining what God has said in his Word and declaring what God has done in his Son and applying this message to the hearts of people. One may or may not yell, pace, or pound a pulpit in announcing the gospel. The Lord has used all sorts of styles and temperaments throughout history to proclaim his Word.

Further, some in the culture react negatively to preaching because of the overall antiauthority mood of the day. But this mood is not new. Just read the opening pages of Genesis. We must remember that our authority as preachers is a derived authority. Our authority comes from God's Word, and if we are heralding his Word, then we should not shy away from preaching.

Finally, some have a negative view of preaching because they have never heard good preaching. Sadly there is a great display of *mediocrity* in pulpits. Outsiders often view preachers as being boring (or fanatical), out of step with culture, and unaware of people's questions and worldviews. But in advocating biblical preaching, I am not advocating poor preaching. I am not advocating dry preaching. I am not advocating insensitivity to people nor being culturally ignorant. Good preaching takes truth to struggle. Good preaching shows an awareness of competing worldviews and cultural issues; it contextualizes the message to a given audience. It establishes points of contact with people and then makes points of conflict with people as a Christ-centered worldview is proclaimed and explained.

A RENEWED VISION OF PREACHING

What is more troubling than the popular opinion of the day is that many seminary students are pessimistic about the word *preaching*. When asking classes, "How many of you want to preach weekly in a local church?" the numbers are usually low. When I was in seminary, professors would try to talk guys *out of preaching*, but now we are trying to talk them *into preaching!*

Now I understand the term *preaching* can be used in a variety of contexts. Sidney Greidanus points out that the New Testament uses "as many as thirty-three different verbs to describe what we usually cover with the single word *preaching*."[2] Indeed, there is a wide array of ways to make disciples by expounding the Scriptures—in villages, in coffee shops, in classes, in homes, in the marketplace, etc. (see Acts 8:4). I get it. I promote it. Many who are making disciples as campus ministers, village evangelists, or marketplace ministers are heroes. I am not discounting these ministries at all. What's more, I think pastors should make disciples in these types of contexts from time to time as well. But still, pastors of churches should value and treasure the opportunity to *preach* the Word weekly in the context of the corporate assembly of the local church (1 Tim 4:13 ESV). And at this point we find many students shirking back not merely from preaching but from the *pastorate* and the *local church*. Many do not have a high view of the church, and they do not aspire to pastor.

While I certainly do not want to push the wrong guys into the pastorate, I do want to encourage those who aspire to pastoral preaching to own it and be devoted to it. We are in desperate need of a new generation of preachers who are passionate about preaching the gospel. The late British preacher Martin Lloyd-Jones said: "What is it that always heralds the dawn of a Reformation or of a Revival? It is renewed preaching. Not only a new interest in preaching but a new kind of preaching."[3] We need to raise up millions of faithful, Christ-centered, people-loving expositors that expound the Word with accuracy and freshness, not ten more sensational conference speakers who say the same things at different events.

How might this happen? We must reaffirm our belief in the power of the preached Word. There seems to be a real absence of this belief. How many church conferences have you attended where little to nothing was said about preaching?

---

[2] Sidney Greidanus, *The Modern Preacher and the Ancient Text* (Grand Rapids: Eerdmans, 1988), 6.
[3] D. Martyn Lloyd Jones, *Preaching and Preachers*, 40th anniversary edition (Grand Rapids: Zondervan, 2011), 31

Recently at a major church planting conference, with thousands in attendance, there was one breakout session on preaching. One! Might I suggest the need to emphasize preaching if you are emphasizing church planting?

Next, we must pray for the Lord of the Word, Lord of the cosmos, and Lord of the church to grant this movement. A renewal of preaching comes from the work of the Spirit.

Additionally, we would also do well to remember the sagely advice from William Perkins's classic work *The Calling of the Ministry*. The old Puritan lamented the "scarcity of true ministers," saying that "good ministers are one in a thousand."[4] He encouraged Christians to realize the importance of good schools and seminaries in order to help raise up competent pastors. Then he said something even more striking. He put the burden on pastors. He said: "Let each minister both in his teaching and his conversation work in such a way that he honors his calling, *so that he may attract others to share his love for it.*"[5] In other words, to attract others to pastoral preaching, we must not settle for *mediocrity* in the pulpit and in the pastorate. We must inspire, emphasize, exemplify, and instruct people in the skill of engaging pastoral preaching.

So I would like to turn your attention to Paul's words to Timothy. We should remember that the best book on preaching the Bible is *the Bible!* John Stott rightly points out, "The secret to effective preaching is not mastering certain techniques; it's being mastered by certain convictions."[6] The Scriptures give us the central convictions we must have to develop and maintain a faithful and effective ministry of the Word.

CONTINUE IN THE WORD OF CHRIST AND
CHERISH THE CHRIST OF THE WORD

Timothy found himself in a situation like ours. Many are misguided. Many reject the claims of Scripture. Many scoff at miracles. Many hate our view of the exclusivity of the gospel. Many laugh at, or are outraged by, our view of marriage. Yet Paul does not tell Timothy to give up on preaching. Paul urges Timothy to "be different" ("But as for you," 2 Tim 3:10; 4:5 HCSB). He urges him to preach the word of truth in a truthless world. Before making this charge, he reminds Timothy to continue learning and loving the inspired Scriptures:

> But as for you, continue in what you have learned and have firmly believed, knowing from whom you learned it and how from childhood you have been acquainted with the sacred writings, which are able to make you wise for salvation

---

[4] William Perkins, *The Art of Prophesying and The Calling of the Ministry*, reprint (Carlisle: The Banner of Truth, 2002), 96.

[5] Ibid., emphasis added.

[6] John Stott, *Between Two Worlds* (Grand Rapids, Eerdmans, 1982), 92.

through faith in Christ Jesus. All Scripture is breathed out by God and profitable for teaching, for reproof, for correction, and for training in righteousness, that the man of God may be complete, equipped for every good work. (2 Tim 3:14–17 ESV)

Timothy had learned "the sacred writings" from "childhood" (v. 15). Both his grandmother Lois and his mother Eunice taught him from his early days (1:5). He also learned from the apostle Paul (e.g., 1:13; 2:2). Now he is charged to keep on learning God's Word and living in God's Word.[7]

I came to faith in college. The Lord used a few teammates to lead me to Jesus. Before then I hated reading, and I had a reading problem. I had to get a tutor in college because I scored so poorly on reading exams. But when Jesus changed my life, he changed my interests, affections, and eventually my capacity to retain information. He made me a student of the Scriptures. As a newly converted sophomore in college, I knew nothing about the Bible. I remember attending Bible studies and asking dumb questions. The leader would ask things like, "What's your favorite verse of the Bible?" But I did not have any verses! (I loved the maps!) But over time the Bible came alive inside of me. I wrote on the margins of my massive study Bible, "It's alive!" Then I went to seminary. They told me, "You need to read books!" And so I did. Now, as a nearly forty-year-old pastor, I still need to continue learning the Bible. By God's grace, on my dying bed I want to say like Paul, "Bring . . . the books" (2 Tim 4:13 ESV).

Do not ever stop meditating on the Scriptures. Make sure the Word is driving you to preach rather than preaching driving you to the Word. The Word must pass through us before it passes from us. Resist becoming "The Sermonator," mechanically churning out sermons instead of daily meeting with Christ in his Word first.

Notice something else in verse 14. Paul says, "Continue in what you have firmly *believed*" (emphasis added). He tells Timothy to be thoroughly convinced of the claims of Scripture. Timothy had become convinced of the truth of God's Word, and now Paul urges Timothy to continue trusting in God's powerful Word.

Do not adjust the Bible; trust the Bible. Regularly remind yourself of why you need the Bible. Continue believing that you need it. Paul tells Timothy three reasons he should continue seeking God's Word.

Because It Leads Us to Jesus

When Paul speaks of the "sacred writings," he is referring to what we call the Old Testament. Paul adds that these Scriptures are "able to make you wise for salvation through faith in Christ Jesus" (2 Tim 3:15 ESV). In other words, the Old

---

[7] Aspects of this exposition can be found in my commentary on 2 Timothy. See Tony Merida, *Christ-Centered Exposition Commentary: Exalting Jesus in 1 & 2 Timothy and Titus* (Nashville: B&H, 2013), 195–207.

Testament points us to Jesus. Read the Bible with this fact in mind. D. A. Carson says, "The entire Bible pivots on one weekend in Jerusalem about two thousand years ago."[8]

The Bible is a book that leads us to Christ. Some are amazed that you could use the Old Testament to lead someone to Christ. But you can! Ask the Ethiopian Eunuch (Acts 8:26–40). The Bible does not tell us everything we *want* to know, but it does tell us everything we *need* to know. It is a book about redemption, of which Jesus is the Hero.

The apostles did pretty well with the Old Testament. Paul did not pass out "Four Spiritual Laws" or "Steps to Peace with God" tracts (as helpful as these may be), but instead he opened up the Scriptures and pointed people to the Messiah (see Acts 13:13–43; 17:2–3; 18:5; 26:22; 28:23; 1 Cor 15:3–4). From Genesis to Revelation, the Bible is a Christian book. God made no mistake in giving us a whole Bible, not just a New Testament. The whole Bible is pointing us to our Redeemer (cf., John 5:39, 46; Luke 24:27, 44). Even the best of men in the Bible fail. The narrative is pointing us to an all-sufficient Prophet, Priest, King, and Sage who never failed. Or, as Homer Simpson once said, "All these people are a mess . . . except this One guy."[9]

Therefore, personally study to see Christ. Rest in and delight in the Messiah. Pastorally, walk the bride down the aisle to Jesus. Make the Hero of the Bible the Hero of your sermons (see Col 1:28).

Because God Speaks to Us from It

Paul states that the Scriptures are inspired or "breathed out" (*theopneustos*) by God (2 Tim 3:16 ESV). Paul does not mean the Bible is "inspired" like an artist or an athlete is "inspired." Many things are "inspiring," but the Bible is "inspired." A better translation may be "expired." God breathed out his Word. We should remember that when we seek God's Word, it's not only that God *was* speaking but that he also *is* speaking to us. When you open the Word of God you in a sense open the mouth of God! We should seek the Scriptures because we want to hear God speak.

Paul also affirms the *total* inspiration of Scripture saying that God breathed out "all Scripture." All of it is important—even Leviticus!

It is trendy today to say, "I'm into Jesus, but I don't like the Bible." But that will not work. When you submit to the lordship of Jesus, you must submit to Jesus's view of the Bible. Jesus quoted Scripture frequently, claiming it was divine and authoritative. He said many powerful truths about Scripture: "Man shall not

---

[8] D. A. Carson, *Scandalous* (Wheaton: Crossway, 2010), 11.

[9] As quoted by Matt Chandler, "God Hears and Responds," *Village Church*, January 16, 2011. Accessed February 25, 2016. http://www.thevillagechurch.net/media/sermons/transcripts/201101161115FMWC21ASA-AA_MattChandler_HabakkukPt2-GodHearsAndResponds.pdf.

live by bread alone; but by every word that comes from the mouth of God" (Matt 4:4 ESV); and "Heaven and earth will pass away, but my words will not pass away" (Matt 24:35 ESV). Jesus also affirmed the authority of the Old Testament by his own use of it. And, as already mentioned, he taught that he was the fulfillment of it (Luke 24:44). Jesus told his disciples not only to avoid being ashamed of him but also to avoid being "ashamed of [his] words" (Mark 8:38 ESV). The fact is, you cannot have Jesus without his words. Try that with your spouse. "I like you, honey, but I don't want you to talk." It will not go so well. You cannot have anyone without his or her words.

In every age the nature of Scripture is questioned. Like Timothy, we must continue learning and believing in the God-breathed nature of the Bible and say with the psalmist, "My heart stands in awe of your words" (Ps 119:161 ESV).

Because God Matures Us by It

Paul has already told us that the Bible is profitable for making us wise for salvation (2 Tim 3:15). But then he adds that it is profitable "for teaching, for reproof, for correction, and for training in righteousness" (v. 16 ESV). The Bible shapes our beliefs as well as our lifestyle. It relates to both doctrine and conduct, and it's *totally sufficient* to shape us into the image of Christ by the power of the Spirit.

Paul adds to his point on the sufficiency of Scripture, saying, "That the man of God may be competent, equipped for every good work" (v. 17 ESV). Scripture is also profitable for *equipping us*. Stott says, "Scripture is the chief means which God employs to bring 'the man of God' to maturity."[10] The Bible grows us personally as we mediate on it, as we behold the glory of Christ in it (2 Cor 3:18).

We need to hear this call to personal, Word-driven *godliness*. It is a righteousness formed by the Word, enabled by the Spirit, focused on the Son. If we do not pursue godliness, then we will not have a ministry. I know a number of guys who are no longer in ministry because they failed to follow this fundamental challenge of continuing in the Scriptures personally and seeking God's power and grace desperately. They were gifted men. They were dynamic leaders. But it does not matter if you cannot keep your pants on; it does not matter if you love money more than people; it does not matter if you do not treasure the glory of God more than the praise of people; it does not matter if you do not delight in God more than power, success, and earthly pleasures.

We must pursue a Word-driven life of godliness not only to be faithful to God and his calling but also in order to make up for our deficiencies. Most pastors have flaws. How do you make up for your weaknesses? While you can hire people to help you, one way to make up for your lack of great ability in the pulpit is by living a godly life. If you are pursuing holiness and you are trying to expound the

---

[10] John Stott, *The Message of 2 Timothy* (Downers Grove: InterVarsity, 1973), 103.

Bible faithfully and lifting up Jesus more than yourself, then people will be blessed by your ministry, even if your sermon delivery is not that polished. People will listen to godly pastors who simply want to bless the congregation by feeding them God's Word. Some of the best preachers I know are not dynamic in delivery. They simply exposit the text faithfully, and they have a contagious walk with Jesus.

In Acts 6:4 the apostles give the pattern of devoting "ourselves to prayer and to the ministry of the word" (ESV). It seems simple and straightforward. Yet it is easy to do a full week of ministry and look back and realize that you have not prayed all week. One can have a full calendar, stay busy, and then on Saturday evening stop and realize that you have not personally mediated on God's Word all week. Let us not attempt to the do the work of the ministry of the Word without being changed personally by the Word. Embrace the utter necessity of a godly life—a praying life—fueled and formed by the sufficient Scriptures.

This charge to continue learning, trusting, and believing the Christ-centered, God-breathed, totally sufficient Scriptures is followed with the charge to preach this life-changing Word.

PREACH THE WORD!

When I was serving as the dean of the chapel at New Orleans Baptist Theological Seminary, President Chuck Kelley gave me a wonderful little gift called a Torah Pointer. On the end of this little ink-pen-looking instrument is a little index finger. In Jewish settings these instruments are used in the reading of the Torah as a sign of respect and carefulness. Dr. Kelley gave me this gift before the audience saying, "Keep your finger on the text when you preach." I keep this little pointer on my desk as a reminder of this task. As I preach, I must be sure I am deriving my points and applications from the text of Scripture. I must not only preach. I must preach *the Word*. Paul charges Timothy with these classic words:

> I charge you in the presence of God and of Christ Jesus, who is to judge the living and the dead, and by his appearing and his kingdom: preach the word; be ready in season and out of season; reprove, rebuke, and exhort, with complete patience and teaching. For the time is coming when people will not endure sound teaching, but having itching ears they will accumulate for themselves teachers to suit their own passions, and will turn away from listening to the truth and wander off into myths. (2 Tim 4:1–4 ESV)

Other religions have preachers. Other religions have missionaries. What makes our task unique is *what* we preach: the Word. Paul tells Timothy to preach it faithfully, consistently, pastorally, patiently, and theologically.

Preach the Word Faithfully (2 Tim 4:1–2a)

Why should we be concerned with faithfulness to God? This opening verse tells us. We preach in the presence of God and Christ Jesus, who is the Judge of the living and the dead, who is coming back to set up his kingdom! We must, then, take the task of preaching seriously. While preaching is certainly a joy, it is also something that should make us tremble (see Jas 3:1; Heb 13:17).

This stunning introduction to preach the Word gives us a much-needed God-centered, Christ-exalting motivation for preaching. We preach in the sight of God. We are never unnoticed by God. We might be unknown by people. So be it. But God is present when we preach.

On one occasion I was scheduled to speak at an orphan-care event. The event was designed to shed some light on the theological motivations that undergird care for the fatherless and also provide practical resources and help to those considering various aspects of orphan care. Many testimonies were shared at the conference, and one was from Noel Piper, the wife of one of my preaching heroes, John Piper. She was sharing about their adoption story, and I was supposed to follow her by expounding Romans 8. When I heard the lineup at this conference, my immediate thought was, *I wonder if John Piper will be there to hear my exposition of Romans 8?* Then I realized how pathetic this question was. Who cares who is present when we open up God's Word! God is present! We must work hard in preparation, as unto the Lord, and preach for the glory of the Lord!

Consider a story about John Broadus—the massively influential preaching professor at The Southern Baptist Theological Seminary. In 1865 the school had only a handful of students. Broadus had only one student in his preaching class—a blind student, Mr. Lunn. The student could not benefit from a written text on homiletics, so Broadus developed more detailed notes than normal. Broadus wrote to his wife saying, "Really, it is right dull to deliver my most elaborate lectures in homiletics to one man, and that a blind man."[11] Yet the Lord used Broadus's faithful labor. From the lectures in this course, Broadus laid the foundation for one of the most influential books ever written on preaching, still used today (though revised), *On the Preparation and Delivery of Sermons.*[12] Whether we preach and teach to 1,000 or one, we should always labor faithfully for the glory of God.

In verse 2 Paul says, "Preach the word." To "preach" means "to herald" or "to proclaim publically" (cf. 1:11). As preachers we herald the news. For us today this means the entire written Word of God. Throughout this section Paul uses various phrases to talk about the truth of God's Word, such as "sacred writings" (3:15),

---

[11] Cited in Thomas J. Nettles, *James Petigru Boyce: A Southern Baptist Statesman* (Phillipsburg, NJ: P&R, 2009), 219.
[12] Ibid.

"Scripture" (3:16), "sound teaching" (4:3), and "the truth" (4:4). We have the holy responsibility and unspeakable privilege of heralding God's timeless truth to people. Like Ezra let us study it, obey it, and teach it (Ezra 7:10; Nehemiah 8). Paul told Timothy earlier, "Until I come, devote yourself to the public reading of *Scripture*, to exhortation, to teaching" (1 Tim 4:13 ESV, emphasis added).

When the Word of God is truly preached, the voice of God is really heard. Our job is not to provide new revelation but to repeat God's revelation in Scripture so people may hear God speak. In the words of J. I. Packer, preaching involves "letting texts talk."[13]

If we are committed to letting texts talk, then we must avoid ranting. Old school ranting involved lifting a phrase or a word out of the text and then building a sermon on that idea. Often it contained good content, but it was not rooted in context. New school ranting happens when you take a text, explain a bit of it, and then bounce out of the text to do twenty minutes of application on a subject that is not really related to the text. I have watched guys preach a sermon on John the Baptist and go on a thirty-minute rant about "manhood." While I believe we must teach biblical manhood (and there is certainly a need to teach it today), we need to make sure our application is established in the text. Otherwise, we fall prey to what Haddon Robinson called "the heresy of application."[14]

To put it in my mentor's words, there's a difference between "good stuff" and "God stuff."[15] These rants might contain some good stuff, but what we have been called to deliver is "God stuff," that is, biblical truth. Let us be more than just good speakers on biblical topics; let us be committed expositors of God's Holy Word.

Preach the Word Consistently (2 Tim 4:2b)

Next, Timothy is told to persist in his faithfulness to God's Word and to "be ready in season and out of season" (v. 2). This charge speaks of urgency and readiness.

Pastors are human, and we will not always feel like "bringing it." But we must remember that the power of our sermon does not lie within us. Powerful preaching happens when the Spirit and the Word work to change lives. Martin Luther described how the Word did the work during the Reformation saying, "I simply taught, preached, wrote God's Word; otherwise I did nothing. . . . I did nothing; the Word did it all. . . . I did nothing; I left it to the Word. . . . But it brings him

---

[13] J. I. Packer, *Engaging the Written Word of God* (Peabody, MA: Hendrickson, 2012), 246.

[14] Haddon Robinson, "The Heresy of Application," *Leadership* (1997): 21.

[15] Jim Shaddix, *The Passion Driven Sermon* (Nashville: B&H, 2003), 65.

[Satan] distress when we only spread the Word, and let it alone do the work."[16] Preach the Word faithfully, and believe that it will do the work.

At times preaching can feel like a hopeless exercise. But we must trust God on this matter. In Acts 19:10 we read that Paul taught daily for two years in the Hall of Tyrannus. What good could come from a little guy pointing people to Jesus from the Scriptures in the powerful city of Ephesus? Read Acts 19–20 and you decide! The gospel changed the lives of people across Asia, and it changes lives today. God has always used the passionate preaching of the Word to stimulate spiritual awakening. John Calvin preached once each day of the week and twice on Sunday during the Genevan Reformation.[17] Through the Spirit-empowered, consistent preaching of God's Word through the reformer, the city was transformed.

Preach the Word Pastorally (2 Tim 4:2c)

The pastor-preacher should apply the Word to the lives of his flock in a variety of ways. Paul gives us three ways of doing it: "reprove, rebuke, and exhort" (4:2). Pastors should know their sheep by name and by need. They should smell like the sheep (cf. Acts 20:17–35). As they understand the needs of the congregation, they should seek to apply the selected text to these needs. Rebellious sheep need to be *rebuked*. Wayward sheep needs to be *corrected*. Fearful, anxious, burdened sheep need to be encouraged.

I often tell students that no matter how big your church gets, you need to stay involved in people's lives: have them over to your home, spend time with them on Sundays, and do some measure of counseling. You should do this not only to be a good pastor but also to learn how to apply the text. Pastoral preaching is different from preaching on the conference circuit because your hearers are not an "audience." They are "your flock" (and you are under the Chief Shepherd). Your job then is not to wow a crowd with a "homerun" each week but to feed, lead, protect, and guide God's people with God's Word.

Preach the Word Patiently (2 Tim 4:2d)

Here is perhaps the most challenging and encouraging part of this charge. We must preach the Word with "great patience" (4:2 HCSB). I am so glad this phrase is in the Bible. Pastors often feel like they are making little progress in the lives of people. But we must remember that sanctification is a slow process. As C. J. Mahaney once said we should probably adjust our expectations and "be amazed

---

[16] Henry Eyster Jacobs, ed., *Works of Martin Luther* (Philadelphia: A. J. Holman Company and the Castle Press, 1915), 2:399–400.

[17] Sinclair Ferguson, "No Little Disturbance." Accessed September 18, 2015. http://www.monergism.com/content/no-little-disturbance-acts-191-20.

that those who heard you last Sunday come back the next Sunday!"[18] It takes time for people to understand, apply, and grow.

So let us trust in the cumulative effect of biblical preaching. Over time, by God's grace, understanding deepens, change is experienced, and the congregation is renewed. I cannot see a big difference in my kids from one day to the next, but when I look at last year's pictures, I am amazed at how much they've grown! So it is with faithful preaching. We do not always see visible results each week, but eventually growth occurs.

How can we grow in patience as pastor-preachers? Since patience is a fruit of the Spirit, then the simple answer is to walk by the Spirit. Commune with God. Abide in Jesus.

As you spend time in God's presence, in unhindered and unhurried prayer and worship, meditate on God's patience with you! The psalmist says, "The LORD is gracious and merciful, slow to anger and abounding in steadfast love" (Ps 145:8 ESV). A lack of patience with God's people reveals pride and self-righteousness in my own life. So work the gospel deeply into your heart daily. Reflect on God's amazing patience. Then, by his grace, display his fatherly patience to his people.

Preach the Word Theologically (2 Tim 4:2e–4)

Paul also adds that Timothy must proclaim the message "with . . . teaching" (v. 2). Interestingly, one of the most famous verses in the Bible about preaching also calls for "teaching." This is important to note because some want to make too sharp a distinction between preaching and teaching, saying preaching is for evangelism while theological teaching is for the discipleship of believers. This is helpful, but it can be pressed too far.

We need to see how these two pastoral activities work together. Preaching is *heralding* the facts, while teaching is *explaining* the facts. When you say, "The tomb is empty! The throne is occupied!" then you are heralding the news. Teaching must follow these news headlines and explain who Jesus is, why Jesus was crucified and buried, and what it means for him to be the King. In other words, if we want to practice verse 2, then we will do both heralding and explaining throughout the sermon.

We desperately need a generation of preachers who preach the Word theologically. The spirit of our day is not unlike that of the first century. Paul says in the next two verses, "For the time is coming when people will not endure sound teaching, but having itching ears they will accumulate for themselves teachers to suit their own passions" (v. 3 ESV). In their fallen condition people drift from healthy teaching. They wander away into myths. Examples of this reality abound today.

---

[18] C. J. Mahaney, "Ordinary Pastors," T4G 2010, http://t4g.org/media/2010/06/ordinary-pastors-session-ix-3.

FAITHFUL AND EFFECTIVE

My seminary president Danny Akin often says, "*What* you say is more important than *how* you say it; but *how* you say it has never been more important."[19] I agree with this statement completely. We could end the discussion with 2 Timothy 3:14–4:4 because *what* we say is most important. We must preach *the Word*. But allow me just to give a few concluding thoughts about *how we say it*. How can we be both *faithful* and *effective*? How can we reach out without selling out? While this subject deserves another chapter, I will simply conclude with some considerations for further investigation.

First, anticipate biblical cluelessness. We can no longer assume that people share our worldview and perspective. Take some time to state your basic framework before dealing with your text and subject. As you prepare, imagine that a person who never entered a Christian worship service will be present (happens regularly at our congregation). Start from the ground up. Assume people will have different ideas about basic concepts like creation, truth, sin, love, salvation, etc. It is not uncommon for highly educated people to be ignorant about basic biblical beliefs and stories. Prepare for them.

Second, prepare to preach to your old self. This tip may not work great for every pastor, but as a guy who started following Jesus later in life, this helps me tremendously. You do not have to water down anything, but you should back away from your sermon and ask, "Would I have understood what I'm about to preach this week?" The longer you preach, the greater tendency to preach to your peers. But they are not there! I try to consider that roughneck twenty-year-old who has an interest in the Bible but does not know anything about it or that educated skeptic or the Indian student who is sitting in her first worship service ever. You do not have to be simplistic, but you do need to be clear and compelling.

Third, address the unbeliever in the introduction and periodically throughout the message. Tim Keller and Mark Dever have taught me much about this need. Try to get everyone on the bus in the introduction. Do not give the outsiders the impression that your sermon is merely for insiders. Classical expository preaching neglected the outsider until the invitation. Seeker preaching neglected the Bible (in many cases). Attempt to do *evangelistic exposition*. Edify and evangelize throughout the message.

After the introduction, have some asides in your sermon that address the unbeliever. Say things like, "Now, if you are an unbeliever, you might be thinking . . ." and then speak to them. You do not have to spend a ton of time on this, and you do not have to answer all of their questions. But you should work to build a culture in your church that says, "We will speak to unbelievers intelligently and

---

[19] I have heard Dr. Akin say this on many occasions, including our cotaught seminar at Southeastern Baptist Theological Seminary.

respectfully." When you do this, you will find that unbelievers will start showing up. This will happen mainly because the believers will start bringing their unbelieving friends. And you will also be indirectly equipping your people to speak to outsiders.

Fourth, illustrate relevantly and deal with important questions in application. Throw sermon illustration books in the trash. Read widely and get engaged in the community. Your best illustrations (and applications) will come from your daily interactions with people. Coach sports. Volunteer at schools. Talk to neighbors. Participate in local events. Be aware of film and music trends. All of these things (and others) are connected to sermon preparation. You tend to preach to the people you talk to each week. So diversify your people context, and in so doing you will begin to illustrate in ways that engage outsiders and help insiders learn how to engage their communities.

Related to this idea, you may even consider having a Q&A time after your sermon. You can do this in a variety of ways: (1) on the spot after the sermon, (2) at a postsermon luncheon, (3) via text message, or (4) via e-mail. Consider using outsiders' questions as a means of creating an evangelistic culture.

Finally, keep the Life Changer at the heart of the sermon. We will not preach life-changing sermons if the Life Changer is not at the core of every sermon. If we want to see renewal through preaching, then exalt Jesus Christ, the Hero of Scripture each week. Look for the innerbiblical connections that culminate in Jesus and make much of him.

Guard What Is Entrusted to You: Counsel to a New Generation of Southern Baptists

Paige Patterson

While I am indebted to President Jason Allen for the opportunity to contribute to the illustrious symposium at Midwestern Seminary and the accompanying book, I must begin with the confession that I do not like the topic assigned. Tapping a veteran of most SBC wars in anyone's recent memory to address the topic of protecting the deposits of a former generation of Southern Baptists might be thought to imply that a younger generation is impervious to the thesaurus of Baptist principles, or worse, that the speaker is a condescending crank determined to resist the changes that are a part of progress. While I cannot be certain I will avoid those sinkholes, I embark on the task assigned with twelve analogies in the hope that whether you agree or dissent you will at least smile at my pedestrian Texas ways. In no particular order of importance, we begin with twelve perspectives, which I believe will be thought-provoking for coming generations of leaders in our churches.

1. Talking About the Gospel Is as Far Removed from Effective Witness as Talking About Race Cars Is from Driving in the Indy 500

Please do not misunderstand. I am thrilled that anyone wants to talk about the gospel. But talk is cheap, and like-minded people can easily sit in pleasant venues and talk about how to define the gospel. To "go out into the highways and along the hedges" and "compel them to come in" (Luke 14:23 NASB) is much more difficult. An etiology of the continual diminishing of baptisms in Baptist churches would include numerous items. Yet I am convinced the major pathology is our obsession with talking extensively about the gospel in our religious conventicles but no longer being willing to do the grinding labor of taking the gospel to the lost.

To reverse this trend, evangelism will have to be reestablished as the major priority of the Great Commission. Church planting is crucial, but one cannot plant a church with unbelievers. Witnessing is hard work. Its doctrinal basis assumes all men are lost outside of Christ and will spend eternity in hell if they are not reborn. Who wants to talk about that in public? Further, evangelism assumes all men can come to Christ through repentance toward God and faith in Christ. It demands that the lost be confronted, however gently, with the claims of Christ. A witnessing church is the product of much concerted intercession, the example of a pastor who establishes the standard by his actions and the focus of a church on those who languish in their sins. However this task may be sugarcoated, it is certain to rub the cultural cat's fur the wrong way and make the church the object of attacks for failure to be open-minded.

May I be so bold as to ask how many of you have shared Christ with someone who is lost during the past month? How many of you have led someone to Christ this year? Ezekiel 3:17–18 (NASB) says:

> "Son of man, I have appointed you a watchman to the house of Israel; whenever you hear a word from My mouth, warn them from Me. When I say to the wicked, 'You will surely die,' and you do not warn him or speak out to warn the wicked from his wicked way that he may live, that wicked man shall die in his iniquity, but his blood I will require at your hand."

My prayer to God is that we will both remember and recover the task of sharing the faith. Quaker philosopher Elton Trueblood, in his two volumes *The Company of the Committed* and *The Incendiary Fellowship*, was remarkably perceptive.

If I do not open the door for another, it may never be opened, for it is possible that I may be the only one who holds this particular key. The worker on the production line may have an entrée to the life of his fellow worker on the line that can never be matched by any pastor or teacher or professional evangelist. The responsibility of each individual Christian is to do that which no other person can do as well as he can.[1]

2. The Culture Is Your Friend in the Same Way a Brown Bear Is Your Buddy

Black bears will maul you but seldom stay with you until you expire. Brown bears, however cuddly though they may appear, have nothing on their minds except that you make a quick journey to confirm that your theory of a Creator is, in fact, true. A while back a deluded couple wanted to prove that brownies were misrepresented and would be good buddies if approached properly. Early in the

---

[1]　Elton Trueblood, *The Company of the Committed* (New York: Harper & Row, 1961), 56.

morning of October 6, 2003, Tim Treadwell and Amie Huguenard discovered that the frequent warnings received from authorities were not "bear fundamentalist" hysteria.[2] On that day I was in Alaska only a few miles from where this couple became the coveted dessert for a brownie on the prowl. The logic seemed natural, but somebody forgot to educate the bear! While all culture is not wicked, the general posture of the culture affirms the reasoning of modernity, encourages the appetites of the flesh, hates the rigors of holy behavior, whitewashes what God calls evil, and delights in affirming that what God says is good is really outrageous prejudice. Candidly I sometimes wish every generation would peruse the Scriptures with the intent of asking, "How did Jesus, the apostles, and the prophets find the reception of the culture?" A contemporary critic of popular culture, Roger Scruton, has observed:

> Pop culture is the spontaneous response to this situation—an attempt to provide easy-going forms of social cohesion, without the costly rites of passage that bring oral and emotional knowledge. It is a culture which has demoted the aesthetic object, and elevated the advert in its place; it has replaced imagination by fantasy and feeling by kitsch; and it has destroyed the old forms of music and dancing, so as to replace them with a repetitious noise, whose invariant harmonic and rhythmic textures sound all about us, replacing the dialect of the tribe with the grammarless murmur of the species, and drowning out the unconfident stutterings of the fathers as they trudge away towards extinction.[3]

Enjoy the genuinely artistic and educational aspects of culture, but remember that a life of holiness is neither ruled nor much motivated by culture. Be sure that Jesus is Lord over culture.

3. Being Saved Means Something Quite Different from Being Picked Up as a Hitchhiker on a Hot Day

Salvation is not simply a rescue from the normal exigencies of life. Salvation is monumental. A person is taken from death to life. He is justified before a God who always judges sin. He is sanctified and made right in his standing in Christ. He is regenerated or made new again, born again. He is removed from the list of God's enemies and made a child of God through adoption. The profundity of this change is unlike anything else that ever happens to a man. Recovering an understanding of what is involved in being saved generates amazement at what our God has effected and propels us into the mission assignment. This action of our Lord is so far-reaching that it occupies the mind of the believer so that he finds spending much time contemplating anything else becomes difficult for him.

---

[2] Kevin Sanders, "Night of the Grizzly: A True Story of Love and Death in the Wilderness," *Bearman's Yellowstone Outdoor Adventures.* Accessed August 6, 2015. http://www.yellowstonebearman.com/Tim_Treadwell.html.

[3] Roger Scruton, *An Intelligent Person's Guide to Modern Culture* (South Bend, IN: St. Augustine's, 2000), 121.

What would happen if our churches gravitated to this perspective? The primary consideration of the church would become the Great Commission not just in theory but also in practice. The most profound rejoicing would occur every time a soul is saved, and our baptismal pools would seldom contain placid water.

4. A Christian Who Has Not Seriously Suffered Is like a Beautiful, New Rolls Royce with No Engine: Beautiful to Behold but Totally Useless

Paul promised that all the godly would suffer (2 Tim 3:12). Suffering turns our faces to the comfort that is in Christ. We fill that which is lacking in the afflictions of Christ (Col 1:24). Discovery is made that the assaults of suffering physically, emotionally, and mentally are inadequate to separate us from the love of Christ. The Scriptures caution about entering too soon into pastoral ministry partly because a youth has seldom suffered enough to have proved the goodness of the Lord in his own life. Frankly that is a major reason future church leaders need seminary. There is not a "fact" associated with the gospel that cannot be learned online or in the crucible of a church ministry, but the ripening of the soul, which is the product of vigorous study in a classroom of one's peers, the injustices sometimes experienced, and the companionship of the called are irreplaceable. One minister said that he did not need seminary because he felt like he was living in the house he was building. How unlike Paul, who, as a student of Gamaliel, nevertheless confined himself for three years in the desert to rethink his theology before he unleashed himself on the churches (Gal 1:17–18). I would never want to be part of a denomination that required seminary for ministry. But neither is the impact of seminary lost on me.

5. Most People Who Say They Believe the Bible Do So in the Same Way They Believe in the Existence of Bhutan. They Seldom Visit and Have Almost No Idea What It Actually Contains

This is why a pastor must teach the whole counsel of God—he must teach and preach through the whole Bible. The frequently repeated refrain that the Bible is not a book of science may be true, but the Bible *is* the book of life and eternity, and how to get along successfully in either place is totally dependent on how much of the Bible is distilled in the mind and heart of the believer. More importantly, the commandments, wisdom, and examples provided by the biblical text must order the life of the minister. His success is not so much determined by his pulpit prowess, his pastoral patience, or his administrative genius, but primarily by his godliness.

6. Mature Elephants Have Less Energy and Seldom Display the Symmetrical Beauty of the Youth of the Heard, but They Can Find Water When the Youth Would Famish, and They Never Fight or Kill Uselessly

The young bull elephant in his cocky, newly discovered strength walks defiantly into the pride of lions, certain he is big enough to handle whatever challenge arises. But this confidence will not save him from serious injury or death. The mature bull is ready but knows that walking a few additional yards out of the path of the lions will save agony for all.

The advent of blogdom has made the airwaves available to all. And everyone has an opinion about just about everything. Who needs a writing seminar? Who wants to labor through a philosophy class? Who needs to have a grasp of theology? Just give me a keyboard. But when the young elephants need water, then the wisdom of the mature elephant who has often traversed the trackless desert to the place where he slakes his thirst is what is needed. For multiplied reasons the young of the herd are essential, but a world of only young elephants is a dangerous world.

7. Ecumenism, in Its Finest Form, Is like Operating a Preservation Farm for Endangered Monkeys by Using a Large Male Lion for Breeding Purposes. The Breeding Process Will Produce No New Monkeys and Will Eventually Result in the Death of Both Monkeys and the Lion

Ecumenism sounds logical, and having peace seems always the best option. The problem is that ecumenism is always a theory based on the least common denominator while Christianity is a faith based on the lordship of Christ, which covers every area of doctrine and practice. Ecumenism never works and eventually reduces its advocates to a mere shell. On the other hand, a recent survey showed that being a Baptist was not a disadvantage in reaching the unchurched. To the contrary, the word *Baptist* stands for something, and that has tracked with many over the generations.[4]

This fact is not to disparage in any way our debt to the Reformers of the sixteenth century. Neither do we turn a deaf ear to the wisdom of the patristic era. We even acknowledge that we stand on the shoulders of Aquinas, Anselm, and a host of others. We, however, must affirm that we are seeking doctrinal purity and that the doctrine of the believers' church witnessed in baptism by immersion is at the heart of the Great Commission.

---

[4] Morgan Lee, "Leaving Baptist in Your Church Name Won't Scare People Away," *Christianity Today*, June 3, 2015. Accessed February 25, 2016. http://www.christianitytoday.com/gleanings/ 2015/june/leaving-baptist-in-your-church-name-wont-scare-people-away.html.

8. The Pastor's Ability to Preach an Engaging Sermon Is Admirable but Is Often like an Aviator Who Knows How to Drop His Ordnance but Is Clueless About How to Take Off or Land

The fine art of being a *poimēn*, a shepherd of the sheep, is lost on many. Being a shepherd certainly means feeding the sheep, but it also means protecting them from the predators, presiding over the births of new lambs, and caring for the wounded. This condition of poor shepherding is ubiquitous, occurring in all age groups, but it is a malady especially epidemic among younger pastors. Unfortunately, I know this from my own experience. Early in my ministry I was doing so much good for God that I totally failed to treasure God's people. I should have been fired.

The shepherd's task includes biblical guidance. This task is partially served by the agency of the pulpit but must also encompass daily care of the flock. Recent confessions from the psychiatric industry, together with its pharmacological side-kick, should remind the pastor that no Freudian-inspired services existed in New Testament times, but pastors were evidently able to care for their sheep. To this model we must return.

These confessions, such as Michael Alan Taylor's *Hippocrates Cried: The Decline of American Psychiatry* and Robert Whitaker's *Anatomy of an Epidemic: Magic Bullets, Psychiatric Drugs, and the Astonishing Rise of Mental Illness in America*, cannot be ignored any longer by thoughtful evangelicals.[5] These tomes are not penned by evangelicals, and some are even written by atheists. But they represent honest, hard-hitting truth that pastors need to hear. The church must recover what it is uniquely prepared to do in pastoral guidance. The Bible is, in fact, sufficient for every need.

9. Arrogance Is as Charming to God's People and as Appealing to God as an Angry Bull Is to a Wounded Cowboy in a Rodeo Arena

Arrogance knows no age restriction, but everyone knows this attitude too often occurs in the younger set. Why? Insufficient experience. Too little knowledge. Inadequate time spent walking with God. I suspect that this last reason pretty much tells the story. Here is why: a man cannot be haughty when he has just been walking with God that morning. Imperfection has been on a stroll with perfection, and the further they hiked, the more obvious the chasm between them appeared. In the end the imperfect one is not so much known by his ascription of praise to the sovereign God (words that anyone can echo) as by the diminution of himself and his humble service to his sovereign Lord. Listen to the humble

---

[5] Michael A. Taylor, *Hippocrates Cried: The Decline of American Psychiatry* (New York: Oxford University Press, 2013); Robert Whitaker, *Anatomy of an Epidemic: Magic Bullets, Psychiatric Drugs, and the Astonishing Rise of Mental Illness in America* (New York: Broadway, 2011).

confession of one of the most pious of preachers and a gallant soul-winner. Robert Murray M'Cheyne wrote these words:

> What a mass of corruption have I been! How great a portion of my life have I spent wholly without God in the world, given up to sense and the perishing things around me! Naturally of a feeling and sentimental disposition, how much of my religion has been, and to this day is, tinged with these colours of earth! Restrained from open vice by educational views and the fear of man, how much ungodliness has reigned within me! How often has it broken through all restraints, and come out in the shape of lust and anger, mad ambitions, and unallowed words! Though my vice was always refined, yet how subtle and how awfully prevalent it was! How complete a test was the Sabbath—spent in weariness, as much of it as was given to God's service! How I polluted it by my hypocrisies, my self-conceits, my worldly thoughts, and worldly friends! How formally and unheedingly the Bible was read—how little was read—so little that even now I have not read it all! How unboundedly was the wild impulse of the heart obeyed! How much more was the creature loved than the Creator!—O great God, that didst suffer me to live whilst I so dishonoured Thee, Thou knowest the whole; and it was Thy hand alone that could awaken me from the death in which I was, and was contented to be.[6]

The Bible makes much of this. Note the difference between the arrogant Joseph who taunts his brethren and the brother who retires to weep when he sees them in Egypt. Seven things the Lord hates, and the first is "a proud look" (Prov 6:17).[7] "The way of a fool is right in his own eyes, but he who heeds counsel is wise" (Prov 12:15). "A soft answer turns away wrath, but a harsh word stirs up anger" (Prov 15:1). "He who has knowledge spares his words, and a man of understanding is of a calm spirit. Even a fool is counted wise when he holds his peace" (Prov 17:27–28a). Those are only a few of such warnings.

My hope for the future of the church is that a recovery of humility and integrity in Christian social media will distinguish the body of believers clearly from the world. And above all, may such genuine piety be observed in our preaching!

10. You Had Just as Soon Attempt to Fuel an Electric Train with an Aspirin as to Attempt to Minister without the Power of God

The enterprise upon which we have embarked is not the running of a Fortune 500 company or even the healing touch of a gracious hospital. Neither is it an Olympic sprint. It is the ambassadorship of God's kingdom. As such, we have no life, no work, no career—nothing of our own. We represent the kingdom of

---

[6] Andrew A. Bonar, *Memoir and Remains of the Rev. Robert Murray M'Cheyne* (repr., Carlisle, PA: Banner of Truth, 1973), 16.

[7] I have used the NKJV translation in this paragraph.

Christ and the best interests of the citizens of that country in a strange land. To do justice to this assignment takes a thousand times more than acquired expertise or relevant experience. In answer to the question, "What are your qualifications for this assignment?" there is only one adequate answer. "I just returned from an hour's walk with my King, and his will and purpose are as follows." In addressing the Corinthian believers, Paul recalled for them his approach:

> And when I came to you, brethren, I did not come with superiority of speech or of wisdom, proclaiming to you the testimony of God. For I determined to know nothing among you except Jesus Christ and Him crucified. I was with you in weakness and in fear and in much trembling, and my message and my preaching were not in persuasive words of wisdom, but in demonstration of the Spirit and of power, so that your faith would not rest on the wisdom of men, but on the power of God. (1 Cor 2:1–5 NASB)

But such a posture does not arise from book knowledge or personal eloquence or cultural affirmation. The power of God is uniquely associated with the presence of God. Without his presence there will be no power. As M'Cheyne said, "Rose early to seek God, and found Him whom my soul loveth. Who would not rise early to meet such company?"[8]

11. When He Comes to a Fence, Before Tearing It Down, a Clever Traveler Will Try to Figure Out Why It Was Built There in the First Place

My generation preached against alcohol, discouraged dancing, and had a number of other commitments to which a younger generation does not adhere. And at times we were, without a doubt, legalistic about these matters. The fences themselves, however, were there for a purpose. One night while in college, my roommate and I water-bombed an open convertible, which we thought contained two lovers. There were six. Making our escape with three men in hot pursuit, I came to a troublesome fence that I always despised, wondering why on earth the farmer had built it there. No choice now, so I vaulted the fence and found myself face-to-face with an astonished, unhappy Black Angus bull who was determined that I achieve intimacy with my Maker in a fresh and comprehensive fashion. My first thought—*Oh, so that's why the farmer built that fence.* The two most devastating industries in America today are the beverage alcohol industry and the porn industry. More sadness, sorrow, fracturing of homes, loss of property, broken relationships, and forfeiture of funds come about as a result of those than any other. How can we not build a fence there?

A recent article documented that 14 percent of American adults have alcohol-related problems. Thirty-three million Americans suffer due to alcohol, and

---

[8] Bonar, *Memoir*, 23.

this says nothing about children and families.[9] And recall that we followers of Christ are responsible not only for the commandments but also for the wisdom of God's Word. And the wisdom literature could not be more lucid. Proverbs 20:1 (KJV) states, "Wine is a mocker, strong drink is raging: and whosoever is deceived thereby is not wise."

12. When You Get into a Texas Shootout, Once You Draw Your Pistol, It Is Too Late to Call Time-out and Say You Changed Your Mind

Another way to express this maxim is to remind ourselves that the law of unintended consequences is the most unobserved law in the ministry today. The question is, If I do what I now contemplate, what will happen that I do not yet see? Some years ago the runner-up award in the competition for the Darwin Awards went to the man who was working high on a water tower. Deciding to save himself the trouble of carefully lowering a heavy ladder below, he dropped it over the edge—forgetting that the ladder was tethered to his own waist for the pull to get it up. I will not here repeat his alleged last words, but I can tell you that he wished he had considered the law of unintended consequences.

Remembering to invoke the law of unintended consequences will save a thousand sorrows. When Charles Darwin published *The Origin of Species*, he probably never thought about Hitler, Stalin, Pol Pot, H. G. Wells, or the Ku Klux Klan; but according to the recent study by Jerry Bergman, all of this and much more may be laid at his feet.[10] What seems so logical at one moment can reap unintended consequences.

A CONCLUDING UNSCIENTIFIC POSTSCRIPT

Doubtless you are relieved my paper ends here. So much more fills my heart, but please allow me to conclude on a different note. While there is much that I hope the younger generation will hold in sacred trust, I am confident today's young leaders will excel. There will be missteps, but Roman 8:28 has not been dropped from the sacred text. A significant number of younger pastors love Jesus profoundly, and they will excel far beyond what we septuagenarians have been able to accomplish. The future is bright with the excitement of the worldwide movement of the hand of God. Before too many days have passed, I will ride off to the big roundup. But when that time comes, I assure you that I will mount up in the quiet confidence that the younger followers of Jesus will handle well the battle on every front. May God bless you every one.

---

[9] Alexandra Sifferlin, "Alcohol Problems Affect About 33 Million U.S. Adults," *Time*, June 3 2015. Accessed February 25, 2016. http://time.com/3907691/alcohol-problems-study.

[10] Jerry Bergman, *The Darwin Effect: It's* [sic] *Influence on Nazism, Eugenics, Racism, Communism, Capitalism and Sexism* (Green Forest, AR: Master, 2014).

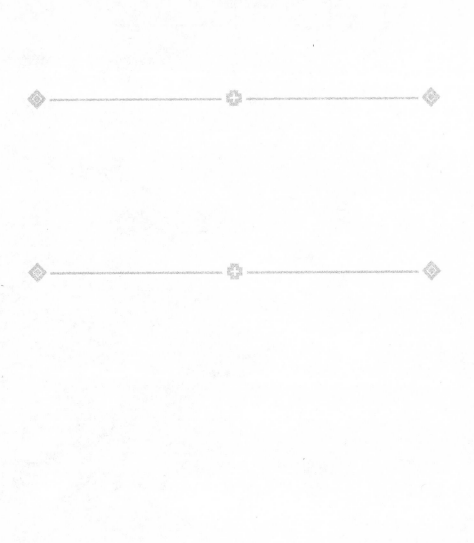

Conclusion

Jason K. Allen

During the SBC's Inerrancy Controversy the convention's annual June meeting became ground zero for denominational conflict. Each year motions were made, resolutions offered, and candidates presented to fill committee assignments and trustee slots. Most every convention maneuver was contested privately, if not publicly.

The most *consequential* moment every year was the presidential election, but the most *influential* moments may have been the Pastors' Conference and convention sermons. After all, Southern Baptists—of all stripes—are people of the Book and intuitively look to the preacher and the preaching of the Word for direction.

Messengers who showed up at the convention looking for direction in navigating the SBC conflict usually found it coming from the pulpit. Messages like Jerry Vines's "A Baptist and His Bible," Adrian Rogers's "The Church Triumphant," Jimmy Draper's "A People of Deep Belief," and W. A. Criswell's "Whether We Live or Die" and "The Curse of Liberalism" were pivotal, memorable moments wherein the preachers pointed out the dangers of liberalism and the necessity of taking action.

The 1988 gathering marked year nine of the controversy, with battle fatigue setting in and no end to the conflict in sight. That year Joel Gregory had been chosen to preach the annual convention sermon, the most coveted preaching slot of them all. Then politically unaligned, Gregory possessed a voice and mind which would make most any preacher envious. God's hand appeared to rest on him.

Gregory's goal was ambitious enough. By citing the high costs of conflict and the benefits of cooperation, he made a compelling, pragmatic case for unity. The sermon was indeed captivating, but its effect proved short-lived. Peace would eventually come, but it would come through the ultimate conservative victory, not by way of pragmatic compromise.

Gregory's sermon lives on, primarily because of its gripping conclusion about "the castle and the wall." In it he told the story of the bizarre ending of one of the great, old castles of Ireland. Gregory recounted:

> It was the ancient home of the Castlereagh family, one of the most princely residences of the Emerald Isle. But the ancient home fell into decay and was no longer inhabited.
>
> The usual happened. When peasants wanted to repair a road, build a chimney or pig-sty, they would scavenge stone from the fine old castle. The stones were already craftily cut, finished and fit. Best of all, they were available without digging and carrying for miles.
>
> One day Lord Londonderry visited his castle. He was the surviving descendant and heir. When he saw the state of his ancestral home, he determined to end immediately the robbery of the building for its stones.
>
> The ruin itself reflected the earlier glories of his family and was one of the treasures of Ireland. He sent for his agent and gave orders for the castle to be enclosed with a wall six feet tall and well-coped. This would keep out the trespassers. He went on his way.
>
> Three or four years later he returned. To his astonishment, the castle was gone, completely disappeared, vanished into the air. In its place there was a huge wall enclosing nothing.
>
> He sent for his agent and demanded to know why his orders had not been carried out. The agent insisted they had been. "But where is the castle?" asked the Lord. "The castle, is it? I built the wall with it, my Lord! Is it for me to be going miles for materials with the finest stones in Ireland beside me?"
>
> Lord Londonderry had his wall—but the castle, without which the wall meant nothing, had disappeared.

Gregory's point could not be missed. What good would erecting a doctrinal wall be, if, in order to build it, one destroyed that which the wall was intended to protect?

In a sense Gregory had a point. After all, as his illustration implied, what good is the wall of sound doctrine if the castle of ministry and missions does not stand behind it. But the point fails the test of Scripture and church history. The castle of doctrine and the wall of ministry and mission do not merely complement each other. They enable and ensure each other. Where there is no wall of doctrinal faithfulness, there will not long be a castle of ministry and missions.

Or, put more bluntly, where there is no confessional faithfulness, there will not long be denominational distinctiveness, and certainly not denominationally vibrant ministry and mission. Where there is no wall, there eventually will be no castle. For the Southern Baptist Convention to flourish in the twenty-first century, we will need both a strong castle and a robust wall. We cannot have the former without the latter. We must not settle for the latter without the former.

The hope of cultivating these dual strengths is precisely what this book has been about. Just as Southern Baptists labor to maintain doctrinal faithfulness, sound Baptist identity, and convictional witness, we must also strive for healthier churches, an increasingly robust and global gospel witness, and a unified, well-funded, and vibrant denomination.

As we do, may Southern Baptists know a doctrinal soundness, enjoy a growing convention of healthy churches proclaiming the Word of God, and spread the gospel of Jesus Christ around the world throughout the twenty-first century.

May God grant it be so.

Appendix A

Cooperative Program Giving: The giving record of Southern Baptists during the fiscal year October 1, 2013–September 30, 2014, is as follows:

	2013-2014	2012-2013	% Change
Total CP as a % of Undesignated Gifts[2]	5.47%	5.50%	-0.03%
Total Receipts[1]	$11,154,665,938	$11,209,655,950	-0.49%
Total Undesignated Gifts	$ 8,748,114,744	$ 8,769,026,657	-0.24%
Total Cooperative Program[2]	$ 478,700,850	$ 482,279,059	-0.74%
State Convention Share of Total CP[2]	$ 297,729,271	$ 298,859,256	-0.38%
SBC Share of Total CP[2]	$ 180,971,579	$ 183,419,803	-1.33%

Trends in Giving: The following five-year record of gifts to Southern Baptist churches and through the Cooperative Program is as follows:

Year	Receipts 1	Change	Gifts	Change	Program 2	Change
2009–10	$11,720,820,320	-1.61%	$8,911,796,522	-0.56%	$495,168,022	-4.84%
2010–11	$11,805,057,705	0.72%	$9,023,216,896	1.25%	$487,884,065	-1.47%
2011–12	$11,521,418,784	-2.40%	$8,891,673,582	-1.46%	$481,409,006	-1.33%
2012–13	$11,209,655,950	-2.71%	$8,769,026,657	-1.38%	$482,279,059	0.18%
2013–14	$11,154,665,938	-0.49%	$8,748,114,744	-0.24%	$478,700,850	-0.74%
Average Change 1970s	9.94%		N/A			8.97%
Average Change 1980s	7.58%		5.10%			6.83%
Average Change 1990s	5.42%		4.91%			2.68%
Average Change 2000s	4.12%		4.82%			2.23%
Average Change						
Last Five Years	-1.30%		-0.48%			-1.64%

Year	SBC $ Share of Total CP²	% Change	SBC % Share of Total CP²	Total CP 2 as a % of	
				Total Receipts¹	Undesig. Gifts
2009–10	$186,520,660	-4.01%	37.67%	4.22%	5.56%
2010–11	$186,386,036	-0.07%	38.20%	4.13%	5.41%
2011–12	$186,640,481	0.14%	38.77%	4.18%	5.41%
2012–13	$183,419,803	-1.73%	38.03%	4.30%	5.50%
2013–14	$180,971,579	-1.33%	37.80%	4.29%	5.47%
Average Change	1970s	8.92%	34.41%	8.94%	N/A
Average Change	1980s	7.98%	37.47%	8.55%	10.50%
Average Change	1990s	2.06%	37.04%	7.00%	8.73%
Average Change	2000s	2.22%	37.16%	5.38%	6.80%
Average Change					
Last Five Years		-1.40%	38.10%	4.23%	5.47%

Notes:

[1.] Due to a change LifeWay made in the ACP information it requested for 2011, Total Gifts were not calculable. Therefore, total receipts are reported above for 2009–2010 through 2013–2014 for comparative purposes. Over the last 20 years total receipts averaged 7.25% more than total gifts.

[2.] For 2009–10 through 2013–2014, in keeping with the Convention approved definition of the Cooperative Program, the total Cooperative Program category does not include church contributions given directly to the national convention that are directed only to the national SBC CP Allocation budget.

Cooperative Program Distribution: Cooperative Program funds received by the Southern Baptist Convention were distributed in keeping with the action of the Southern Baptist Convention when the 2013–2014 Southern Baptist Convention Cooperative Program Allocation Budget was approved. The 2013–2014 SBC Cooperative Program funds distributed include funds received from state conventions and identified by them as Cooperative Program Allocation Budget funds.

DISBURSEMENTS—SBC COOPERATIVE
PROGRAM ALLOCATION BUDGET

Southern Baptist Statistics: A summary of the statistical record for the Southern Baptist Convention for 2013–2014 is as follows. (See last page of appendix for chart of Southern Baptist Statistics by State Convention.)

Southern Baptist Convention Statistical Summary: 2014

Item/Statistic	2014–2013	2014–2013	2014–2013 Numeric Change	2014–2013 Percent Change
State Conventions	42	42	0	0.00%
Associations	1,157	1,161	-4	-0.34%
Churches	46,499	46,125	374	0.81%
Total Membership[1]	15,499,173	15,735,640	-236,467	-1.50%
Baptisms	305,301	310,368	-5,067	-1.63%
Ratio of Baptisms : Total Membership	1:51	1:51	–	–
Weekly Worship Attendance	5,674,469	5,834,707	-160,238	-2.75%
Church-type Missions Operating[2]	4,595	4,789	-194	-4.05%
Undesignated Receipts	$8,748,114,744	$8,769,026,657	-$20,911,913	-0.24%
Cooperative Program[3]	– www.sbc.net/ cp/statistics.asp	–	–	–

Notes:

[1] Georgia Baptist Convention calculated total membership based on change in resident membership.

[2] Some state conventions no longer use the designation of church-type mission to categorize congregations which are not self-determining, self-sustaining, and self- propagating. This practice has impacted the number of churches and church-type missions.

[3] Cooperative Program as reported on the Annual Church Profile is not included in this table. Cooperative Program, based on the actual amount given through the state convention, is provided in the SBC Annual in the Executive Committee Annual Report.

Other 2014 Items—Not Asked by All State Conventions[1]

Item/Statistic	2014	2013
Other Additions[2]	276,021	279,915
Total Receipts[2]	$ 11,154,665,938	$ 11,209,655,950
Total Mission Expenditures[3]	$ 1,230,258,151	$ 1,294,701,479
Great Commission Giving[4]	$ 637,498,179	$ 777,452,820

Notes:

[1] Totals for items in this table have incomplete data for 2014 due to the fact that not all state conventions asked the item or did so in a way not comparable with the standard definition. Similar actions occurred in 2013. Thus, comparisons between the two years may not be appropriate. See the Notes in the 2013 SBC Statistical Summary for specific details to determine if a comparison is desirable.

[2] California Southern Baptist Convention did not ask this item or the information necessary to obtain the item.

[3] California Southern Baptist Convention, Georgia Baptist Convention, and the Baptist General Convention of Oklahoma did not ask this item or the information necessary to obtain the item.

[4] Alabama State Board of Missions, Arkansas Baptist State Convention, Missouri Baptist Convention, and the Baptist General Convention of Oklahoma did not ask this item or the information necessary to obtain the item.

Prepared by: LifeWay Insights, LifeWay Christian Resources, One LifeWay Plaza, Nashville, TN 37234-0127, June 8, 2015

CHURCH PLANTS PLUS NEW AFFILIATES FOR 2014, SBC: 1,193**

Source: Reports from State Directors of Missions compiled by the North American Mission Board, Alpharetta, GA

** Note: 2010 was the first year an SBC ID # was requested for each reported congregation. In 2014, partners reported 985 new church starts and 208 new affiliations.

	2014	2013	Change	% Change
International Missionaries	4,839	4,846	-7	-0.14%
North American Missionaries	2,178	2,406	-228	-9.48%

Special Missions Offerings: Southern Baptists contributed a special missions offering total of $184,040,974 through the SBC Executive Committee for North American and International Missions in 2013-2014. The record is as follows:

	2013–2014	2012–2013	Change Gain (Loss)	Percentage Change
Lottie Moon Christmas Offering for International Missions	$128,366,852	126,754,910	1,611,942	1.27%
Annie Armstrong Easter Offering for North American Missions	55,674,122	54,957,016	717,106	1.30%
Total	$184,040,974			

Global Hunger Relief Funds: Southern Baptists contributed a total of $3,857,233 for global hunger relief through the SBC Executive Committee in 2013–2014. The record is as follows:

2013–2014	2012–2013	Percent Change	
Received by Executive Committee	$3,857,233	$4,290,625	-10.10%
Forwarded to International Mission Board	$3,023,839	$3,301,538	-8.41%
Forwarded to North American Mission Board	$ 833,394	$ 908,087	-8.23%

Southern Baptist Statistics by State Convention: 2014[1]

SBC and State Conventions	Associations	Churches[2]	Baptisms	Other Additions[3]	Total Membership	Total Receipts[3]	Total Mission Expenditures[3]
Alabama	75	3,215	17,355	21,668	998,236	$718,690,841	$85,300,583
Alaska	4	84	517	609	12,563	$13,363,256	$1,835,004
Arizona	13	414	2,516	2,060	87,488	$83,914,539	$8,850,542
Arkansas	42	1,434	11,273	10,726	500,002	$325,560,460	$46,243,488
California[4]	29	1,742	12,496	See Footnote 4	385,727	See Footnote 4	See Footnote 4
Colorado	11	278	1,663	1,473	38,824	$46,392,813	$5,749,655
Dakota	7	81	182	318	4,541	$5,548,751	$707,984
District of Columbia		135	163	99	6,626	$6,981,619	$623,191
Florida[5]	49	2,593	58,401	21,546	1,106,969	$765,798,008	$77,556,158
Georgia[6]	92	3,320	27,742	28,761	1,407,341	$1,034,019,996	See Footnote 6
Hawaii-Pacific	6	114	850	553	16,203	$22,073,816	$2,567,675
Illinois	34	906	4,428	2,531	192,851	$122,247,612	$13,941,965
Indiana	14	392	2,187	2,203	89,760	$60,863,468	$6,346,075
Iowa	5	97	638	475	12,310	$17,361,897	$2,282,301
Kansas-Nebraska	13	312	2,646	1,582	89,529	$64,618,201	$8,512,230
Kentucky	70	2,484	14,180	11,937	712,976	$385,315,672	$51,390,291
Louisiana	40	1,439	10,614	9,533	516,668	$396,650,057	$45,276,287
Maryland-Delaware	11	536	1,704	1,220	97,732	$93,130,786	$10,896,348
Michigan	14	264	904	697	26,824	$19,113,925	$3,124,976
Minnesota-Wisconsin	8	126	313	333	14,823	$14,436,124	$1,669,088
Mississippi	66	2,100	11,318	14,088	651,473	$517,835,405	$73,784,296
Missouri	61	1,837	8,448	8,743	553,559	$331,042,843	$43,002,622
Montana	5	129	611	369	10,292	$10,906,419	$1,430,331
Nevada	4	156	1,137	1,338	28,648	$28,163,466	$2,585,744
New England	7	236	1,606	544	27,286	$19,077,935	$2,549,950
New Mexico	13	314	2,698	2,713	76,934	$58,884,829	$8,276,626
New York	10	376	2,603	558	36,909	$24,101,577	$1,929,888
North Carolina	79	4,147	18,655	17,882	1,188,807	$855,409,479	$98,361,726
Northwest	14	424	1,679	1,735	55,253	$61,923,331	$8,067,703

SBC and State Conventions	Associations	Churches[2]	Baptisms	Other Additions[3]	Total Membership	Total Receipts[3]	Total Mission Expenditures[3]
Ohio	15	616	4,113	2,557	119,056	$84,818,613	$10,406,746
Oklahoma[7]	43	1,723	11,979	10,666	676,732	$420,257,024	See Footnote 7
Pennsylvania-South Jersey	8	261	1,806	1,316	26,578	$18,767,405	$2,564,466
Puerto Rico-US Virgin Islands	4	44	183	52	3,642	$1,712,996	$188,739
South Carolina	42	2,119	17,464	14,491	664,818	$557,355,146	$60,427,609
Tennessee	67	3,026	22,986	21,023	1,057,660	$754,702,098	$96,700,513
Texas[8]	112	5,971	44,718	47,966	2,797,743	$2,251,178,603	$236,165,987
BGCT	101	4,171	32,214	34,836	2,146,257	$1,674,139,857	$177,721,234
SBTC	108	2,335	23,435	22,051	1,150,868	$1,068,543,344	$105,399,126
Utah-Idaho	11	133	344	392	15,008	$14,107,566	$1,989,879
Virginia[9]	41	1,863	11,112	10,438	599,251	$514,210,381	$52,717,021
BGAV	41	1,302	5,351	5,620	406,422	$313,142,684	$32,468,000
SBCV		622	6,671	5,587	222,627	$225,873,339	$23,500,993
West Virginia	10	193	710	470	28,641	$20,251,041	$3,454,929
Wyoming	8	81	292	254	10,268	$9,261,693	$1,518,955
Subtotal	1,157	46,311	347,075	285,609	15,475,731	$11,266,359,931	$1,129,203,916
Adjustments[10]		188	-41,774	-9,588	23,442	-$111,693,993	$ 101,054,235
Grand Total For SBC[2]	1,157	46,499	305,301	276,021	15,499,173	$11,154,665,938	$1,230,258,151

Notes:

[1] All information as of June 8, 2015.

[2] Some state conventions no longer use the designation of church-type mission to categorize congregations which are not self-determining, self-sustaining, and self-propagating. This practice has impacted the number of churches and church-type missions.

[3] Total impacted by incomplete data from some state conventions. See body of table and notes for details. Care should be exercised in comparing SBC totals to previous years.

[4] California Southern Baptist Convention did not ask the following items or the information necessary to obtain the items: Other Additions, Total Receipts, and Total Mission Expenditures.

[5] There are 1,654 church-type missions located in Haiti which are recorded as cooperating with the Florida Baptist Convention (FBC) during the 2014 reporting year. Statistics for these missions are included in the FBC's total for the following items reported in this table: number of baptisms and number of total members. These missions are not considered a part of the Southern Baptist Convention (SBC) and the statistics for these missions are not included in the reported SBC totals (Grand Total for SBC).

[6] Georgia Baptist Convention did not ask the following item or the information necessary to obtain the item: total mission expenditures. Total membership was calculated based on change in resident membership.

[7] Baptist General Convention of Oklahoma did not ask the following item or the information necessary to obtain the item: total mission expenditures.

[8] Two conventions exist within the state of Texas. The Texas summary line does not show the arithmetic sum of the two state convention figures, because some congregations are affiliated with both state conventions, and their numbers are reflected in the totals for both state conventions.

[9] Two conventions exist within the state of Virginia. The Virginia summary line does not show the arithmetic sum of the two state convention figures, because some congregations are affiliated with both state conventions, and their numbers are reflected in the totals for both state conventions.

[10] This line includes four types of adjustments to the data:

[a] The removal of duplicate data caused by 716 congregations that are affiliated with more than one state convention.

[b] The removal of data from 66 congregations affiliated with a state convention but not affiliated with the SBC.

[c] The addition of data from 1,332 congregations affiliated with the SBC but not affiliated with a state Convention.

[d] The addition of data "pulled forward" from previous ACP reporting cycles for 9,731 congregations that did not report in 2014.

Prepared by: LifeWay Insights, LifeWay Christian Resources, One LifeWay Plaza, Nashville, TN 37234-0127, June 8, 2015

Appendix B

PENETRATING THE LOSTNESS

Embracing a Vision for a Great Commission
Resurgence Among Southern Baptists

Final Report of the Great Commission Task Force
of the
Southern Baptist Convention
(as amended and adopted by the Southern
Baptist Convention, June 16, 2010)

RECOMMENDATIONS TO THE
SOUTHERN BAPTIST CONVENTION

1. That the messengers to the Southern Baptist Convention, meeting in Orlando, Florida, June 15–16, 2010, adopt the following as the mission statement of the Southern Baptist Convention:

   As a convention of churches, our missional vision is to present the Gospel of Jesus Christ to every person in the world and to make disciples of all the nations.

2. That the messengers to the Southern Baptist Convention, meeting in Orlando, Florida, June 15–16, 2010, adopt the following as Core Values for our work together:

CHRIST-LIKENESS—We depend on the transforming power of the Holy Spirit, the Word of God and prayer to make us more like Jesus Christ.

TRUTH—We stand together in the truth of God's inerrant Word, celebrating the faith once for all delivered to the saints.

UNITY—We work together in love for the sake of the Gospel.

RELATIONSHIPS—We consider others more important than ourselves.

TRUST—We tell one another the truth in love and do what we say we will do.

FUTURE—We value Southern Baptists of all generations and embrace our responsibility to pass this charge to a rising generation in every age, faithful until Jesus comes.

LOCAL CHURCH—We believe the local church is given the authority, power, and responsibility to present the Gospel of Jesus Christ to every person in the world.

KINGDOM—We join other Christ-followers for the Gospel, the Kingdom of Christ, and the glory of God.

3. That the messengers to the Southern Baptist Convention, meeting in Orlando, Florida, June 15–16, 2010, request the Executive Committee of the Southern Baptist Convention to consider recommending to the Southern Baptist Convention the adoption of the language and structure of Great Commission Giving as described in this report in order to enhance and celebrate the Cooperative Program and the generous support of Southern Baptists channeled through their churches, and to continue to honor and affirm the Cooperative Program as the most effective means of mobilizing our churches and extending our outreach. We affirm that designated gifts to special causes are to be given as a supplement to the Cooperative Program and not as a substitute for Cooperative Program giving. We further request that the boards of trustees of the International Mission Board and North American Mission Board, in consultation with the Woman's Missionary Union, consider the adoption of the Lottie Moon and Annie Armstrong offering goals as outlined in this report.

4. That the messengers to the Southern Baptist Convention, meeting June 15–16, 2010, request the Executive Committee of the Southern Baptist Convention to consider any revision to the ministry assignment of the North American Mission Board that may be necessary in order to accomplish the redirection of NAMB as outlined in this report; and that the Board of Trustees of the North American Mission Board be asked to consider the encouragements found within this report in all matters under their purview.

5. That the messengers to the Southern Baptist Convention, meeting June 15–16, 2010, request that the Executive Committee of the Southern Baptist Convention and the International Mission Board of the Southern Baptist Convention consider a revised ministry assignment for the International Mission Board that would remove any geographical limitation on its mission to reach unreached and underserved people groups wherever they are found.

6. That the messengers to the Southern Baptist Convention, meeting June 15–16, 2010, request the Executive Committee of the Southern Baptist Convention to consider working with the leadership of the state conventions in developing a comprehensive program of Cooperative Program promotion and stewardship education in alignment with this report.

7. That the messengers to the Southern Baptist Convention, meeting June 15–16, 2010, in Orlando, Florida, request the Executive Committee of the Southern Baptist Convention to consider recommending an SBC Cooperative Program Allocation Budget that will increase the percentage allocated to the International Mission Board to 51 percent by decreasing the Executive Committee's percentage of the SBC Allocation Budget by 1 percent.

Contributors

Editor

Jason K. Allen, president, Midwestern Baptist Theological Seminary

Contributors

Daniel L. Akin, president, Southeastern Baptist Theological Seminary

Jason K. Allen, president, Midwestern Baptist Theological Seminary

Paul Chitwood, executive director, the Kentucky Baptist Convention

David S. Dockery, president, Trinity International University

Jason G. Duesing, provost and associate professor of historical theology, Midwestern Baptist Theological Seminary

Kevin Ezell, president, the North American Mission Board of the Southern Baptist Convention

Ronnie W. Floyd, president, the Southern Baptist Convention and pastor, Cross Church

Christian T. George, assistant professor of historical theology and curator of the Spurgeon Library, Midwestern Baptist Theological Seminary

Collin Hansen, editorial director, The Gospel Coalition

Tony Merida, pastor for preaching and vision, Imago Dei Church and associate professor of preaching, Southeastern Baptist Theological Seminary

R. Albert Mohler Jr., president, The Southern Baptist Theological Seminary

Frank S. Page, president and CEO, the Executive Committee of the Southern Baptist Convention

L. Paige Patterson, president, Southwestern Baptist Theological Seminary

David J. Platt, president, the International Mission Board of the Southern Baptist Convention

Thom S. Rainer, president and CEO, LifeWay Christian Resources

Owen D. Strachan, associate professor of Christian theology and director of the Center for Theological and Cultural Engagement, Midwestern Baptist Theological Seminary

Walter R. Strickland II, instructor of theology and special advisor to the president for diversity, Southeastern Baptist Theological Seminary

Justin Taylor, executive vice president of book publishing and book publisher, Crossway

John L. Yeats, executive director, the Missouri Baptist Convention and recording secretary, the Southern Baptist Convention

John Mark Yeats, dean, Midwestern College and associate professor of church history, Midwestern Baptist Theological Seminary

Name and Subject Index

CPSIA information can be obtained
at www.ICGtesting.com
Printed in the USA
LVHW112331120921
697683LV00001B/70